Genetic Disorders Sourcebook,
  1st Edition
Genetic Disorders Sourcebook,
  2nd Edition
Head Trauma Sourcebook
Headache Sourcebook
Health Insurance Sourcebook
Health Reference Series Cumulative
  Index 199~

Podiatry Sourcebook
Pregnancy & Birth Sourcebook
Prostate Cancer
Public Health Sourcebook
Reconstructive & Cosmetic Surgery
  Sourcebook
Rehabilitation Sourcebook
Respiratory Diseases & Disorders

Healthy Agi
Healthy Chi
Healthy Hea
Heart Disea
  Sourceboc
Household S
Immune Sys
Infant & To
Injury & Tra
Kidney & U
  Disorders
Learning Di
  1st Edition
Learning Di
  2nd Editic
Liver Disorc
Lung Disorc
Medical Tes
Men's Healt
Mental Heal
  1st Editio
Mental Hea
  2nd Editic
Mental Reta
Movement
Obesity Sou
Ophthalmic
Oral Health
Osteoporosi
Pain Source
Pain Source
Pediatric Ca
Physical &
  Sourceboc

cs

es

st Edition
nd Edition
rcebook

ourcebook
Sourcebook
ok

es
ens
eens
tion

ion

Vegetarian
SOURCEBOOK

Health Reference Series

First Edition

Vegetarian
SOURCEBOOK

*Basic Consumer Health Information about
Vegetarian Diets, Lifestyle, and Philosophy,
Including Definitions of Vegetarianism and
Veganism, Tips about Adopting Vegetarianism,
Creating a Vegetarian Pantry, and Meeting
Nutritional Needs of Vegetarians, with Facts
Regarding Vegetarianism's Effect on Pregnant
and Lactating Women, Children, Athletes,
and Senior Citizens*

*Along with a Glossary of Commonly Used
Vegetarian Terms and Resources for Additional
Help and Information*

Edited by
Chad T. Kimball

Omnigraphics

615 Griswold Street • Detroit, MI 48226

Bibliographic Note

Because this page cannot legibly accommodate all the copyright notices, the Bibliographic Note portion of the Preface constitutes an extension of the copyright notice.

Edited by Chad T. Kimball

Health Reference Series

Karen Bellenir, *Managing Editor*
David A. Cooke, MD, *Medical Consultant*
Elizabeth Barbour, *Permissions Associate*
Dawn Matthews, *Verification Assistant*
Carol Munson, *Permissions Assistant*
Laura Pleva Nielsen, *Index Editor*
EdIndex, Services for Publishers, *Indexers*

* * *

Omnigraphics, Inc.

Matthew P. Barbour, *Senior Vice President*
Kay Gill, *Vice President — Directories*
Kevin Hayes, *Operations Manager*
Leif Gruenberg, *Development Manager*
David P. Bianco, *Marketing Consultant*

* * *

Peter E. Ruffner, *Publisher*

Frederick G. Ruffner, Jr., *Chairman*

Copyright © 2002 Omnigraphics, Inc.

ISBN 0-7808-0439-2

Library of Congress Cataloging-in-Publication Data

Vegetarian sourcebook : basic consumer health information about vegetarian diets, lifestyle, and philosophy, including definitions of vegetarianism and veganism, tips about adopting vegetarianism, creating a vegetarian pantry, and meeting nutritional needs of vegetarians, with facts regarding vegetarianism's effect on pregnant and lactating women, children, athletes, and senior citizens; along with a glossary of commonly used vegetarian terms and resources for additional help and information / edited by Chad T. Kimball.-- 1st ed.
    p. cm.-- (Health reference series)
  Includes bibliographical references and index.
  ISBN 0-7808-0439-2 (lib. bdg. : alk. paper)
    1. Vegetarianism--Popular works. I. Kimball, Chad T. II. Health reference series (Unnumbered)

RM236 .V436 2002
613.2'62--dc21
                                                                    2002070236

Printed in the United States

Table of Contents

Part III: Vegetarian Food Choices

Part IV: Special Groups

Part V: Vegetarian Philosophy and Controversies

Part VI: Additional Help and Information

Preface

About This Book

Studies show that 12.4 million Americans consider themselves to be vegetarians. Many people are interested in the vegetarian diet but are unsure whether such eating habits are healthy. Some are concerned about protein requirements, availability of ingredients, and proper vitamin intake, while others are concerned about the effects of a vegetarian diet on growing children and family life.

This *Sourcebook* describes various types of vegetarian diets and gives practical advice for safely incorporating them into everyday life, including creating a vegetarian pantry and obtaining sufficient amounts of various nutrients, vitamins, and minerals. It provides details to help readers understand the advantages and disadvantages of eating vegetarian. It also includes information about the feasibility and healthfulness of vegetarianism for pregnant and lactating mothers, children, teenagers, the elderly, and other special groups. Other common concerns such as finding vegetarian items on a menu and determining which food ingredients contain animal products are also discussed. Additionally, this *Sourcebook* includes cookery information, a glossary, and a resource listing for additional help and information.

How to Use This Book

This book is divided into parts and chapters. Parts focus on broad areas of interest. Chapters are devoted to single topics within a part.

Part I: Vegetarian Fundamentals provides an overview of vegetarian diets, including the history, advantages, and challenges associated with vegetarianism. It gives general guidance for switching to and maintaining a healthy vegetarian diet.

Part II: Vegetarian Nutrition explains the nutritional advantages of following a vegetarian diet, addresses questions regarding cancer and heart disease in vegetarians, and examines vegetarian-specific nutritional concerns. These include concerns about iron, zinc, protein, and calcium deficiency, and getting enough vitamin D and vitamin B_{12}.

Part III: Vegetarian Food Choices discusses common foods that make up vegetarian diets and gives general cookery advice. It also offers information on foods which contain animal products, as well as lists vegetarian and non-vegetarian items at popular restaurants and fast food chains.

Part IV: Special Groups offers advice regarding the unique needs of pregnant and lactating women, children, teenagers, athletes, and the elderly who desire to healthfully follow a vegetarian diet.

Part V: Vegetarian Philosophy and Controversies explores controversial issues such as environmental reasons for vegetarianism, eating disorders in vegetarian teens, and vegetarian diets in the light of the evolution of the human digestive tract.

Part VI: Additional Help and Information includes a glossary of vegetarian-related terms, an extensive list of animal ingredients and their alternatives, information about the vegetarian food guide pyramid, a directory of resources, and a list references for additional reading.

Bibliographic Note

This volume contains documents and excerpts from publications issued by the following U.S. government agencies: Department of Health and Human Services (DHHS) and the U.S. Food and Drug Administration (FDA).

In addition, this volume contains copyrighted documents from the following organizations, individuals, and publications: American Council on Science and Health (ACSH); American Dietetic Association (ADA); *American Journal of Clinical Nutrition;* Celestial Arts/Ten Speed Press; Cornell University; Elson Haas, MD; European Vegetarian Union; IDEA Health and Fitness Source; *Lifelines*; Loren Cordain, PhD; Michael Garnett; Nava Atlas; North American Vegetarian Society

(NAVS); People for the Ethical Treatment of Animals (PETA); Random House; Toronto Vegetarian Association; Vegan Society; Vegan.com; *Vegetarian 5-Ingredient Gourmet*; Vegetarian Nutrition Dietetic Practice Group; Vegetarian Society UK; and *Vegetarian Times*.

Full citation information is provided on the first page of each chapter. Every effort has been made to secure all necessary rights to reprint the copyrighted material. If any omissions have been made, please contact Omnigraphics to make corrections for future editions.

Acknowledgements

In addition to the organizations, agencies, and individuals listed above, special thanks go to many others who worked behind the scenes to help bring this book to fruition. They include permissions associate Liz Barbour, verification assistant Dawn Matthews, document engineer Bruce Bellenir, indexer Edward J. Prucha, and operations manager Kevin Hayes.

Note from the Editor

This book is part of Omnigraphics' *Health Reference Series*. The *Series* provides basic consumer health information about a broad range of medical concerns. The information is intended to help facilitate communication between people and their health care providers. It is not intended to serve as a tool for diagnosing illness, in prescribing treatments, or as a substitute for the physician/patient relationship. The editorial staff and Omnigraphics encourage all persons concerned about medical symptoms or the possibility of disease to seek professional care from an appropriate health care provider.

Our Advisory Board

The *Health Reference Series* is reviewed by an Advisory Board comprised of librarians from public, academic, and medical libraries. We would like to thank the following board members for providing guidance to the development of this series:

Dr. Lynda Baker,
Associate Professor of Library and Information Science,
Wayne State University, Detroit, MI

Nancy Bulgarelli,
William Beaumont Hospital Library, Royal Oak, MI

Karen Imarisio,
Bloomfield Township Public Library, Bloomfield Township, MI

Karen Morgan,
Mardigian Library, University of Michigan-Dearborn,
Dearborn, MI

Rosemary Orlando,
St. Clair Shores Public Library, St. Clair Shores, MI

Medical Consultant

Medical consultation services are provided to the *Health Reference Series* editors by David A. Cooke, MD. Dr. Cooke is a graduate of Brandeis University, and he received his MD degree from the University of Michigan. He completed residency training at the University of Wisconsin Hospital and Clinics. He is board-certified in Internal Medicine. Dr. Cooke currently works as part of the University of Michigan Health System and practices in Brighton, MI. In his free time, he enjoys writing, science fiction, and spending time with his family.

Health Reference Series *Update Policy*

The inaugural book in the *Health Reference Series* was the first edition of *Cancer Sourcebook* published in 1989. Since then, the *Series* has been enthusiastically received by librarians and in the medical community. In order to maintain the standard of providing high-quality health information for the layperson the editorial staff at Omnigraphics felt it was necessary to implement a policy of updating volumes when warranted.

Medical researchers have been making tremendous strides, and it is the purpose of the *Health Reference Series* to stay current with the most recent advances. Each decision to update a volume will be made on an individual basis. Some of the considerations will include how much new information is available and the feedback we receive from people who use the books. If there is a topic you would like to see added to the update list, or an area of medical concern you feel has not been adequately addressed, please write to:

Editor
Health Reference Series
Omnigraphics, Inc.
615 Griswold Street
Detroit, MI 48226

The commitment to providing on-going coverage of important medical developments has also led to some format changes in the *Health Reference Series*. Each new volume on a topic is individually titled and called a "First Edition." Subsequent updates will carry sequential edition numbers. To help avoid confusion and to provide maximum flexibility in our ability to respond to informational needs, the practice of consecutively numbering each volume has been discontinued.

Part One

Vegetarian Fundamentals

Chapter 1

More People Are Trying Vegetarian Diets

Perceiving plant foods as beneficial because they are high in dietary fiber and, generally, lower in saturated fat than animal foods, many people are turning to vegetarian diets.

Grain products, for instance, form the base of the US Department of Agriculture and Department of Health and Human Services' (USDA, DHHS) Food Guide Pyramid, which recommends 6 to 11 daily servings of bread, cereal, rice, and pasta. Daily intakes advised for other foods are: 3 to 5 servings of vegetables; 2 to 4 servings of fruits; 2 to 3 servings of milk, yogurt and cheese; and 2 to 3 servings of meat, poultry, fish, dry beans, eggs, and nuts. The guide advises using fats, oils and sweets sparingly.

And, who hasn't seen signs in their grocer's produce section urging consumers to eat "5 a day for better health"? This slogan reflects a major government-industry campaign to help people eat more fruits and vegetables as part of a high-fiber, low-fat diet that emphasizes variety.

The campaign is consistent with the USDA-DHHS Dietary Guidelines for Americans, which states, "Most Americans of all ages eat fewer than the recommended number of servings of grain products, vegetables, and fruits, even though consumption of these foods is

Farley, Dixie, "More People Trying Vegetarian Diets," *FDA Consumer*, October 1995, revised January 1996, FDA (Food and Drug Administration) Pub. No. 96-2296, http://www.fda.gov/fdac/features/895_vegdiet.html. Reviewed in April, 2001 by Dr. David A. Cooke, MD, Diplomate, American Board of Internal Medicine.

associated with a substantially lower risk for many chronic diseases, including certain types of cancer." Also noted: "Most vegetarians eat milk products and eggs, and as a group, these lacto-ovo-vegetarians enjoy excellent health."

But health benefits are not the only reason vegetarian diets attract followers. Certain people, such as Seventh-day Adventists, choose a vegetarian diet because of religious beliefs. Others give up meat because they feel eating animals is unethical. Some believe it's a better use of the Earth's resources to eat low on the food chain—that is, to eat plant foods, rather than the animals that eat the plant foods. And many people eat plant foods simply because they are less expensive than animal foods.

It's wise to take precautions, however, when adopting a diet that entirely excludes animal flesh and dairy products, called a vegan diet. (See "Vegetarian Varieties.")

"The more you restrict your diet, the more difficult it is to get the nutrients you need," says John Vanderveen, PhD, director of the Food and Drug Administration's (FDA) Office of Plant and Dairy Foods and Beverages. "To be healthful, vegetarian diets require very careful, proper planning. Nutrition counseling can help you get started on a diet that is nutritionally adequate."

If appropriately planned, vegan diets, though restrictive, can provide adequate nutrition even for children, according to the American Dietetic Association and the Institute of Food Technologists.

Plant Food Benefits

Registered dietitian Johanna Dwyer, of Tufts University Medical School and the New England Medical Center Hospital, Boston, summarizes these plant food benefits:

> "Data are strong that vegetarians are at lesser risk for obesity, atonic [reduced muscle tone] constipation, lung cancer, and alcoholism. Evidence is good that risks for hypertension, coronary artery disease, type II diabetes, and gallstones are lower. Data are only fair to poor that risks of breast cancer, diverticular disease of the colon, colonic cancer, calcium kidney stones, osteoporosis, dental erosion, and dental caries are lower among vegetarians."

According to Dwyer, vegetarians' longevity is similar to or greater than that of non-vegetarians, but is influenced in Western countries by vegetarians' "adoption of many healthy lifestyle habits in addition to diet, such as not smoking, abstinence or moderation in the use of alcohol, being physically active, resting adequately, seeking ongoing health surveillance, and seeking guidance when health problems arise."

Can Veggies Prevent Cancer?

The National Cancer Institute, in its booklet *Diet, Nutrition, & Cancer Prevention: A Guide to Food Choices*, states that 35 percent of cancer deaths may be related to diet. The booklet states:

- Diets rich in beta-carotene (the plant form of vitamin A) and vitamin C may reduce the risk of certain cancers.

- Reducing fat in the diet may reduce cancer risk and, in helping weight control, may reduce the risk of heart attacks and strokes.

- Diets high in fiber-rich foods may reduce the risk of cancers of the colon and rectum.

- Vegetables from the cabbage family (cruciferous vegetables) may reduce the risk of colon cancer.

The U.S. Food and Drug Administration (FDA), in fact, authorized several health claims on food labels relating low-fat diets high in some plant-derived foods with a possibly reduced risk of cancer.

While FDA acknowledges that high intakes of fruits and vegetables rich in beta-carotene or vitamin C have been associated with reduced cancer risk, it believes the data are not sufficiently convincing that either nutrient by itself is responsible for the association. Nevertheless, since most fruits and vegetables are low-fat foods and may contain vitamin A (as beta-carotene) and vitamin C, the agency authorized a health claim relating diets low in fat and rich in these foods to a possibly reduced risk of some cancers.

Another claim may relate low-fat diets high in fiber-containing vegetables, fruits and grains to a possible reduction in cancer risk. (The National Cancer Institute recommends 20 to 30 grams of fiber a day.) Although the exact role of total dietary fiber, fiber components, and other nutrients and substances in these foods is not fully understood, many studies have shown such diets to be associated with reduced risk of some cancers.

Lowering Heart Disease Risk

FDA also notes that diets high in saturated fats and cholesterol increase blood levels of total cholesterol and LDL (low density lipoprotein) cholesterol, and thus the risk for coronary heart disease. (The National Cholesterol Education Program recommends a diet with no more than 30 percent fat, of which no more than 10 percent comes from saturated fat.) For this reason, the agency authorized a health claim relating diets low in saturated fat and cholesterol to a possibly reduced risk of coronary heart disease.

Another claim may relate diets low in fat and high in fruits, vegetables, and grain products that contain fiber, particularly soluble fiber, to a possibly reduced risk of coronary heart disease. However, the agency recognizes that it is impossible to adequately distinguish the effects of fiber, including soluble fiber, from those of other food components.

With respect to increasing fiber in the diet, Joanne Slavin, PhD, RD, of the University of Minnesota, gives this advice: "The current interest in dietary fiber has allowed recommendations for fiber supplementation to outdistance the scientific research base. Until we have a better understanding of how fiber works its magic, we should recommend to American consumers only a gradual increase in dietary fiber from a variety of sources."

Precautions

The American Dietetic Association's position paper on vegetarian diets states, "Because vegan diets tend to be high in bulk, care should be taken to ensure that caloric intakes are sufficient to meet energy needs, particularly in infancy and during weaning." Dwyer and Suzanne Havala, also a registered dietitian, updated the paper in the 1993 issue of the association's journal.

It's generally agreed that to avoid intestinal discomfort from increased bulk, a person shouldn't switch to foods with large amounts of fiber all at once. A sensible approach is to slowly increase consumption of grains, legumes, seeds, and nuts. "Some may choose to eliminate red meat but continue to eat fish and poultry occasionally, and such a diet is also to be encouraged," Jack Zeev Yetiv, MD, PhD, in his book *Popular Nutritional Practices: A Scientific Appraisal*.

As with any diet, it's important for the vegetarian diet to include many different foods, since no one food contains all the nutrients required for good health. "The wider the variety, the greater the chance of getting the nutrients you need," says FDA's Vanderveen.

In its position paper on vegetarian diets, the American Dietetic Association states that, with a plant-based daily diet, eating a variety of foods and sufficient calories for energy needs will help ensure adequate intakes of calcium, iron and zinc. (See "Replacing Animal Sources of Nutrients.")

The mixture of proteins from grains, legumes, seeds, nuts, and vegetables provides a complement of amino acids so that deficits in one food are made up by another. Not all types of plant foods need to be eaten at the same meal, since the amino acids are combined in the body's protein pool.

"Soy protein," the paper states, "has been shown to be nutritionally equivalent in protein value to proteins of animal origin and, thus, can serve as the sole source of protein intake if desired."

The Institute of Food Technologists also recommends careful diet planning for vegetarians. This is especially important when the diet excludes dairy foods, to ensure adequate intake of calcium, iron, riboflavin, and vitamin D. For these vegetarians, the institute recommends calcium supplements during pregnancy, when breast-feeding, and for infants and children.

The institute and the American Dietetic Association say a vitamin D supplement may be needed if sunlight exposure is limited. (Sunlight activates a substance in the skin and converts it into vitamin D.)

They also point out that vegan diets should include a reliable source of vitamin B_{12} (see "Replacing Animal Sources of Nutrients"), because this nutrient occurs only in animal foods. Vitamin B_{12} deficiency can result in irreversible nerve deterioration.

The need for vitamin B_{12} increases during pregnancy, breast-feeding, and periods of growth, Dwyer says. In a recent issue of *Annual Review of Public Health*, she writes that elderly people also should be especially cautious about adopting vegetarian diets because their bodies may absorb vitamin B_{12} poorly.

Unless advised otherwise by a doctor, those taking dietary supplements should limit the dose to 100 percent of the U.S. Recommended Daily Allowances.

With the array of fruits, vegetables, grains, and spices available in US grocery stores and the availability of vegetarian cookbooks, it's easy to devise tasty vegetarian dishes that even non-vegetarians can enjoy.

However, the key to any healthful diet—vegetarian or non-vegetarian—is adherence to sound nutrition principles.

Replacing Animal Sources of Nutrients

Vegetarians who eat no animal products need to be more aware of nutrient sources. Nutrients most likely to be lacking and some non-animal sources are:

- vitamin B_{12}—fortified soy beverages and cereals

- vitamin D—fortified soy beverages and sunshine

- calcium—tofu processed with calcium, broccoli, seeds, nuts, kale, bok choy, legumes (peas and beans), greens, lime-processed tortillas, and soy beverages, grain products, and orange juice enriched with calcium

- iron—legumes, tofu, green leafy vegetables, dried fruit, whole grains, and iron-fortified cereals and breads, especially whole-wheat. (Absorption is improved by vitamin C, found in citrus fruits and juices, tomatoes, strawberries, broccoli, peppers, dark-green leafy vegetables, and potatoes with skins.)

- zinc—whole grains (especially the germ and bran), whole-wheat bread, legumes, nuts, and tofu

- protein—tofu and other soy-based products, legumes, seeds, nuts, grains, and vegetables

American Dietetic Association Recommendations

For people who follow vegetarian diets, the American Dietetic Association has these recommendations:

- Consult a registered dietitian or other qualified nutrition professional, especially during periods of growth, breast-feeding, pregnancy, or recovery from illness.

- Minimize intake of less nutritious foods such as sweets and fatty foods.

- Choose whole or unrefined grain products instead of refined products.

- Choose a variety of nuts, seeds, legumes, fruits, and vegetables, including good sources of vitamin C to improve iron absorption.

- Choose low-fat or nonfat varieties of dairy products, if they are included in the diet.

- Avoid excessive cholesterol intake by limiting eggs, if they are included in the diet, to three or four egg yolks per week.

- For infants, children, and teenagers, ensure adequate intakes of calories, vitamin D, calcium, iron, and zinc. (Intakes of vitamin D, calcium, iron, and zinc are usually adequate when a variety of foods and sufficient calories are consumed.)

- If exclusively breast-feeding premature infants or babies beyond 4 to 6 months of age, give vitamin D and iron supplements to the child from birth or at least by 4 to 6 months, as your doctor suggests.

- Usually, take iron and folate (folic acid) supplements during pregnancy.

In addition, for vegans:

- Use properly fortified food sources of vitamin B_{12}, such as fortified soy beverages or cereals, or take a supplement.

- If sunlight is inadequate, take a vitamin D supplement during pregnancy or while breast-feeding.

Vegetarian Varieties

The American Dietetic Association describes three types of vegetarians. They are listed here by the extent to which the diet includes animal foods:

- lacto-ovo-vegetarian—dairy foods and eggs
- lacto-vegetarian—dairy foods, but no eggs
- vegan—no animal foods of any type

Chapter 2

Vegetarian Diets: The Pluses and the Pitfalls

People are attracted to vegetarian diets. It's no wonder. Health experts for years have been telling us to eat more plant foods and less fat, especially saturated fat, which is found in larger amounts in animal foods than plant foods.

C. Everett Koop, MD, former surgeon general of the Public Health Service, in his 1988 Report on Nutrition and Health, expressed "major concern... [about Americans'] disproportionate consumption of foods high in fats, often at the expense of foods high in complex carbohydrates and fiber—such as vegetables, fruits, and whole-grain products—that may be more conducive to health."

And, while guidelines from the U.S. departments of Agriculture and Health and Human Services advise 2 to 3 daily servings of milk and the same of foods such as dried peas and beans, eggs, meat, poultry and fish, they recommend 3 to 5 servings of vegetables, 2 to 4 of fruits, and 6 to 11 servings of bread, cereal, rice, and pasta—in other words, 11 to 20 plant foods, but only 4 to 6 animal foods.

It's wise to take precautions, however, when adopting diets that entirely exclude animal flesh or dairy products.

"The more you restrict your diet, the more difficult it is to get all the nutrients you need," says Marilyn Stephenson, RD, of the Food and Drug Administration's (FDA) Center for Food Safety and Applied

Farley, Dixie, *FDA Consumer*, May 1994, FDA (Food and Drug Administration) Pub. No. 93-2258, http.//www.pueblo.gsa gov/cic text/food/veg-diet/veg-diet.txt, updated in April, 2001 by Dr. David A. Cooke, MD, Diplomate, American Board of Internal Medicine.

Nutrition. "To be healthful, vegetarian diets require very careful, proper planning. Nutrition counseling can help you get started on a diet that is nutritionally adequate." Certain people, such as Seventh-day Adventists, choose a vegetarian diet because of religious beliefs. Others give up meat because they feel that eating animals is unkind. Some people believe it's a better use of the Earth's resources to eat low on the food chain; the North American Vegetarian Society notes that 1.3 billion people could be fed with the grain and soybeans eaten by US livestock. On the practical side, many people eat plant foods because animal foods are more expensive. "I'm a vegetarian because I just plain enjoy the taste of vegetables and pasta," says Judy Folkenberg of Bethesda, MD. Reared on a vegetarian diet that included eggs and dairy products, Folkenberg added fish to her diet five years ago. "I love crab cakes and shrimp," she says.

Just as vegetarians differ in their motivation, their diets differ as well. In light of these variations, it's not surprising that the exact number of vegetarians is unknown. In a National Restaurant Association Gallup Survey in June 1991, 5 percent of respondents said they were vegetarians, yet 2 percent said they never ate milk or cheese products, 3 percent never ate red meat, and 10 percent never ate eggs.

Risks

Vegetarians who abstain from dairy products or animal flesh face the greatest nutritional risks because some nutrients naturally occur mainly or almost exclusively in animal foods.

Vegans, who eat no animal foods (and, rarely, vegetarians who eat no animal flesh but do eat eggs or dairy products), risk vitamin B_{12} deficiency, which can result in irreversible nerve deterioration. The need for vitamin B_{12} increases during pregnancy, breast-feeding, and periods of growth, according to Johanna Dwyer, DSc, RD, of Tufts University Medical School and the New England Medical Center Hospital, Boston. Writing in the *American Journal of Clinical Nutrition*, Dwyer concluded that elderly people also should be especially cautious about adopting vegetarian diets because their bodies may absorb vitamin B_{12} poorly.

Ovo-vegetarians, who eat eggs but no dairy foods or animal flesh, and vegans may have inadequate vitamin D and calcium. Inadequate vitamin D may cause rickets in children, while inadequate calcium can contribute to risk of osteoporosis in later years. These vegetarians are susceptible to iron deficiency anemia because they are not only missing the more readily absorbed iron from animal flesh, they are also likely to be eating many foods with constituents that inhibit iron absorption—soy protein, bran, and fiber, for instance.

Vegans must guard against inadequate calorie intake, which during pregnancy can lead to low birth weight, and against protein deficiency, which in children can impair growth and in adults can cause loss of hair and muscle mass and abnormal accumulation of fluid. According to the Institute of Food Technologists and the American Dietetic Association, if appropriately planned, vegan diets can provide adequate nutrition even for children.

Some experts disagree. Gretchen Hill, PhD, associate professor of food science and human nutrition at the University of Missouri, Columbia, believes it's unhealthy for children to eat no red meat.

"My bet is those kids will have health problems when they reach 40, 50 or 60 years of age," she says, "mostly because of imbalances with micronutrients [nutrients required only in small amounts], particularly iron, zinc and copper." While meat is well-known as an important source of iron, Hill says it may be even more valuable for copper and zinc. Copper not only helps build the body's immunity, it builds red blood cells and strengthens blood vessels. "A lot of Americans are marginal in this micronutrient," she says, "and, as a result, are more susceptible to diseases. Children can't meet their zinc needs without eating meat."

Also, vegetarian women of childbearing age have an increased chance of menstrual irregularities, Ann Pedersen and others reported in the *American Journal of Clinical Nutrition*. Nine of the study's 34 vegetarians (who ate eggs or dairy foods) missed menstrual periods, but only 2 of the 41 non-vegetarians did. The groups were indistinguishable when it came to height, weight and age at the beginning of menstruation.

Can Veggies Prevent Cancer?

The National Cancer Institute states in its booklet *Diet, Nutrition & Cancer Prevention: The Good News* that a third of cancer deaths may be related to diet. The booklet's "Good News" is: Vegetables from the cabbage family (cruciferous vegetables) may reduce cancer risk, diets low in fat and high in fiber-rich foods may reduce the risk of cancers of the colon and rectum, and diets rich in foods containing vitamin A, vitamin C, and beta-carotene may reduce the risk of certain cancers.

Despite studies showing lower rates of cancers in people who consume diets high in fruits in vegetables, it has been very difficult to determine exactly what accounts for this benefit. It does not appear to be as simple as more vitamins or fiber. Studies which added specific vitamins or vitamin combinations to participants' diets have not shown reduced risks of cancer. Perhaps there are as yet unidentified substances present in these foods which are responsible for their benefits.

As for increasing fiber in the diet, Joanne Slavin, PhD, RD, of the University of Minnesota, gives this advice: "Animal studies show that soluble fibers are associated with the highest levels of cell proliferation, a precancerous event. The current interest in dietary fiber has allowed recommendations for fiber supplementation to outdistance the scientific research base. Until we have a better understanding of how fiber works its magic, we should recommend to American consumers only a gradual increase in dietary fiber from a variety of sources."

Unfortunately, despite ten years and multiple research trials, the effect of fiber on cancer has not been settled. Several studies looking specifically at the effect of increasing dietary fiber on colon cancer have shown no real benefit of the extra fiber. However, it is possible that these studies did not last long enough, or that a high-fiber diet may need to be followed for decades in order to help. Therefore, the jury is still out on this question.

FDA acknowledges that high intakes of fruits and vegetables rich in beta-carotene or in vitamin C have been associated with reduced cancer risk. But the agency believes the data are not sufficiently convincing that either nutrient by itself is responsible for this association.

Pointing out that plant foods' low fat content also confers health benefits, FDA states in its proposed rule that diets low in fat give protection against coronary heart disease and that it has tentatively determined, "Diets low in fat are associated with the reduced risk of cancer."

FDA notes that diets high in saturated fats and cholesterol increase levels of both total and LDL (low density lipoprotein) cholesterol, and thus the risk for coronary heart disease, and that high-fat foods contribute to obesity, a further risk factor for heart disease. (The National Cholesterol Education Program recommends a diet with no more than 30 percent fat, of which no more than 10 percent comes from saturated fat.)

For those reasons, the agency would allow some foods to be labeled with health claims relating diets low in saturated fat and cholesterol to decreased risk of coronary heart disease and relating diets low in fat to reduced risk of breast, colon and prostate cancer. "Examples of foods qualifying for a health claim include most fruits and vegetables; skim milk products; sherbets; most flours, grains, meals, and pastas (except for egg pastas); and many breakfast cereals," the proposed rule states.

Dwyer, in her article, summarizes these plant food benefits:

> "Data are strong that vegetarians are at lesser risk for obesity, atonic [reduced muscle tone] constipation, lung cancer, and alcoholism. Evidence is good that risks for hypertension, coronary artery disease, type II diabetes, and gallstones are lower. Data are only fair to poor that risks of breast cancer, diverticular disease of the colon, colonic cancer, calcium kidney stones, osteoporosis, dental erosion, and dental caries are lower among vegetarians."

Death rates for vegetarians are similar or lower than for non-vegetarians, Dwyer reports, but are influenced in Western countries by vegetarians' "adoption of many healthy lifestyle habits in addition to diet, such as not smoking, abstinence or moderation in the use of alcohol, being physically active, resting adequately, seeking ongoing health surveillance, and seeking guidance when health problems arise."

Slow Switching

It's generally agreed that to avoid intestinal discomfort from increased bulk, a person shouldn't switch to foods with large amounts of fiber all at once. A sensible approach to vegetarian diets is to first cut down on the fattiest meats, replacing them with cereals, fruits and vegetables, recommends Jack Zeev Yetiv, MD, PhD, in his book *Popular Nutritional Practices: A Scientific Appraisal.* "Some may choose to eliminate red meat but continue to eat fish and poultry occasionally, and such a diet is also to be encouraged."

Changing to the vegetarian kitchen slowly also may increase the chances of success.

"If you suddenly cut out all animal entrees from your diet, it's easy to get discouraged and think there's nothing to eat," says lifelong veggie-eater Folkenberg. "I build my meals around a starchy carbohydrate such as pasta or potatoes. Even when I occasionally cook seafood, I center on the carbohydrate, making that the larger portion. Shifting the emphasis from animal to plant foods is easier after you've found recipes you really enjoy." Because vegans and ovo-vegetarians face the greatest potential nutritional risk, the Institute of Food Technologists recommends careful diet planning to include enough calcium, riboflavin, iron, and vitamin D, perhaps with a vitamin D supplement if sunlight exposure is low. (Sunlight activates a substance in the skin and converts it into vitamin D.)

For these two vegetarian groups, the institute recommends calcium supplements during pregnancy, infancy, childhood, and breast-feeding. Vegans need to take a vitamin B_{12} supplement because that vitamin is found only in animal food sources. Unless advised otherwise by a doctor, those taking supplements should limit the dose to 100 percent of the National Academy of Sciences' Recommended Dietary Allowances.

Vegans, and especially children, also must be sure to consume adequate calories and protein. For other vegetarians, it is not difficult to get adequate protein, although care is needed in small children's diets. Nearly every animal food, including egg whites and milk, provides all eight of the essential amino acids in the balance needed by humans and therefore constitutes "complete" protein. Plant foods contain fewer of these amino acids than animal foods.

The American Dietetic Association's position paper on vegetarian diets states that a plant-based diet provides adequate amounts of amino acids when a varied diet is eaten on a daily basis. The mixture of proteins from grains, legumes, seeds, and vegetables provide a complement of amino acids so that deficits in one food are made up by another. Not all types of plant foods need to be eaten at the same meal, since the amino acids are combined in the body's protein pool.

Frances Lappe, in *Diet for a Small Planet*, writes that to gain the greatest use of all the amino acids, it's best to consume complementary proteins within three to four hours. High amounts of complete proteins can be gained by combining legumes with grains, seeds, or nuts.

Also available are various protein analogs. These substitute "meats"—usually made from soybeans—are formed to look like meat foods such as hot dogs, ground beef, or bacon. Many are fortified with vitamin B_{12}.

As with any diet, it's important for the vegetarian diet to include many different foods, since no one food contains all the nutrients required for good health. "The wider the variety, the greater the chance of getting the nutrients you need," says FDA's Stephenson.

The American Dietetic Association recommends:

- minimizing intake of less nutritious foods such as sweets and fatty foods

- choosing whole or unrefined grain products instead of refined products

- choosing a variety of nuts, seeds, legumes, fruits, and vegetables, including good sources of vitamin C to improve iron absorption

- choosing low-fat varieties of milk products, if they are included in the diet

- avoiding excessive cholesterol intake by limiting eggs to two or three yolks a week

- for vegans, using properly fortified food sources of vitamin B_{12}, such as fortified soy milks or cereals, or taking a supplement

- for infants, children and teenagers, ensuring adequate intakes of calories and iron and vitamin D, taking supplements if needed

- consulting a registered dietitian or other qualified nutrition professional, especially during periods of growth, breast-feeding, pregnancy, or recovery from illness

- if exclusively breast-feeding premature infants or babies beyond 4 to 6 months of age, giving vitamin D and iron supplements to the child from birth or at least by 4 to 6 months, as your doctor suggests

- usually, taking iron and folate (folic acid) supplements during pregnancy.

With the array of fruits, vegetables, grains, and herbs available in U.S. grocery stores and the availability of vegetarian cookbooks, it's easy to devise tasty vegetarian dishes.

People who like their entrees on the hoof also can benefit from adding more plant foods to their diets. You don't have to be a vegetarian to enjoy dishes from a vegetarian menu.

Vegetarian Varieties

The Institute of Food Technologists, in its journal, Food Technology, describes six types of vegetarians. They are listed here by degree of exclusion of animal foods and by the foods included in the diet:

- semi-vegetarian—dairy foods, eggs, chicken, and fish, but no other animal flesh

- pesco-vegetarian—dairy foods, eggs, and fish, but no other animal flesh
- lacto-ovo-vegetarian—dairy foods and eggs, but no animal flesh
- lacto-vegetarian—dairy foods, but no animal flesh or eggs
- ovo-vegetarian—eggs, but no dairy foods or animal flesh
- vegan—no animal foods of any type

Chapter 3

American Dietetic Association Statement on Vegetarian Diets

Scientific data suggest positive relationships between a vegetarian diet and reduced risk for several chronic degenerative diseases and conditions, including obesity, coronary artery disease, hypertension, diabetes mellitus, and some types of cancer. Vegetarian diets, like all diets, need to be planned appropriately to be nutritionally adequate.

It is the position of The American Dietetic Association (ADA) that appropriately planned vegetarian diets are healthful, are nutritionally adequate, and provide health benefits in the prevention and treatment of certain diseases.

Vegetarianism in Perspective

The eating patterns of vegetarians vary considerably. The lacto-ovo-vegetarian eating pattern is based on grains, vegetables, fruits, legumes, seeds, nuts, dairy products, and eggs, and excludes meat, fish, and fowl. The vegan, or total vegetarian, eating pattern is similar to the lacto-ovo-vegetarian pattern except for the additional exclusion of eggs, dairy, and other animal products. Even within these patterns, considerable variation may exist in the extent to which animal products are avoided. Therefore, individual assessment is required to accurately evaluate the nutritional quality of a vegetarian's dietary intake.

Studies indicate that vegetarians often have lower morbidity (1) and mortality (2) rates from several chronic degenerative diseases than do nonvegetarians. Although nondietary factors, including physical activity and abstinence from smoking and alcohol, may play a role, diet is clearly a contributing factor.

In addition to the health advantages, other considerations that may lead a person to adopt a vegetarian diet pattern include concern for the environment, ecology, and world hunger issues. Vegetarians also cite economic reasons, ethical considerations, and religious beliefs as their reasons for following this type of diet pattern. Consumer demand for vegetarian options has resulted in increasing numbers of food services that offer vegetarian options. Presently, most university food services offer vegetarian options.

Health Implications of Vegetarianism

Vegetarian diets low in fat or saturated fat have been used successfully as part of comprehensive health programs to reverse severe coronary artery disease. Vegetarian diets offer disease protection benefits because of their lower saturated fat, cholesterol, and animal protein content and often higher concentration of folate (which reduces serum homocysteine levels), antioxidants such as vitamins C and E, carotenoids, and phytochemicals. Not only is mortality from coronary artery disease lower in vegetarians than in nonvegetarians, but vegetarian diets have also been successful in arresting coronary artery disease. Total serum cholesterol and low-density lipoprotein cholesterol levels are usually lower in vegetarians, but high-density lipoprotein cholesterol and triglyceride levels vary depending on the type of vegetarian diet followed.

Vegetarians tend to have a lower incidence of hypertension than nonvegetarians. This effect appears to be independent of both body weight and sodium intake. Type 2 diabetes mellitus is much less likely to be a cause of death in vegetarians than nonvegetarians, perhaps because of their higher intake of complex carbohydrates and lower body mass index.

Incidence of lung and colorectal cancer is lower in vegetarians than in nonvegetarians. Reduced colorectal cancer risk is associated with increased consumption of fiber, vegetables, and fruit. The environment of the colon differs notably in vegetarians compared with nonvegetarians in ways that could favorably affect colon cancer risk. Lower breast cancer rates have not been observed in Western vegetarians, but cross-cultural data indicate that breast cancer rates are lower in populations that consume plant-based diets. The lower estrogen levels in vegetarian women may be protective.

A well-planned vegetarian diet may be useful in the prevention and treatment of renal disease. Studies using human being and animal models suggest that some plant proteins may increase survival rates and decrease proteinuria, glomerular filtration rate, renal blood flow, and histologic renal damage compared with a nonvegetarian diet.

Nutrition Considerations for Vegetarians

Plant sources of protein alone can provide adequate amounts of essential amino acids if a variety of plant foods are consumed and energy needs are met. Research suggests that complementary proteins do not need to be consumed at the same time and that consumption of various sources of amino acids over the course of the day should ensure adequate nitrogen retention and use in healthy persons. Although vegetarian diets are lower in total protein and a vegetarian's protein needs may be somewhat elevated because of the lower quality of some plant proteins, protein intake in both lacto-ovo-vegetarians and vegans appears to be adequate.

Plant foods contain only non-heme iron, which is more sensitive than heme iron to both inhibitors and enhancers of iron absorption. Although vegetarian diets are higher in total iron content than nonvegetarian diets, iron stores are lower in vegetarians because the iron from plant foods is more poorly absorbed. The clinical importance of this, if any, is unclear because iron deficiency anemia rates are similar in vegetarians and nonvegetarians. The higher vitamin C content of vegetarian diets may improve iron absorption.

Although plant foods can contain vitamin B_{12} on their surface from soil residues, this is not a reliable source of B_{12} for vegetarians. Much of the vitamin B_{12} present in spirulina, sea vegetables, tempeh, and miso has been shown to be inactive B_{12} analog rather than the active vitamin. Although dairy products and eggs contain vitamin B_{12}, research suggests that lacto-ovo-vegetarians have low blood levels of vitamin B_{12}. Supplementation or use of fortified foods is advised for vegetarians who avoid or limit animal foods.

Because vitamin B_{12} requirements are small, and it is both stored and recycled in the body, symptoms of deficiency may be delayed for years. Absorption of vitamin B_{12} becomes less efficient as the body ages, so supplements may be advised for all older vegetarians.

Lacto-ovo-vegetarians have calcium intakes that are comparable to or higher than those of nonvegetarians. Calcium intakes of vegans, however, are generally lower than those of both lacto-ovo-vegetarians and omnivores. It should be noted that vegans may have lower calcium needs than nonvegetarians because diets that are low in total protein and more alkaline have been shown to have a calcium-sparing effect. Furthermore, when a person's diet is low in both protein and sodium and regular weight-bearing physical activity is engaged in, his or her calcium requirements may be lower than those of a sedentary person who eats a standard Western diet. These factors, and genetic influences, may help explain variations in bone health that are independent of calcium intake.

Because calcium requirements of vegans have not been established and inadequate calcium intakes are linked to risk for osteoporosis in all women, vegans should meet the calcium requirements established for their age group by the Institute of Medicine. Calcium is well absorbed from many plant foods, and vegan diets can provide adequate calcium if the diet regularly includes foods rich in calcium. In addition, many new vegetarian foods are calcium-fortified. Dietary supplements are advised for vegans only if they do not meet calcium requirements from food.

Vitamin D is poorly supplied in all diets unless vitamin D-fortified foods are consumed. Vegan diets may lack this nutrient because fortified cow's milk is its most common dietary source. However, vegan foods supplemented with vitamin D, such as soy milk, and some cereals, are available. Furthermore, findings indicate that sunlight exposure is a major factor affecting vitamin D status and that dietary intake is important only when sun exposure is inadequate. Sun exposure to hands, arms, and face for 5 to 15 minutes per day is believed to be adequate to provide sufficient amounts of vitamin D. People with dark skin or those who live at northern latitudes or in cloudy or smoggy areas may need increased exposure. Use of sun screen interferes with vitamin D synthesis. If sun exposure is inadequate, vitamin D supplements are recommended for vegans. This is especially true for older persons who synthesize vitamin D less efficiently and who may have less sun exposure.

Studies show zinc intake to be lower or comparable in vegetarians compared with nonvegetarians. Most studies show that zinc levels in hair, serum, and saliva are in the normal range in vegetarians. Compensatory mechanisms may help vegetarians adapt to diets that may be low in zinc. However, because of the low bioavailability of zinc from plant foods and because the effects of marginal zinc status are poorly understood, vegetarians should strive to meet or exceed the Recommended Dietary Allowances for zinc.

Diets that do not include fish or eggs lack the long-chain n-3 fatty acid docosahexanoic acid (DHA). Vegetarians may have lower blood lipid levels of this fatty acid, although not all studies are in agreement with this finding. The essential fatty acid linolenic acid can be converted to DHA, although conversion rates appear to be inefficient and high intakes of linoleic acid interfere with conversion. The implications of low levels of DHA is not clear. However, it is recommended that vegetarians include good sources of linolenic acid in their diet.

Vegetarianism throughout the Life Cycle

Well-planned vegan and lacto-ovo-vegetarian diets are appropriate for all stages of the life cycle, including during pregnancy and lactation. Appropriately planned vegan and lacto-ovo-vegetarian diets satisfy nutrient needs of infants, children, and adolescents and promote normal growth. Dietary deficiencies are most likely to be observed in populations with very restrictive diets. All vegan children should have a reliable source of vitamin B_{12} and, if sun exposure is limited, vitamin D supplements or fortified foods should be used. Foods rich in calcium, iron, and zinc should be emphasized. Frequent meals and snacks and the use of some refined foods and foods higher in fat can help vegetarian children meet energy needs. Guidelines for iron and vitamin D supplements and for the introduction of solid foods are the same for vegetarian and nonvegetarian infants. When it is time for protein-rich foods to be introduced, vegetarian infants can have pureed tofu, cottage cheese, and legumes (pureed and strained). Breast-fed vegan infants should receive a source of vitamin B_{12} if the mother's diet is not supplemented and a source of vitamin D if sun exposure is inadequate.

Vegetarian diets are somewhat more common among adolescents with eating disorders than in the general adolescent population; therefore, dietetics professionals should be aware of young clients who greatly limit food choices and who exhibit symptoms of eating disorders. However, recent data suggest that adopting a vegetarian diet does not lead to eating disorders. With guidance in meal planning, vegetarian diets are appropriate and healthful choices for adolescents.

Vegetarian diets can also meet the needs of competitive athletes. Protein needs may be elevated because training increases amino acid

Table 3.1. Food sources of nutrients that are often of concern for vegetarians. (Continued on next page.)

Calcium,	Milligrams per serving
Legumes (1 c cooked)	
Chickpeas	78
Great northern beans	121
Navy beans	128
Pinto beans	82
Black beans	103
Vegetarian baked beans	128
Soy foods	
Soybeans, 1 c cooked	175
Tofu, ½ c	120–350
Tempeh ½ c	77
Textured vegetable protein, ½ c	85
Soymilk, 1 c	84
Soy milk, fortified, 1 c	250–300
Soynuts, ½ c	252
Nuts and seeds (2 Tbsp)	
Almonds	50
Almond butter	86
Vegetables (½ c cooked)	
Bok choy	79
Broccoli	89
Collard greens	178
Kale	90
Mustard greens	75
Turnip greens	125
Fruits	
Dried figs, 5	258
Calcium-fortified orange juice, 1 c	300
Other Foods	
Blackstrap molasses, 1 Tbsp	187
Cow's milk, 1 c	300
Yogurt, 1 c	275–400

metabolism, but vegetarian diets that meet energy needs and include good sources of protein (e.g., soy foods, legumes) can provide adequate protein without use of special foods or supplements. For adolescent athletes, special attention should be given to meeting energy, protein, and iron needs. Amenorrhea may be more common among vegetarian than nonvegetarian athletes, although not all research supports this finding. Efforts to maintain normal menstrual cycles might include

Table 3.1. Food sources of nutrients that are often of concern for vegetarians. (Continued on next page.)

Iron	Milligrams per serving
Breads, cereals, and grains	
Whole wheat bread, 1 slice	0.9
White bread, 1 slice	0.7
Bran flakes, 1 c	11.0
Cream of wheat, ½ c cooked	5.5
Oatmeal, instant, 1 packet	6.3
Wheat germ, 2 Tbsp	1.2
Vegetables (½ c cooked)	
Beet greens	1.4
Sea vegetables	18.1–42.0
Swiss chard	1.9
Tomato juice 1 c	1.3
Turnip greens	1.5
Legumes (½ c cooked)	
Baked beans, vegetarian	0.74
Black beans	1.8
Garbanzo beans	3.4
Kidney beans	1.5
Lentils	3.2
Lima beans	2.2
Navy beans	2.5
Soy foods (1/2 c cooked)	
Soybeans	4.4
Tempeh	1.8
Tofu	6.6
Soy milk, 1 c	1.8
Nuts/seeds (2 Tbsp)	
Cashews	1.0
Pumpkin seeds	2.5
Tahini	1.2
Sunflower seeds	1.2
Other foods	
Blackstrap molasses, 1 Tbsp	3.3

increasing energy and fat intake, reducing fiber, and reducing strenuous training.

Lacto-ovo-vegetarian and vegan diets can meet the nutrient and energy needs of pregnant women. Birth weights of infants born to well nourished vegetarian women have been shown to be similar to birthweight norms and to birth weights of infants of nonvegetarians. Diets of pregnant and lactating vegans should be supplemented with

Table 3.1. Food sources of nutrients that are often of concern for vegetarians. (Continued from previous page.)

Vitamin D	Micrograms per serving
Fortified, ready-to-eat cereals, 3/4 c	1.0–2.5
Fortified soy milk or other nondairy milk 1 c	1.0–2.5

Vitamin B$_{12}$	Micrograms per serving
Ready-to-eat breakfast cereals, 3/4 c	1.5–6.0
Meat analogs (1 burger or 1 serving according to package)	2.0–7.0
Fortified soy milk or other nondairy milks, 8 oz	0.2–5.0
Nutritional yeast (Red Star Vegetarian Support Formula, formerly T6635a), 1 Tbsp	4.0

Linolenic acid	Grams per serving
Flax seed, 2 Tbsp	4.3
Walnuts, 1 oz	1.9
Walnut oil, 1 Tbsp	1.5
Canola oil, 1 Tbsp	1.6
Linseed oil, 1 Tbsp	7.6
Soybean oil, 1 Tbsp	0.9
Soybeans, ½ c cooked	0.5
Tofu, ½ c	0.4

Zinc	Milligrams per serving
Breads, grains, and cereals	
Bran flakes, 1 c	5.0
Wheat germ, 2 Tbsp	2.3
Legumes (½ c cooked)	
Adzuki beans	2.0
Chickpeas	1.3
Lima beans	1.0
Lentils	1.2
Soy foods (½ c cooked)	
Soybeans	1.0
Tempeh	1.5
Tofu	1.0
Textured vegetable protein	1.4
Vegetables (½ c cooked)	
Corn	0.9
Peas	1.0
Sea vegetables	1.1–2.0
Dairy foods	
Cow's milk, 1 c	1.0
Cheddar cheese, 1 oz	0.9
Yogurt, 1 c	1.8

2.0 micrograms and 2.6 micrograms, respectively, of vitamin B_{12} daily and, if sun exposure is limited, with 10 micrograms vitamin D daily. Supplements of folate are advised for all pregnant women, although vegetarian women typically have higher intakes than nonvegetarians.

Meal Planning for Vegetarian Diets

A variety of menu-planning approaches can provide vegetarians with adequate nutrition. In addition, the following guidelines can help vegetarians plan healthful diets.

- Choose a variety of foods, including whole grains, vegetables, fruits, legumes, nuts, seeds and, if desired, dairy products and eggs.

- Choose whole, unrefined foods often and minimize intake of highly sweetened, fatty, and heavily refined foods.

- Choose a variety of fruits and vegetables.

- If animal foods such as dairy products and eggs are used, choose lower-fat versions of these foods. Cheeses and other high-fat dairy foods and eggs should be limited in the diet because of their saturated fat content and because their frequent use displaces plant foods in some vegetarian diets.

- Vegans should include a regular source of vitamin B_{12} in their diets along with a source of vitamin D if sun exposure is limited.

- Solely breast-fed infants should have supplements of iron after the age of 4 to 6 months and, if sun exposure is limited, a source of vitamin D. Breast-fed vegan infants should have vitamin B_{12} supplements if the mother's diet is not fortified.

- Do not restrict dietary fat in children younger than 2 years. For older children, include some foods higher in unsaturated fats (e.g., nuts, seeds, nut and seed butters, avocado, and vegetable oils) to help meet nutrient and energy needs.

Chapter 4

Frequently Asked Questions about Going Vegetarian

Why Become Vegetarian?

There are as many reasons for becoming vegetarian as there are vegetarians; it's a highly personal and individual decision to make. But in a survey conducted on behalf of The Vegetarian Society the majority of people said that they gave up meat and fish because they did not morally approve of killing animals, or because they objected to the ways in which animals are kept, treated, and killed for food.

With the growing awareness of the importance of healthy food, many people are also becoming vegetarian because it matches the kind of low fat, high fiber diet recommended by dietitians and doctors. Concern about the environment is another factor as people become more aware of the effect raising animals for their meat is having on the environment. Or you may be concerned about wasting world food resources by using land to raise animals for meat instead of growing crops that can feed more people directly.

What Is a Vegetarian?

A vegetarian is someone who does not eat meat, fish, poultry or any slaughterhouse by-product such as gelatin. Vegetarians live on a

Excerpted from "Information Sheet: Going Vegetarian," Vegetarian Society UK, http://www.vegsoc.org/info/goingveg.html, copyright 2001, reprinted with permission. Some words have been changed to conform to American spelling conventions. Material may be viewed in its original format on the Vegetarian Society of the UK website: http://www.vegsoc.org.

diet of grains, pulses, nuts, seeds, vegetables, and fruit, with or without free-range eggs, milk and milk products. Vegetarians not eating anything containing dairy products or eggs are called vegans.

Isn't It Hard Being a Vegetarian?

Not at all. Vegetarian food is widely available in shops and restaurants, it's easy to cook and you're probably already eating many vegetarian meals without even putting your mind to it. It's no sacrifice to give up meat when there are so many delicious recipes and so many tasty foods to experiment with. Plus you'll have the satisfaction of knowing that you're eating a healthy diet that doesn't involve the killing of animals or the abuse of the world's resources.

Where Will I Buy All This New Food for My Vegetarian Diet?

Exactly the same place you used to buy food—in markets, supermarkets, corner shops. Vegetarian food, both in its "raw state" as grains, pulses and vegetables, and as pre-cooked meals, is widely available nowadays.

What Do I Say to My Family and Friends?

Don't get caught up in arguments, just gather all the information about vegetarianism so you can calmly explain your decision. Then try introducing them to some of the delicious meat-free meals you're enjoying and see if you can win them over by setting a good example.

Aren't Vegetarians Being Hypocritical because They Still Wear Leather or Exploit Cows for Their Milk?

There is a very valid argument for becoming vegan—for giving up all dairy products, eggs, and any other animal by-products. But realistically speaking, few people can go from being a meat eater to a vegan overnight. Vegetarianism is a very important halfway house. And even if you never go on to being vegan, you've already made an impact and saved the lives of many animals simply by giving up meat. Far from being hypocritical, you're making an effort to change the way you live for the better. How far you go with vegetarianism is up to you, but however small the step you take, it's not wasted. And don't feel that you have to become a perfect vegetarian overnight. If you forget to check the ingredients list and realize that you've just eaten something containing gelatin, don't feel that you've failed. Take it one step at a time and enjoy learning more about the vegetarian lifestyle. The important thing is that you're doing something!

Aren't All Vegetarians Pale and Unhealthy?

This old stereotype has taken a long time to die out. In fact, people who follow a varied, well-balanced vegetarian diet are in line with the current nutritional recommendations for a low fat, high fiber diet. That's why medical studies are proving that vegetarians are less likely to suffer from such illnesses as heart disease, cancer, diet-related diabetes, obesity and high blood pressure. So, if for no other reason, go vegetarian as a favor to your body!

What Happens If I Have to Try to Get a Vegetarian Meal in a Restaurant?

There are very few restaurants now that don't offer at least one vegetarian option. Vegetarianism is such a growing movement, restaurateurs can't afford to ignore it. In the unlikely event that a restaurant doesn't have anything for you, don't be put off, especially with the offer of a fish or chicken dish which are "practically vegetarian"— they're not!! Simply ask politely if they can make something specially for you. If they can't be bothered, why give them the benefit of your business when there are plenty of other places all too willing to help.

Isn't Vegetarian Food Boring?

Vegetarians don't eke out a miserable existence on a few limp lettuce leaves and some boiled rice. And a proper vegetarian meal doesn't mean taking the meat away and leaving the side vegetables. With the hundreds of different vegetables, grains, fruit, pulses and nuts, and seeds that exist, you could live to be 100 without exhausting all the possibilities for imaginative, nutritious meals! And as vegetarian food tends to be cheaper than a meat-based diet, you can afford to treat yourself to more expensive delicacies such as asparagus.

Won't It Take a Long Time to Prepare the Food?

Just because there are so many wonderful vegetarian dishes to try, doesn't mean you have to become an expert cook and spend hours in the kitchen. You can easily cook good, wholesome vegetarian meals in under half an hour, and don't forget that most manufacturers now also offer a wide range of ready-made vegetarian dishes.

But How Will I Get Enough of the Vital Nutrients Such as Iron and Protein?

A well-balanced vegetarian diet provides all the nutrients you need for good health. In the case of protein, it's not only found in meat. It's also present in adequate quantities in dairy products, eggs and nuts, as well as in combinations of foods such as pulses and grains. In fact it would be very difficult to design a vegetarian diet that doesn't include enough protein.

Useful Tips on Going and Staying Vegetarian

- Treat yourself to a vegetarian cookbook for inspiration and advice. There are a wide range covering recipes for beginners, advanced cooks, slimmers, diabetics. Most also give dietary advice.

- Find out more about the subject.

- Start gradually. Adapt familiar meals such as lasagna and shepherd's pie by using textured vegetable protein (TVP). Although fully vegetarian, it has the look, taste, and texture of mince or meat chunks, according to which variety you buy. It is available from health food stores. If you don't buy the flavored variety, be aware that you need to add seasoning of some kind or it will remain bland and uninteresting.

- Buy vegetarian cheese. It's not an unfamiliar product as cheese is probably already on your shopping list. But whereas some cheeses are made with an ingredient from the stomachs of slaughtered calves, vegetarian cheese uses vegetable-derived rennet. Every supermarket now stocks at least one kind of vegetarian cheese, and many of the more unusual varieties such as Stilton and Brie are also now available in vegetarian versions.

- Buy free-range eggs. Again, eggs are another staple ingredient in many people's diets so it won't take much effort to pick up the free-range variety instead of the battery produced.

- Read the labels. Although you may get the odd shock when you realize that a food product that seems vegetarian in fact contains something such as gelatin or animal fat, there are plenty of others you'd be surprised and pleased to find out are suitable for you.

- Legumes. Forget the dried variety if you find them difficult to prepare—go for the canned variety of kidney beans, chick peas, etc.

- Adapt familiar dishes. If you're the only vegetarian in your family and it's too difficult or expensive to cook totally separate meals, adapt a meat dish. A casserole, for instance, can be made with beans and vegetables in one pan. Then the meat can be cooked separately and given just to the meat eaters. Or use TVP and see if anyone notices the difference.

- Don't be put off by unfamiliar foods. Tofu, for instance, is a boon to vegetarians, especially new ones. This by-product of soya beans is incredibly versatile and easy to use. And if you use the plain variety, don't think that you've done something wrong when it appears tasteless in the finished recipe—it's meant to absorb the flavor of other ingredients. Or you can buy the smoked or marinated versions.

- Explore health food stores. They'll have vegetarian products you haven't seen before, and the assistants will be able to answer your questions about products suitable for your new lifestyle.

Chapter 5

Making the Change to a Vegetarian Diet

If your usual eating pattern has often included animal foods, and you are ready to move toward vegetarian alternatives, the suggestions below may help ease the transition.

There are many different ways to plan a healthy vegetarian diet. The most important rule is to include a wide variety of whole grains, legumes, vegetables and fruits in different meals. Nuts and seeds may be included, too. Lacto-ovo vegetarians also choose to include eggs and low-fat dairy products in their diet. Vegans omit all products derived from animals.

Vegetarian diets may include familiar foods such as cereals, bean soup, potatoes, peanut butter sandwiches, and spaghetti—as well as the less familiar—such as bulgur, adzuki beans, TVP (textured vegetable protein, derived from soy), and soymilk. Experimentation with new foods can provide nutritional benefits as well as enhance your eating enjoyment.

Foods to Ease the Transition

Some foods made from soybeans, wheat protein and other vegetable sources can ease the change to a vegetarian diet because they mimic

Reeser, Cyndi, MPH, RD, LD and Lisa Ford, RD, "Vegetarian Nutrition Dietetic Practice Group, Making the Change to a Vegetarian Diet," http://www.andrews.edu/NUFS/Change%20to%20a%20vegn%20diet.htm, 2001. This fact sheet is reprinted with permission from *Vegetarian Nutrition Update*, the official newsletter of the Vegetarian Nutrition Dietetic Practice Group of the American Dietetic Association. © 1995.

meat and dairy products in the diet. Meat analogs are made to look and taste like different types of meat. Some mimic sausages, hot dogs, hamburgers, or chicken patties. Soymilk, soy yogurt, and soy cheese are available for people who don't use dairy products or who wish to add some variety to their diet. Tofu can be pureed and seasoned to make a filling for lasagna or stuffed shells. Textured vegetable protein (TVP) has the look and texture of ground beef and can be used to make sloppy joes, spaghetti sauce, or tacos.

A Gradual Approach Is Easiest

Some people decide to trade in their usual diet for a vegetarian plan all at once. Others prefer a more gradual approach. This allows a comfortable transition and allows time to find plenty of new ways to meet nutrient needs. The goal is to make changes that you can live with and which are nutritionally sound. The following plan outlines an easy transition to a vegetarian diet.

1. Take stock of your current diet.
   - Make a list of the foods and menus that you normally eat.
   - Identify the foods and meals that are vegetarian, and build from these as a foundation.
   - Some examples include spaghetti with marinara sauce, bean burritos, or cheese sandwiches.
   - Plan to eat a vegetarian meal several times a week using foods you know and enjoy.

2. Add more vegetarian meals by revising favorite recipes that are meat-based.
   - For example, chili can be made using beans, TVP or tofu in place of ground beef.
   - The beef in spaghetti sauce can be replaced with TVP or sauteed vegetables.

3. Expand your options by finding new recipes in cookbooks and trying different products from the store.
   - Many vegetarian meals can be made without a recipe or without much time invested in the kitchen. Try seasoned rice mixes, spaghetti with sauce from a jar, vegetable chow mein, burritos with canned refried beans, vegetarian

baked beans with rice. Try various brands of veggie
burgers and meatless hot dogs.

4. Make a list of vegetarian meals that you can eat away from
home.

- Inventory your options at the cafeteria, nearby restaurants, carry-outs, and convenience stores. Look for vegetarian soups, salad bars, pasta salads, pasta primavera,
vegetable pizza, and baked potatoes. Chinese, Thai, Indian, and Middle Eastern restaurants have numerous vegetarian entrees. Choices from a convenience store may
include a bean burrito or a microwavable frozen entree.

- Plan vegetarian meals to go, using leftovers from a home-
cooked or restaurant meal. Other vegetarian brown bag
ideas include bean or vegetable soup in a thermos, peanut
butter and banana sandwiches, bean dip with pita bread
or crackers, or cheese with bread and fruit.

5. Eliminate meat at breakfast.

- Try some of the meat analogs that look and taste like bacon or sausage, to make the change easier.

6. Take stock of your menu once again. Do your meals include the
following? If not, make a list of ways to add more of these foods:

- A variety of grains, legumes and soy products, vegetables,
and fruits? (Aim for 2 to 3 servings of legumes and other
meat alternates daily.)

- Some fresh fruits and vegetables daily? (Aim for 5 to 9
servings/day.)

- Primarily whole grains with little processing? (Aim for 6
to 11 servings/day.)

- Low-fat dairy products, if following a lacto-ovo vegetarian
or lacto vegetarian plan? (Aim for 2 to 3 servings/day.)

If You Don't Eat Dairy Foods

Calcium is found in a wide variety of plant foods. It is easy to obtain adequate calcium without including dairy foods. If you choose to
eliminate dairy from your diet, it is a good idea to first identify other
foods that provide calcium and to start including them in meals. Some

good choices are calcium-fortified soymilk, calcium-fortified cereals, calcium-fortified juice, tofu, tempeh, TVP, leafy green vegetables, broccoli, Chinese cabbage (bok choy), vegetarian baked beans, almond butter, figs, and tahini.

If You Don't Eat Eggs

A variety of foods can replace eggs in a recipe, depending on the dish. Applesauce, mashed bananas, prune puree, soymilk, yogurt, juice, or water can replace the moisture eggs provide in baked goods, but not necessarily their binding qualities. Powdered egg replacer (primarily potato starch) works in muffins and other baked goods. Some commercial fat replacer products also successfully replace eggs. Rolled oats, pureed beans, tofu, or ground flaxseed all work well as binding agents in vegetable patties. Adapting recipes to egg-free versions requires some experimentation. Vegan cookbooks provide recipes developed without eggs.

Meal Planning Made Easy

Most people think of meat first when it comes to menu planning. Instead of thinking about a "meat replacement" think in terms of a wide variety of entrees. The center of a meal can be a favorite soup, sandwich or casserole. Grains should play the biggest role in the diet so consider grain-based entrees as often as possible, such as soup with macaroni, barley or rice, a noodle casserole, or herb-flavored rice or pasta. Then add vegetables, fruits, beans (and nuts or seeds if desired) to complete the meal.

Some Tips for Introducing Variety into Vegetarian Meals

- Aim for variety, even when you serve favorite entrees over and over again, by serving different side dishes, snacks, and desserts.

- Be creative in planning meals. Increase intake of beans and vegetables by eating these foods at lunch time rather than just for dinner. Make it a goal to serve a vegetable every day for lunch and two for dinner.

- If beans are a new addition to your menus, introduce them gradually by having a few spoonfuls on a salad, a small cup of bean soup at lunch, or a bean casserole at dinner. Puree beans with herbs, lemon juice or other seasonings to create a sandwich spread or dip. A mixture of lentils or beans with rice, onions, parsley and vegetables makes a colorful main dish salad, with the dressing of your choice.

- Plan a meal around a vegetable. A baked potato can be a hearty entree; serve it with baked beans, a sauce of stewed tomatoes or a few tablespoons of salsa. Or make a simple meal of sauteed vegetables and pasta.

- Try new foods often. Experiment with a variety of grains such as quinoa, couscous, bulgur, barley, and wheat berries. Try fruits and vegetables that are popular in different international cuisines, such as bok choy and sea vegetables (e.g. nori, kombu, hiziki, etc.).

To Ensure Healthy Eating

Variety is the best insurance that your diet will be healthy.

- Accentuate the positive. Focus more on healthy foods that fit into a vegetarian plan instead of foods to avoid.

- Base your diet on plant foods. Eating too much milk, cheese, and yogurt may raise the fat content of the diet and displace fiber-rich foods. Once you are past the initial transition phase and have made the change to vegetarianism, use dairy foods in moderation, not as the center of meals.

- Be relaxed about protein. As long as calories are sufficient and the diet is varied, vegetarians easily meet protein needs. Grains, beans, vegetables, and nuts all provide protein. It isn't necessary to have a "high-protein" food like cheese, soy, beans, or meat analogs at each meal. Vegetarians do not need to eat special combinations of foods to meet protein needs.

- Be aware of fat. Even vegetarians can get too much fat if the diet contains large amounts of nuts, oils, processed foods, sweets, margarine, salad dressings, high fat dairy products, or eggs.

Resources

Davis B, Melina V. *Becoming Vegan*. Summertown, Tennessee: Book Publishing Co.; 2000.

Melina V, Davis B, Harrison V. *Becoming Vegetarian*. Summertown, Tennessee: Book Publishing Company, 1995.

Messina M, Messina V, Mangels R. *The Dietitian's Guide to Vegetarian Diets: Issues and Applications, 2nd ed*. Gaithersburg, Maryland: Aspen Publishers, Inc., 2001.

Messina V, Messina M. *The Vegetarian Way*. New York: Crown Publishers, 1996.

Wasserman D, Mangels R.. *Simply Vegan, 3rd ed*. Baltimore, Maryland: The Vegetarian Resource Group, 1999.

Chapter 6

Creating a Vegetarian Pantry

Whether you are a newcomer to a vegetarian diet, or someone who wants to have a greater variety of healthy ingredients at hand, this list can serve as your handy guideline. Now, no matter how time-crunched life gets, you can be sure that a healthy, nearly effortless meal awaits at the end of the day!

Basic Pantry Staples

Non-Perishable Dry Goods

Beans, canned: Look for good-quality beans, without additives, or better yet, organic canned or jarred beans from natural food stores or co-ops, including your favorites from the following:

- Black beans
- Black-eyed peas
- Chickpeas (garbanzos)
- Great northern beans (cannellini)
- Pink beans
- Pinto beans
- Red or kidney beans

From VEGETARIAN 5-INGREDIENT GOURMET by Nava Atlas, copyright 2001 by Nava Atlas. Used by permission of Broadway Books, a division of Random House, Inc. Original document can be found at http://www.vegkitchen.com/Veg_pantry.htm.

Beans, dried: If you're inclined to cook beans from scratch, I don't object! Black beans, adzuki beans, and navy beans are particularly good cooked from scratch; there's also pink, kidney, red, and large white beans; brown and red lentils, and split peas.

Chilies, green, in 4 or 7-ounce cans, chopped, mild or hot, as preferred.

Grains: If you are going to store whole grains at room temperature, don't buy more than what you will use up in about 3 months. During hot summer months, refrigerate them.

- Barley
- Bulgur
- Couscous
- Rice (long-grain brown, basmati, arborio, quick-cooking, etc.)
- Quinoa
- Wild rice

Herbs and spices, dried: Keep a good range of commonly used varieties on hand; seasoning blends, especially an all-purpose salt-free herb-and-spice blend, a good-quality curry powder, as well as an Italian herb seasoning blend, are especially useful.

Oils:

- Dark sesame oil
- Extra-virgin olive oil
- Light olive oil

Pastas and noodles: Keep a good supply of different sizes and shapes of pasta in your pantry. Some useful shapes to have on hand include angel hair, thin spaghetti, spirals (rotini), ziti or penne, fettuccine, and linguine. A few Asian noodles, such as udon, soba, and rice vermicelli, are available in natural food stores and are nice to have on hand too.

Soy sauce: Sometimes marketed under the name tamari or shoyu; buy a good natural brand for best flavor.

Tomato products, canned:

- Diced, in 14- to 16-ounce cans

- Crushed or pureed, in 14, 16, and 28-ounce cans
- Tomato sauce.

Vinegars:

- Balsamic (dark and/or white)
- Red wine or white wine vinegar
- Rice vinegar (for Asian-style cooking)

Prepared Condiments, Sauces, and Such

- Barbecue sauce (great for broiling or stir-frying tofu, tempeh, or seitan)
- Pasta (marinara) sauce (this comes in so many natural and flavorful varieties)
- Pizza sauce
- Salad dressings (choose natural, low-fat varieties of your favorites; I find red wine vinaigrette, balsamic vinaigrette, and ranch most useful)
- Salsa, tomato-based, mild to hot as you prefer
- Salsa, tomatillo (Salsa verde)
- Thai peanut sauce
- Stir-fry sauce

Pantry Vegetables

- Garlic
- Onions (yellow, red, or both)
- Potatoes, white (red-skinned are an excellent all-purpose potato)
- Potatoes, sweet (for fall and winter)

Refrigerator Staples

Refrigerator staples are more subjective to define than pantry staples. That being the case, this is a fairly short list, concentrating on the ingredients that I feel are essential to have on hand to ensure flexibility in meal preparation. This doesn't include fruits and vegetables, which you should buy as often as you need them.

- Butter or margarine (both to be used quite sparingly; I like natural soy based margarines; look for a brand that is free of hydrogenated oils and trans-fatty acids)

- Cheeses, shredded (low-fat if preferred, or soy cheese)
- Parmesan cheese, grated fresh (or if you prefer, try Parmesan-style soy cheese)
- Ketchup
- Lemons
- Mayonnaise (preferably commercially prepared tofu mayonnaise)
- Milk, low-fat, or soy milk
- Mustard, prepared (Dijon-style is excellent)
- Tofu (in various forms including silken, soft, firm or extra-firm, and baked.)
- Yogurts, plain and flavored

Freezer Staples

- Burger and hot dog rolls (for veggie burgers and soy hot dogs, of course)
- Hero or sub rolls
- Pastas, frozen (any of ravioli, tortellini, cavatelli, gnocchi)
- Pita bread
- Pizza crusts
- Soy bacon
- Soy hot dogs
- Tortillas, corn and flour
- Vegetables of your choice (corn kernels, green beans, green peas, and chopped spinach are useful)
- Veggie burgers

Fresh Fruits and Vegetables

Though fresh produce is undoubtedly a staple in this book's recipes and menus, it would be cumbersome to list all those used. Produce is the food I shop for most frequently, since I like to have it as fresh as possible. Though the seasonality of produce has been stretched by imports, I like to stick with what is truly seasonal as much as possible. Please support family farms by shopping at local farm stands and farmers markets if you have access to them. Cast a vote for organic produce (as well as organic eggs and dairy products) by buying them as often as you can; they are more expensive, to be sure, but if there is more of a demand, prices will come down.

Part Two

Vegetarian Nutrition

Chapter 7

Vegetarian Nutrition Overview

We as a nation have some catching up to do: Our per person consumption of vegetables, whole grains and beans is only a fraction of that of other nations such as China. The burgers and phenomenally fatty or seductively sweetened offerings at fast food establishments are very popular. There is vast room for improvement in American public health, and a vegetarian way of eating can help. This chapter can begin to show the way toward making wise food choices, based on the most recent scientific evidence.

Carbohydrates

A vegetarian diet is usually rich in carbohydrates, which are the most efficient source of body fuel. Simple sugars, as found in fresh fruits and vegetables, are the instant energy form of carbohydrate. Starches are the complex form which, when supplied by whole natural foods, provides sustenance over an extended period. Complex carbohydrates are found in whole grains (such as products made from brown rice or whole wheat), legumes and vegetables, particularly the

The information in this chapter is reprinted with permission from, "Good Nutrition: A Look at Vegetarian Basics," by Bob LeRoy, RD, MS, EdM, Nutrition Advisor, North American Vegetarian Society. © NAVS (revised 2002). This brochure was produced by the North American Vegetarian Society, a non-profit, educational organization serving vegetarians and the public since 1974. For more information, contact the North American Vegetarian Society at P.O. Box 72, Dolgeville NY 13329, (518) 568-7970, navs@telenet.net, or visit their website at www.navsonline.org.

starchy vegetables such as potatoes, yams, corn, winter squash and various root vegetables.

Wrongly maligned as fattening, carbohydrates are actually filling. Like proteins, they contain approximately four calories per gram; fats have almost nine. A man who needs 3,000 calories daily would have to eat 29 potatoes or 37 apples or 46 oranges to maintain his body weight if no other foods were used.

Carbohydrates are not as easily turned into body fat, as are dietary fats, because carbohydrates burn more efficiently as fuel in times of demand. Excess carbohydrate calories are stored in the liver and muscles as glycogen (an energy reserve for work and exercise) until storage limits are reached. In contrast, dietary fat circulates through the blood and readily becomes part of fat tissues.

Nutritionally inferior foods such as white rice, white flour, white sugar, and the breads and other foods made with them have given their quality cousins a bad reputation. These highly processed items are not recommended, but even they can be handled by the body more effectively than fatty foods.

Whole grains still retain their naturally occurring vitamins, minerals, phytochemicals, and fiber, and are preferred sources of complex carbohydrates. These include whole wheat products, rolled oats, brown rice, whole corn meal products, popcorn, whole rye products, buckwheat, unpearled barley, millet, and the less familiar amaranth, kamut, quinoa, grain sorghum, spelt, teff and triticale. Most of the world's traditional caloric staple foods appear on this list.

Legumes, also important providers of complex carbohydrates worldwide, include members of the pea family (green and yellow peas, chickpeas, lentils, green soybeans) and many beans commonly used in the U.S.: aduki, black, black-eyed, fava, great northern, lima, mung, pink, pinto, red chili, red kidney, white navy. Yellow soybeans and peanuts are two legumes of different composition: they furnish more calories from fat than from complex carbohydrates.

Whole grains, legumes, and starchy vegetables are more useful in helping keep blood sugar levels stable than are any other foods. They give support to physical energy and alertness through gradual effects over many hours.

The largest section of the U.S. Department of Agriculture Food Pyramid is devoted to foods supplying most of their calories as complex carbohydrates. The American Dietetic Association, National Institutes of Health, and American Academy of Pediatrics have formally declared that most of our calories should NOT come from protein, fat, or sugars and sweeteners. The medical and sports medicine professions have since the mid-1980s agreed that even for diabetes patients and athletes, more than half the daily calories should be drawn from complex carbohydrates.

Protein

We break down the proteins in our foods into their amino acid building blocks, which our bodies use to construct tissue proteins, hormones, enzymes and other substances crucial to our existence. When we take in more protein than we need for these purposes, we burn the excess as fuel. This surplus protein is not as desirable an energy source as is either carbohydrate or fat, since in using its calories we must discard its nitrogen-related portions. Thus we burden the liver and kidneys with additional excretion tasks.

How much protein do we need? This may be the most discussed nutrition question in society, but we can study many different scientific observations and eventually combine them into one easy-to-remember guideline. First, it is important to note that international organizations dealing with hunger and malnutrition problems have long shared this consensus: protein deficiency basically only appears as a public health problem when there is calorie deficiency, or else the range of foods available is terribly narrow. This means that when people simply have enough food to eat, overall, and any modest range and variety of food choices, they tend not to experience protein deficiency. Thus it would make sense to describe our protein needs as a percentage of our total calorie needs.

Assuming that we have sufficient food, and some diversity of it, how much of that food needs to provide us protein? One suggestion comes from the makeup of human breast milk: 6.1 to 7.5 percent of its calories are derived from protein. The World Health Organization has stated that, given adequate total calories, a minimum of 5 percent of those calories must come from protein... but a 10 percent level is more desirable. If we look back through several decades of recommendations made by major national and international nutrition bodies throughout the world, we find that nearly every guideline for adequate protein consumption has fallen into the range of 8 to 10 percent of overall calories.

As a final reference on desired protein quantity, let's examine the U.S. Recommended Dietary Allowances. RDAs show figures for total calories and for grams of protein in each of 18 different age- and gender-sorted groups. One gram of protein from commonly available foods would supply us anywhere from 2.44 to 4.36 calories, according to

USDA. data. We may assume that a diet of mixed foods will provide approximately 3.5 to 3.75 calories for each gram of protein (an all-plant-based diet would offer no mor e than 3.5). Thus, we can see what percentage of calories from protein the RDAs actually propose for each group of people.

Infants are assigned 5.75 to 7.5 percent of calories from protein, much like the content of breast milk. Children up through 10 are matched with 4 to 5.25 percent of calories from protein. Females 11 to 50 receive 7 to 8.52 percent of calories from protein, and under pregnancy or lactation conditions this increases to 8.04 to 9.03 percent. Males 11 to 50 are assigned 6.3 to 8.15 percent. Persons over 50 are given the recommendation of 9.21 to 10.27 percent of calories from protein. Clearly, there is extensive evidence that a range of 8 to 10 percent of calories derived from protein should be adequate for the broad spectrum of people who are eating varied diets with enough food, and who are not suffering from unusual illnesses.

In addition, there is currently widespread agreement in the nutrition profession that when protein is drawn from a wide variety of natural foods, not just from one or two food families such as starchy root vegetables, the quality of the overall protein consumed will be adequate. There is no longer much support for the idea that meticulous simultaneous combining of different proteins is necessary.

How do we obtain 8 to 10 percent of calories from protein on a plant-based diet? Effortlessly! Protein is not confined to a few headline-making foods, but is distributed through all whole natural foods. Look at these examples of protein in plant-derived foods:

- 10 to 36%—dark green leafy vegetables
- 25 to 43%—mushrooms, asparagus, sprouts
- 16 to 39%—(fresh or dried) beans, peas, other legumes
- 11 to 20%—flax, sunflower, pumpkin and sesame seeds
- 6.6 to 11%—onions, turnips, rutabagas, carrots, Jerusalem artichokes, peppers, pumpkin
- 15 to 36%—other cabbage-family vegetables
- 7.2 to 15%—whole grains, carob, most sea vegetables
- 13 to 15%—tomatoes, beets, okra, celery, cucumbers, eggplant, radishes, summer squash
- 4.6 to 16%—nuts
- 6 to 9%—oranges, strawberries, figs, potatoes, parsnips, butternut/acorn/Hubbard squash

Obviously, any diverse random mixture of whole natural vegetarian foods will supply enough protein to meet this guideline. Only sweet potatoes and some other starchy roots, plus coconuts, avocados and most fruits contain a lower percentage of their calories as protein than do the foods above. We must remember, though, that refined concentrated-fat and concentrated-sweetened foods have had virtually all their original protein content removed, and these relatively junky foods will not contribute to our protein needs.

Fats

Fats enhance flavor of foods and increase satiety by slowing the emptying of the stomach. In our bodies they transport fat-soluble vitamins such as D, K and the antioxidants A and E, and they are integral parts of mammary tissue and of all cell membranes. The essential fatty acids linoleic and alpha-linolenic acid must be supplied by our food. A balanced diet of vegetables, fruits, whole grains, beans, seeds and unprocessed nuts can provide these antioxidants and essential fats without burdening us with many fat calories. However, in reality, most people in the U.S. take in nearly all of their fats from animal-derived foods and processed vegetable oils, and they over consume them in alarming amounts. Thus, we need guidance both about reducing fats in our diets and about shifting toward different kinds.

Fats and Our Blood

Major sources of fat in the typical diet are animal products such as meat, fish, poultry, cheese, whole milk, eggs, butter and lard, and refined vegetable fats (margarine and shortenings, salad and cooking oils, hardened fats used as ingredients). Animal fats, coconut and palm oil, and cocoa butter are mostly saturated. In essence, this means that these fats are solid at room temperature, and physiologically, it means that they are one of the greatest factors in raising blood cholesterol levels. They help clog arteries and increase the likelihood of death by heart attack. Coronary heart disease, stroke and male impotence are all illnesses of impaired blood circulation usually caused by buildup of fatty plaques on artery walls.

Cholesterol is manufactured in the livers of most animals and is used for hormone production. We humans make all that we need; yet most people get a daily overload from eating meat, fish, poultry, eggs, and dairy products. Extra cholesterol resists breakdown, deposits in tissues and contributes to atherosclerotic plaque. Vegetarians generally have lower levels of serum cholesterol than do meat-eaters, and vegans (who eat no animal products) have the lowest of all. Food processors often take unsaturated vegetable oils and pump additional hydrogen into them to give them solidity, as in the production of margarine and shortening. These hydrogenated fats (also known as trans fatty acids) are seen as ingredients in countless baked goods and some peanut butters. Scientific consensus is that they worsen blood cholesterol content and increase coronary artery disease risk just as do naturally saturated fats.

Another primary risk factor for heart disease is obesity. Vegetarian diets tend to make weight control a bit easier because they are usually less calorie-dense than the diets of non-vegetarians. This means that a similarly sized plate of food would, on the average, contain fewer calories. This is partly because the two kinds of food most associated with vegetarians—vegetables and fruits—have very high water content and so by their nature are extremely low-calorie foods. This is also due to the fact that fat contains more than twice as many calories by weight as does either protein or carbohydrate. Because most animal-based foods are very high in fat, the move toward vegetarian eating usually involves some further calorie reduction.

Yet another primary risk factor for heart disease is high blood content of homocysteine. This amino acid, made in the body from other sulfur-containing amino acids, seems to initiate some artery wall damage, paving the way for buildup of fatty cholesterol-laden plaques. Homocysteine levels generally remain well under control if enough folic acid, vitamin B_6, and vitamin B_{12} are consumed. Folic acid and vitamin B_6 are plentifully supplied by a diet rich in vegetables, whole grains and beans. Vitamin B_{12} sources are discussed under "Vitamins." An excess supply of sulfur-containing amino acids can be promoted by over-consumption of proteins, particularly of animal-derived proteins.

Vitamins

With two exceptions, all known vitamins are amply provided by plant foods. The list below illustrates this for most vitamins. We should explain two families of vegetables mentioned in the list:

1. Dark Green Leafy Vegetables: examples include kale, collard greens, bok-choi, spinach, very dark lettuces, leeks, scallions, parsley, watercress, arugula, escarole, chicory greens, dill, fennel/anise, basil, cilantro, chives, mint, chard, beet greens,

52

turnip greens, mizuna, mustard greens, dandelion, garlic scapes (greens), broccoli rabe.

2. Cabbage Family: examples include kale, collard greens, bok-choi, broccoli, broccoli rabe, cauliflower, green cabbage, red cabbage, savoy cabbage, nappa/Chinese cabbage, brussels sprouts, kohlrabi, rutabagas, turnips, turnip greens, mizuna, mustard greens, and the sprouts of broccoli, cabbage, rutabaga or turnip seeds.

List of Vitamins and Plant Foods

Vitamin A. dark green leafy vegetables; deep-yellow fleshed root vegetables (e.g. carrots, sweet potatoes), squashes (e.g. butternut) and fruits (e.g. apricots, peaches, cantaloupes); red peppers; broccoli

B vitamins. dark green leafy vegetables, sprouts and nutritional yeast are good sources of a broad spectrum of B vitamins. Specific vitamins follow.

- Thiamin: beans and peas, peanuts, sunflower and sesame seeds, whole grains, some nuts, laver sea vegetable, asparagus, okra, Jerusalem artichokes, cabbage-family vegetables, garlic, potatoes

- Riboflavin: mushrooms, almonds, whole grains, sea vegetables, beans and peas, okra, asparagus, cashews, avocado, broccoli, sweet potatoes, bok-choi, bananas, peanuts

- Niacin: peanuts, sea vegetables, mushrooms, seeds, beans and peas, potatoes, almonds, whole grains, asparagus, sweet corn, avocado, dried apricots, dates, cashews, prunes

- Pyridoxine (B_6): sea vegetables, legumes, walnuts, peanuts, bananas, potatoes, sweet potatoes, figs, avocado, whole grains, cauliflower, cabbage, beets, watermelon, tomatoes, raisins, prunes, okra, oranges

- Pantothenic acid and biotin: beans, peanuts, oats and other whole grains, cauliflower, pecans, walnuts, almonds, mushrooms, avocado, sweet potatoes

- Folic acid: beans and legumes, whole grains, asparagus, avocado, brussels sprouts and other cabbage-family vegetables, mushrooms, almonds, walnuts, pecans, beets, parsnips, tomatoes, peanuts, sunflower and sesame seeds, okra, onions, sweet potatoes, some fruits

Vitamin C. dark green leafy vegetables, sweet peppers, broccoli and other cabbage-family vegetables, sprouts, citrus fruits, tomatoes, berries, tropical fruits, asparagus, okra, fresh beans and peas

Vitamin E. dark green leafy vegetables; sprouts other than alfalfa; sweet potatoes; pumpkin and sunflower seeds; mango; whole soybean products such as tempeh; cabbage-family vegetables; asparagus; whole grains; avocado; walnuts; sea vegetables; peanuts; pecans; almonds; parsnips; tomatoes

Vitamin K. dark green leafy vegetables, cabbage-family vegetables, legumes, asparagus, some sea vegetables.

There are many more plant-derived sources of these vitamins than those listed above.

Two vitamins merit extra attention. The first, vitamin D, is actually a family of hormones. It is vital to calcium metabolism and a deficiency can lead to rickets in children. The source of vitamin D intended by nature is sunlight's action on the skin. Because this fat-soluble vitamin is stored in the body, reasonable time spent in the sunshine during the warm months should provide enough to last the winter. Dark-skinned children and those who live in far northern latitudes or in cloudy or smoggy areas should be sure to use reliable dietary sources of vitamin D. Though the vitamin D added to cow's milk is well publicized, there is no need to use this product. Vitamin D_2, or ergocalciferol, is commercially produced from plant sources and added to many vegetarian foods and supplements. Vegetarians should avoid vitamin D_3, or cholecalciferol (also a common ingredient or supplement), normally derived from animal body parts. Nutritionists recommend that we do not take in more than the Recommended Daily Allowance of 5 mcg (10 after age 50) due to toxicity risks. We should be aware that many foods fortified with vitamin D have been found to contain (in error) amounts greater than those stated on their labels.

The second, vitamin B_{12}, is essential for the nervous system, for energy metabolism, for the health of our DNA and red blood cells, and for cell division throughout the body. In recent years, it has been clarified that it (along with folic acid and vitamin B_6) is also crucial to holding down our levels of amino acid homocysteine by assisting conversion to other sulfur-containing amino acids. Excess homocysteine in the blood is likely to cause oxidative damage in cells and blood vessels, increasing risk of coronary artery diseases and some kinds of cancer.

Attention to this vitamin is necessary for all people, regardless of the kind of diet they choose to eat. Though it is required in microscopic amounts, the consequences of its deficiency may be extremely serious. Nervous system symptoms of deficiency may remain hidden for years. Erroneous information about sources of the vitamin is widespread and often falsely reassuring.

Tempeh, sea vegetables, mushrooms and sprouts had been publicized as practical B_{12} providers, but later research has shown them not to be reliable sources.

It is clear that each of us should take supplemental forms of the vitamin. Active B_{12}, generally labeled as cyanocobalamin, is produced commercially via bacterial fermentation, and not taken from animal tissue. It is available alone in pills, as part of multivitamin preparations, and as an added ingredient in many packaged vegetarian foods. The solo pill form is regarded as most reliable in terms of potency; the megadoses of other vitamins which may be present in a multivitamin can interfere with absorption or usage of B_{12}. A once or twice weekly dosage would seem adequate for nearly all people without current deficiency or digestive disorders to maintain their vitamin B_{12} levels long-term. However, anyone with possible doubts about past B_{12} history is strongly urged to take supplements daily for a transition period of at least a few years.

Minerals

Minerals help in the body's acid-base balance, aid in the maintenance of osmotic pressure, assist in blood clotting, provide a medium for nerve transmission and muscle contraction, and much more. They are generally plentiful in a varied vegetarian diet of natural foods.

Well Supplied, without Worry about Absorption Rates

Whole grains, beans, nuts, and seeds, all-important mineral sources, contain something called phytate phosphorus, which partly reduces the percentage we absorb of certain alkaline minerals from our food. Calcium, iron, magnesium and zinc are among these minerals. This lowering of absorption is not a serious issue, as exemplified by tests involving calcium. Research studies have found the calcium absorption percent for various whole wheat and soy products at least comparable to that for cow's milk. Also, sprouting or fermenting any of these items enhances its absorbability of these minerals. Thus, when we use soy or multi-grain tempeh, sourdough whole grain breads, brown rice amasake, yogurt from soy or nuts, or sprouted beans/peas/grains, we're digesting an even greater share of these minerals than we would have by eating the original ingredients. Overall, whole grains, beans, nuts, and seeds do make a significant contribution to our mineral needs, especially if we choose a wide variety of them.

The only other foods documented as showing a much lower absorption rate for these alkaline minerals are the excess oxalate ones. Those few commonly used in the U.S. are spinach, chard, beet greens, rhubarb, unhulled sesame seeds, beets, parsley, and a few weeds. These are still nutritious foods, but we simply don't digest as much of their mineral content as we'd expect. We should let them be modest parts of our diet, not the dominant foods, not relying upon them as major mineral sources. Spinach and parsley shouldn't be the only salad greens we ever use!

We will examine individually some minerals of special interest.

Calcium provides the mineral matrix for teeth and bones, and it plays a role in blood clotting, nervous system activity, muscle relaxation, and enzyme activity. It is important to the health of the heart, and seems to help control the risk of certain types of cancer.

Calcium is an essential mineral we all must ensure that we get from our diet, but someone eating a wide variety of natural plant-based foods generally has no need to take calcium supplements. The richest calcium sources on the planet are dark leafy greens (they're also what cows use), but many vegetables, fruits, legumes, whole grains and unprocessed nuts/seeds make a significant contribution to our calcium supply. Seeking diversity of whole plant-derived foods is more beneficial than is eating a narrow-range or junk-based diet after we've identified one calcium powerhouse food. At least 11 vegetables commonly used in the U.S. contain more calcium per calorie than do any (even the skim) cow's milk products; these are bok-choi, turnip greens, watercress, mustard greens, collard greens, kale, chicory greens, dandelion, escarole, dark lettuces, and fennel/anise. Twenty-seven common vegetables, plus carob, oranges, tangerines, papayas, currants, figs, and several seaweeds, have a greater calcium-to-protein ratio than does any dairy food. This is important to note because the amount of protein eaten is one of the main factors causing the body to need more calcium. Kale, turnip greens, broccoli, and related vegetables have even demonstrated a higher calcium absorption percentage than has cow's milk.

Iron is the central element in the hemoglobin molecules which carry oxygen through our blood. It also plays a part in our muscle cells energy systems, in our immune system, and in some brain and nervous system functioning. It is well publicized that meat does contain iron, but also true that cow's milk products are quite deficient in it. Dairy products have been further incriminated in scientific research as the cause of hypochromic microcytic anemia in infants, an iron deficiency anemia arising through intestinal bleeding. Because of this and because of the extensive scientific evidence linking dairy products to infant insulin-dependent diabetes, the American Academy of Pediatrics recommended that unmodified cow's milk not be given to infants under one year of age.

The 25 or 30 foods showing the greatest iron content per calorie would all be fresh vegetables, except that a few sea vegetables like dulse, kombu kelp or alaria/wakame would be included. Dark green leafy vegetables, other than the higher-oxalate spinach, chard, beet greens, and parsley, should be seen as the finest sources among common foods. Iron absorption is increased when foods high in vitamin C are used simultaneously, but in the case of most fresh vegetables and fruits, each food is already a useful source of both these nutrients anyway. Eating a wide variety of vegetables, fruits, whole grains, and legumes, with optional addition of nut/seed foods, offers easy opportunities to meet normal iron needs.

Zinc is a part of over 80 enzymes, does teamwork with many vitamins, is involved with protein, fat, and carbohydrate metabolism, and plays a key role in our immune and reproductive systems. Deficiency, likely seen in conjunction with other conditions such as alcoholism or rheumatoid arthritis, may cause retarded growth and wound healing, nervous disorders, and impairment of the senses of taste and smell.

People relying mainly on refined foods, such as white flour, white rice, concentrated fats and sweeteners, may have difficulty meeting requirements for zinc. However, the amount of zinc per calorie found in vegetables, whole grains, legumes and nut/seed foods varies surprisingly little. Simply emphasizing a wide variety of whole, natural plant-derived foods and avoiding empty calorie foods should serve zinc needs well. When zinc deficiencies have been found in studies throughout the world, they have occurred with people unable to get enough or sufficiently varied food or people who lost large amounts of minerals due to sweat dehydration, parasites or unusual illness. Dark green leafy vegetables, other than the higher-oxalate spinach, chard, beet greens and parsley, are, as expected, very useful common sources, along with sprouts made from beans. Pumpkin seeds, sunflower seeds, and nutritional yeast are often publicized as helpful supplemental foods for zinc, but along these lines the most impressive example would be sea vegetables such as dulse, kombu kelp or alaria/wakame.

Iodine is crucial to our energy metabolism via its role in thyroid gland functioning. Our iodine needs are small but must be supplied by what we eat. More so than with other minerals, iodine has its content in foods varying widely according to production conditions. Traditionally, foods grown farthest from oceans have been most likely to be iodine deficient. Recent generations in the U.S. have looked toward the table salt condiment (whether iodized or sea salt) as providing some assurance that enough iodine was being consumed. Drastic overuse of table salt in the U.S. has increased risk of high blood pressure and osteoporosis, and it is desirable to cut back somewhat on this sodium use. An additional iodine source would be sea vegetables such as dulse, kombu kelp or alaria/wakame. Very modest use of any of these would provide plenty of iodine.

Antioxidants and Other Phytochemicals

Extensive scientific research over the last 20 years has shown that many more substances found in plant-derived foods are actually highly beneficial to human health. These naturally occurring chemicals, present in microscopic amounts, and not classified as vitamin or mineral, are known as phytochemicals. Many of them have shown the effect of lowering blood cholesterol levels. Many of them act as antioxidants in our bodies, particularly protecting us from damage in our cell membranes, just as do the vitamins A, C, and E. This means that they help prevent destructive oxidizing chemicals like free radicals from attacking us where we are most vulnerable. Their work helps to resist cancer development, and to slow down the progress of aging and of degenerative diseases.

Thousands of health-promoting phytochemicals have been discovered, mainly in fresh vegetables and fruits, and new ones emerge every month. This chart shows many for which some research has demonstrated cancer-fighting properties. We should explain two families of vegetables mentioned in the chart:

1. Celery family: examples include celery, carrots, parsley, dill, parsnips, fennel/anise, cilantro, celeriac, caraway

2. Onion family: examples include garlic, red/white/yellow onions, scallions, leeks, chives, shallots, garlic scapes (greens)

Fiber

A lack of what Grandma called roughage has been linked with ills ranging from constipation to colon cancer to varicose veins to heart and artery disease. Fiber refers to many kinds of non-digestible non-calorie-supplying carbohydrates. It is what prolongs and gradualizes digestion/absorption of starches in whole grains, legumes and starchy vegetables, thereby allowing them to have a stabilizing influence on blood sugar levels and a sustained energy effect. Farther down the tract: just as increased fat content of one's diet slows down passage of digested food through the colon, increased fiber speeds it up. Thus it reduces absorption of any toxins or cancer-causing agents there may be, and it reduces re-absorption of a woman's estrogen, helping to control one risk factor for breast cancer. Fiber is absent in animal-origin foods.

Attempting to make up for the lack of fiber in the typical meats-and-sweets meals, many people have tried to aid their elimination by supplementing their diets with products famous for high-fiber content. Usually these have not been fresh foods, but dry foods, e.g. dried prunes and the various processed bran items made from wheat and oats. If these foods are eaten in their dried form, not well rehydrated, their fiber probably won't work its expected wonders on intestinal movement. It will probably cause some dehydrating effect and discomfort. Fiber demands a watery intestinal environment. Take note that vegetables and fruits contain all the fiber we'd ever want, plus abundant water built in from the start. Also note: if we're interested in wheat bran or oat bran, why not eat whole wheat or whole oatmeal (or any other whole grains or legumes), which give us the benefit of all the vitamins, minerals and other nutrients which were scooped out to produce the bran? Fiber is easily and deliciously available from all plant-origin whole foods.

Putting It All Together

It's easy to meet all our nutritional requirements on a plant-based diet. The Physicians Committee for Responsible Medicine has proposed

Table 7.1. Food Sources of Phytochemicals

Phytochemicals Linked to Cancer-Preventive Effects	Usual Food Pigment	Foods Generally Recognized as Significant Sources
lutein and 100s of miscella. carotenoids	orange/yellow	dark greens + same foods as for plant vitamin A
anthocyanins (polyphenolic flavonoids)	blue/purple	blueberries, other berries, grapes, plums
indole-3-carbinol, other indoles		cabbage-family
sulphoraphane	blue/purple	cabbage-family
other glucosinilates and aromatic isothiocyanates	blue/purple	cabbage-family
coumarins		celery-family, citrus
rutin and flavone flavonoids		celery-family, citrus, olives, buckwheat, asparagus, rose hips, some other fruits
d-limonene and limonoid monoterpenes		citrus
d-carvone and other monoterpenes		citrus, onion-family, ginger, dill, mint, caraway
diphenolic lignans		flaxseed, whole grains, legumes, other seeds
allylic sulfides		garlic and onion-family
thiosulfinates		garlic and onion-family

triterpenes		garlic and onion-family, licorice root, legumes
quercetin and flavonol flavonoids		grapes, olives, cranberries, greens, buckwheat
proanthocyanidin flavonoids	blue/purple/red	grapes, cranberries, blueberries, apples, rhubarb, barley, rose hips, legumes, sorghum
chlorophyllin	green	green peas
tannins, catechins, other polyphenols		legumes, c. sinensis green tea, grapes, carob
lectins		legumes
Bowman-Birk protease inhibitor		soybeans, lima beans, peanuts, other legumes
genistein, daidzein, diphenolic isoflavores		soybeans, other legumes, licorice root
lycopene carotenoids	red, purple-red	tomatoes, red cabbage, watermelon, red grapefruit, guava, some berries and other fruits
phenolic acids and phenolic curcurmin		turmeric, ginger, raspberries, grapes, cherries, strawberries, other fruits, garlic, onion family, legumes, whole grains, nuts, vegetables, cumin

61

the following new four food groups to help us plan our daily menu for optimum health and nutrition: 1) Vegetables, 2) Fruits, 3) Whole grains, 4) Legumes.

Fresh vegetables and fruits are nature's most magnificent sources of phytochemicals, antioxidants and cancer-preventive factors. Whole grains and legumes are the greatest storehouses of complex carbohydrates, our bodies ' optimum fuel. All four groups provide us generously with fiber, which is unavailable in animal-origin foods, plus vitamins and minerals. Using these four groups will offer us an inviting adventure of diversity and flavor while reducing our risks of numerous degenerative diseases.

Chapter 8

Nutritional Concerns for Vegetarians and Vegans

Chapter Contents

Section 8.1

An Overview of Vegetarian-Specific Nutritional Needs

Excerpted from *Staying Healthy with Nutrition* copyright © 1992 by Elson M. Haas, MD. Reprinted by permission of Celestial Arts, Berkeley, CA. Revised in April, 2002, by Dr. David A. Cooke, MD, Diplomate, American Board of Internal Medicine. Original text can be found at http://www.healthy.net/asp/templates/article.asp?PageType=article&ID=2045.

Vegetarianism has a long history, and a primarily vegetarian diet is still the most common type on the planet. Even in America, most people's diets were mainly vegetarian until the turn of the twentieth century, when beef consumption began to increase; it continued to increase steadily until only recently.

A change to a vegetarian diet automatically reduces intake of both protein and saturated fats unless there is a marked increase in consumption of dairy foods and eggs. One of the biggest problems with the contemporary American diet, which I have discussed earlier, is the focus on (or obsession with) protein as the staple of the diet. This is probably responsible for the increase in cardiovascular diseases and cancer because it also naturally increases the intake of saturated fats. We need to return to a focus on whole grains, legumes, and vegetables to give us the high complex carbohydrate, high fiber, high nutrient, and low fat diet that is so essential to good health and longevity.

Among the potential disadvantages of vegetarianism are that a no flesh food product diet often makes it more difficult to balance our intake all of the necessary nutrients, particularly protein, vitamin B_{12}, iron, and zinc. Calcium deficiency, in general a big concern, seems not to be as common in vegetarians as had been thought. Adequate protein can easily be obtained, as discussed later in this section. Vitamin B_{12}, or cobalamin, is consistently a problem for vegetarians, especially for the pure vegetarian, or vegan, who eats no animal foods at all—not even milk products or eggs. Vitamin B_{12} is most plentiful in red meats, and some is found in other animal foods, but most plant proteins are fairly low in this "red" vitamin. Brewer's yeast, tempeh (fermented soybeans), and some sprouts have small amounts of B_{12}.

Vitamin B_{12} deficiency leads to poor metabolism of protein, fats, and carbohydrate; problems in building the coverings of nerves; and a low red blood cell count, called pernicious anemia. Fortunately, though, B_{12} is stored in the tissues at levels high enough to last for several years of low intake. Extra B_{12} as a supplement (the sublingual tablets are currently the best source of oral B_{12}) will usually prevent any deficiency unless there are problems with the stomach making intrinsic factor or with the liver's ability to store this vitamin.

A vegetarian diet can also be an important part of a good therapeutic plan for many problems. It is more cleansing or detoxifying than the usual higher fat and higher protein diets, because it usually contains a greater percentage of dietary fiber and the watery fruits and vegetables. In terms of the body's nutritional cycles of cleansing, building, and balancing, the vegetarian regime is very effective in cleansing, beneficial in balancing if it is well planned and implemented, and generally less effective in its building powers. (For that reason, I do not recommend a vegan diet for children or teenagers or during pregnancy or lactation, where I feel more building and strengthening are needed. The lacto-ovo type of vegetarianism, though, should work fine.) It might be wise for all of us to eat a vegetarian diet every so often, such as a day or two a week, one week a month, or even more often during spring and summer. Variations of the vegetarian diet can be used for detoxification. A fast or cleansing diet may be a useful remedy for many types of congestive problems. With sickness, though, I usually suggest more complex carbohydrates in the diet, with higher intake of water and water containing foods; this helps avoid dehydration and usually improves vitality.

The vegetarian diet composed of organically grown foods comes the closest to following the general nutritional guidelines recommended throughout this book. A high fiber, high complex carbohydrate, nutrient rich diet composed mainly of whole grains, legumes, vegetables, fruits, nuts, and seeds will provide all the nutrients we need. Whether vegetarian or not, this should be the basic foundation of all health oriented diets. It is also more alkaline and higher in most vitamins and minerals than any other type of diet. Only small amounts of milk products, eggs, or various animal fleshes might be added to the vegetarian diet to make it easier to obtain the necessary calcium, iron, and B_{12}.

Protein is always the big topic of discussion when it comes to vegetarianism. Eating complementary proteins, such as grains or seeds with legumes, or eggs or dairy foods with any of the vegetable proteins, is the usual suggestion for obtaining adequate protein. This is because each specific vegetable protein is low in one or two of the essential amino acids so that when eaten alone it does not provide equivalent levels of all the essential amino acids required to build our tissue proteins. When we eat some legumes, which are high in lysine and isoleucine and low in tryptophan and methionine, with grains, which have the opposite strengths and weaknesses, we obtain all of our essential amino acids in more equal levels. If the digestion of proteins and the assimilation of amino acids and peptides is normal, then a minimum daily requirement of protein should be in the range of 40–50 grams (about 1½ ounces).

Several noted authors have recently suggested that we do not need to be as concerned about complementary proteins as was previously thought. Frances Lappe, who proposed the idea of complementing proteins in *Diet for a Small Planet*, now suggests that our body can find the needed amino acids when any plant protein food has been eaten over the day. Though I have felt that this might be true, I have not seen any conclusive research, which might be hard to conduct, about this issue. On the other hand, it would seem that when there is any malnutrition and subsequent deficiency or low body stores of certain nutrients, in this case amino acids, it would be more difficult to manufacture necessary body proteins from consistent meals containing incomplete proteins eaten over several days. In that situation, or when food intake analyses or blood tests suggest inadequate protein intake or assimilation, we then must focus more on protein consumption and, possibly, digestion. Otherwise, a balanced vegetarian diet should pose no concerns about adequacy of protein intake.

Given the current knowledge and an attitude of "better safe than sorry," I still suggest combining vegetable proteins at meals or at least in the same day to create a complete profile of essential amino acids. Protein deficiency, though much rarer than most people fear, can cause some problems. With a more stressful lifestyle or a high level of athletic activity, protein needs may be increased, and thus, more high protein foods are required. Fatigue is a common problem in vegetarians with low protein diets. Weight loss and low body weights are also more likely with this type of diet. Another concern I have is that amino acids and proteins are very important to the immune system. I commonly see lower white (and red) blood cell counts in vegetarians, likely due to not having all the cell building nutrients available, particularly protein. If the immune system is weakened by a low nutrient availability, especially in combination with high stresses, infectious disease is much more likely. In the digestive analyses of my patients I also see a higher amount of parasites and intestinal yeast overgrowth present in the vegetarians. This may be due to the lower protein and higher sweet diet which appears more common with inadequate protein intake—more vegetable based foods are higher in carbohydrates and sweet flavors, plus many vegetarians crave sweet foods. It may also result from a more alkaline system, which supports growth of parasites and yeasts, or low immunity. In most of these cases, I recommend a higher protein, wholesome food diet. I may even suggest the additional L-amino acids to ensure that all are present for immune functions, though most amino acid formulas are not "vegetarian derived."

There is also some concern that a high fiber vegetarian diet does not provide enough of the important minerals such as zinc, manganese, copper, iron, and calcium, or that the phytic acid in grains combines with these minerals in the intestinal tract and reduces their absorption. Recent research described in Dr. Stuart Berger's *How to Be Your Own Nutritionist* suggests that after a few weeks of high fiber vegetarianism, our body improves its absorption of zinc, iron, calcium, and copper. In any event, I recommend a good mineral supplement program to ensure that we ingest enough of these nutrients. The mineral intake should be in balance, because a high amount of one mineral may interfere with the absorption of the others; this is especially true for zinc and copper or calcium and magnesium.

As part of the supplement program, I suggest a general multiple nutrient formula, vegetarian-derived, of course. Additional calcium/magnesium is suggested if there is low intake of dairy products. Extra vitamin D will enhance calcium absorption, and this is particularly important during the less sunny months and for those who avoid the sunshine. I encourage taking extra zinc (and copper and manganese to balance with zinc) because it is so important and dietary deficiencies are common, even in vegetarians. I often suggest additional iron, especially if the red blood cell count is low; menstruating women frequently need higher amounts of iron. It is wise for vegetarians to have blood counts done occasionally (every year or two) to make sure that anemia is not developing.

In regard to supplemental vitamin B_{12}, I suggest it for all strict vegetarians. It is contained in almost all multiple formulas, though even higher amounts are often wise, at least several times yearly for a month or so. Vitamin B_{12} may often help with problems of fatigue. If there is any problem with absorption (this can be checked by monitoring blood levels), vitamin B_{12} injections would be indicated. An amino acid formula or protein powder may also be useful if there is any fatigue, excessive weight loss, or concern about inadequate protein ingestion, digestion, or assimilation.

The following table offers a basic supplement plan as insurance for those on a vegetarian diet. Some naturalists do not like to take "vitamins," as they are not whole foods, but extracts of foods or synthetic preparations, but in many instances I feel that they are indicated. They are suggested here as a means for prevention of depletions and deficiency diseases. If we eat very well, balance our foods, maintain low stress levels, stay attuned to our body functions, and occasionally test body nutrient states and biochemical functions, then we might be able to avoid supplementation. However, I recommend at least short-term periods, several times yearly, of more intense nutrient intake to ensure proper availability of all the micronutrients.

Section 8.2

Iron and Zinc Deficiency

Excerpted from Kannan, Srimathi, PhD, "Factors in Vegetarian Diets Influencing Iron and Zinc Bioavailability." This article is reprinted with permission from *Vegetarian Nutrition Update*, the official newsletter of the Vegetarian Nutrition Dietetic Practice Group of the American Dietetic Association. © 1998. The full text of this article, including references, can be found at http://www.andrews.edu/NUFS/FeZnbioavail.htm.

Whole grain products and legumes provide a rich variety of phytochemicals and antioxidants that reduce the risk of cardiovascular disease, hypertension, cancer, and diabetes. Furthermore, these foods are often good sources of iron and zinc. These minerals, however, may be poorly available from certain plant foods. Therefore, vegetarians may need guidance on appropriate diet planning and food selection in order to achieve an adequate intake of bioavailable iron and zinc. This text will review the dietary components and food processing methods that enhance iron and zinc absorption.

Plant sources of iron include green leafy vegetables, legumes, soy foods, nuts, whole-grain and fortified breads, cereals, and pasta, while plant sources for zinc include cereals, nuts, legumes, and soy products. There are two kinds of iron, heme and non-heme iron. In plant foods, iron exists in the less bioavailable non-heme form. Relative to heme iron, non-heme iron is far more sensitive to the enhancers and inhibitors of iron absorption, and also to physiological iron need. Hence, non-heme iron will actually protect individuals against iron overload.

Absorption Promoters and Inhibitors

Bioavailability of non-heme iron and dietary zinc is greatly influenced by both dietary inhibitors and enhancers. This may place certain segments of the vegetarian population at risk for iron and zinc deficiency. The balance between absorption facilitators and inhibitors, along with the existing iron/zinc status of the individual determines the bioavailability of iron and zinc from individual foods or from a meal. Amino acids (especially cysteine), ascorbic acid, citric acid, and fructose enhance iron absorption. Inhibitors of iron include phytate, polyphenols and fiber, oxalate and, to a certain extent, calcium.

Promoters of zinc absorption include amino acids such as histidine and cysteine. The relatively high absorption of zinc from breast milk compared to cow's milk or soy protein-based infant formula has been explained by the presence of zinc-binding proteins in human milk which are more easily digested than casein in cow's milk. Alternatively, the higher content in breast milk of the amino acids histidine and cysteine may also provide a partial answer. While phytate has been singled out as the most potent dietary inhibitor of zinc bioavailability, other known inhibitors include oxalate, fiber, EDTA (ethylenediaminetetraacetic acid), and polyphenols (such as tannins).

Role of Ascorbic acid and Other Absorption Promoters

Ascorbic acid is the most potent enhancer of iron absorption. By adding substantial quantities of ascorbic acid to a plant-based meal, iron absorption may be increased as much as 6-fold. This influence is most pronounced in meals that contain high levels of phytates and polyphenols. The solubilizing effect of ascorbic acid counterbalances the negative consequences of dietary fiber and phytic acid.

In iron deficient individuals, vitamin C greatly enhances iron absorption from foods when consumed in the same meal. In individuals with normal iron status, vitamin C has a lesser effect on improving iron absorption. The absorption-enhancing effect is much smaller when the vitamin C is taken 4 to 8 hours before the meal. Both synthetic and dietary ascorbic acid enhance iron absorption. For meals consumed in the morning, the iron-enhancing effect of vitamin C is high. With meals consumed later in the day, the effect may be somewhat dampened.

When food is held at warm temperatures, ascorbic acid is oxidized and the iron absorption enhancing effect is decreased. Ascorbic acid also increases the iron bioavailability of those iron compounds used in fortification. Citric, malic, or tartaric acids found in fruits and vegetables improve iron absorption two- to four-fold. Lactic acid, found in sauerkraut, also enhances iron absorption. There is limited information about the influence of vitamin C on zinc bioavailability.

Polyphenols

Polyphenols commonly present in many vegetables include phenolic acids, flavonoids, and their polymerization products. There are numerous kinds of phenolic compounds in beverages such as tea and coffee, herbal teas, cocoa and red wine. These compounds form insoluble complexes with iron and may exist as an "iron-tannin" complex and thus inhibit iron absorption. The relative order of polyphenol content per cup of beverage follows the following order: black tea>coffee>cocoa>herbal teas. There is reason to believe that in iron deficient individuals, drinking polyphenol-containing cocoa, tea, or coffee beverages along with a phytate-containing wheat-, rice-, or maize-based meal may further compromise iron status. For clients with severe iron deficiency, use of herbal teas may be the preferred option. Similarly, phenolics present in vegetables such as butter beans, spinach and lentils may strongly inhibit iron absorption from a composite meal.

Phytates

Phosphorus in unrefined cereals, legumes, nuts, seeds, and tubers is mostly present as phytic acid (phytate). Since phytate is negatively charged it complexes with positively charged Fe or Zn ions, and in doing so it inhibits the uptake of these minerals. Only the hexa- and penta- phosphate esters of inositol in foods appear to be potent inhibitors of both iron and zinc absorption. Through some food processing methods such as fermentation these phosphate esters can be hydrolyzed to substances containing fewer phosphate groups.

Phytate may be of minor significance in affecting the zinc status of most vegetarians. Phytate/zinc molar ratio and Ca/phytate/Zn molar ratios are of importance. From high phytate meals, zinc absorption is typically less than 15%. Exact critical molar phytate to zinc ratios that compromise zinc bioavailability have yet to be quantified. The phytate:zinc molar ratio is calculated as the millimoles of phytate intake per day divided by the daily intake of zinc in millimoles. Zinc absorption impairment may occur at molar phytate:zinc ratios above 10:1, but whether this poses a threat to the zinc status is unknown. Typical ratios range from 8–12 for American vegetarian women and 9–23 for vegetarian men. Calcium potentiates this inhibitory effect.

Overcoming the Phytate Factor

Food processing, for example sprouting beans, can dephytinize food products, thus improving iron and zinc bioavailability. Additionally, vitamin C content is greatly increased with sprouting. Vitamin C level increases 17.5 times in the germinated lentil and 8.5 times in germinated mung bean. Also, 100 g of germinated lentils and mung beans supply 90% and 96% of the RDA for iron for adult men and 41% and 43% of the allowance for women. Twenty percent of the daily zinc allowance can be met by consuming 100 g of germinated lentils and mung beans. Soaking oats followed by sprouting the oats reduces phytate content and doubles the amount of absorbed zinc in comparison with untreated oats. In short, iron and zinc absorption is improved when leavened products are used rather than unleavened ones. During sourdough fermentation the lactic acid which is formed may improve mineral absorption.

For many vegetarians, soy protein is a major component of their diets. Soy has a high quality protein and is an excellent source of the health-promoting phytochemical, genestein. However, most forms of soy (soy flour, soy protein isolate, and tofu processed with calcium sulfate) reduce the absorption of non-heme iron and zinc, due mainly to the presence in soy of phytic acid. The inhibitory effect can be largely eliminated by using fermented soy-based products (for example, soy sauce, tempeh, natto, miso), silken tofu (made from using glucono-delta-lactone as the coagulant) or alternatively, iron- and zinc-fortified soy products (such as fortified soy infant formula). Fermentation reduces the phytate content by two mechanisms—it releases endogenous phytases and incorporates yeast during the process. Adding substantial amounts of vitamin C-rich foods to a soy-based meal will also greatly enhance iron absorption and counteract the inhibitory effects of soy.

Dietary Fiber

Vegetarians may need specific guidelines for selecting a diet that would accommodate the recommended fiber intake without compromising their iron status. Dietary fiber per se does not markedly impact iron absorption. The effects seen with fiber-rich diets are compounded by the quantity of minerals and protein in the diet, the presence of phytate or oxalic acid, and also the type of fiber present.

High fiber foods are often associated with a diminished zinc absorption. However, refined foods that are low in fiber have substantially lower levels of zinc, so that while the relative zinc absorption from low fiber foods is improved, the overall total zinc absorption is greater from the high fiber foods. For example, almost 40 percent of the zinc in white bread is absorbed, while only 17 percent is absorbed from whole grain bread. However, the total amount of zinc absorbed from whole grain bread is almost 50 percent more than that absorbed from white bread because whole grain bread contains more than three times the level of zinc found in the white bread.

Another matter of concern, relates to the issue of consuming fiber supplements along with a low zinc diet. This may pose a risk to one's zinc nutritional status, and is a relevant issue for certain segments of the population, such as the elderly.

Fiber may have a greater effect on iron and zinc balance in infants and children compared with adults. In adults, up to 32 g per day of dietary fiber and 2 g per day of phytic acid may exert no adverse effects on iron and zinc bioavailability. Among children, up to 25 g per day of dietary fiber and 1 g per day of phytic acid is unlikely to have a deleterious effect on iron and zinc bioavailability.

Calcium

The influence of calcium on iron and zinc bioavailability remains controversial. The level of iron inhibition by calcium depends on the quantity of calcium consumed, the meal size and the meal composition. The inhibition may be more pronounced in small, single-food meals than in complex meals. Lacto-ovo-vegetarians, who consume diets which are generous in dairy products, should be advised to eat substantial amounts of iron-rich vegetables, grains, and legumes to minimize the inhibitory effect of calcium, and also to consume plenty of vitamin C-rich fruits to facilitate absorption of the non-heme iron. Vitamin C appears to enhance iron retention when calcium is consumed at the same meal.

Maximum iron absorption occurs when iron and calcium intakes are separated. This may not seem practical when consuming iron-fortified cereals with milk. However, preliminary studies show that iron absorption may not be greatly affected in this case. Generally, iron absorption from a meal is not greatly affected by the time of day at which the meal is consumed. Also, in clients with borderline iron deficiency, prolonged and excessive use of antacids, such as calcium carbonate, should be discouraged.

Other Influences

Food treatments have a major influence on food composition and subsequently on mineral availability. Interactions with dietary components during food processing, and the thermal effects induced by heating and cooking foods may positively or negatively impact on iron and zinc availability. Maillard browning reactions take place commonly in heat-processed foods, such as milk and milk-based food products, breads, roasted coffee, and breakfast cereals. Maillard reaction products can chelate zinc and decrease zinc retention. These products have little influence on the overall zinc nutrition of individuals consuming zinc adequate diets. Individuals with borderline zinc intakes need to be cognizant about these factors.

Another matter of real concern, is the consumption of large amounts of non-heme iron (in the form of a supplement). Non-heme iron has an adverse effect upon zinc absorption. Conversely, large zinc intakes can also effect iron absorption.

Conclusion

Vegetarian diets generally contain adequate amounts of iron and zinc. A well-planned vegetarian diet can readily meet physiological needs for both iron and zinc. Studies have shown that the incidence of iron-deficiency anemia among long-term vegetarians is similar to that of nonvegetarians. Furthermore, the serum zinc levels and the zinc levels in hair and saliva of vegetarians (measures of the zinc status of an individual) were found to be within the normal range for each of these parameters.

Sub-optimal iron and zinc status may be of some concern in pregnant and lactating women, young children, adolescents, and the elderly. Consuming balanced meals that comprise a variety of foods (including whole or fortified grains, and legumes) is a very important element for meeting iron and zinc requirements of all those age groups.

The potential for iron and zinc deficiency can be diminished by paying careful attention to the dietary factors that enhance and inhibit the bioavailability of iron and zinc. Dietitians should help parents of vegetarian children identify a variety of zinc-rich foods to include in their children's diets, such as fortified cereals, cheese, legumes, and peanut butter.

It is important to emphasize that the health benefits and advantages associated with consuming a vegetarian diet outweigh the concerns mentioned above. Nevertheless, dietetics professionals should assist the client in making appropriate food choices so as to minimize the influence of inhibitors and to maximize the use of promoters of

Table 8.1. Use of Iron Supplements

Take between meals

Use a ferrous supplement, rather than ferric iron

Avoid taking with dairy products, whole grain products, a calcium or magnesium supplement, and tea or coffee.

Table 8.2. Recommendations for Optimizing Iron and Zinc Bioavailability in Vegetarians

1. Emphasize variety in the diet, especially foods that are micronutrient-dense.
2. Include plenty of sprouted lentils, chickpeas and beans.
3. Include consumption of fermented soy foods.
4. Choose dried fruits for dessert.
5. Eat plenty of fresh fruits and dark green leafy vegetables.
6. Avoid consuming phytate-rich foods and calcium-rich dairy foods in the same meal.
7. Avoid consuming calcium- and iron-rich foods in the same meal.
8. Drink tea and coffee at times other than at mealtime.
9. Pay special attention to vitamin C-rich foods.
10. Evaluate on a regular basis iron, zinc, calcium, and phytate intake.
11. Use iron and zinc fortified foods, if required.

iron and zinc absorption. In addition, the diet may be supplemented with fortified foods and beverages.

Vegetarians may also be advised on the appropriate use of iron supplements (Table 8.1). Clients may be encouraged to use iron cookware, such as an iron skillet. Further recommendations for optimizing iron and zinc availability from vegetarian diets appears in Table 8.2. Additionally, meal scores are available to rank foods in terms of non-heme iron availability. Published lists of iron- and zinc-rich foods for vegetarians are available.

During counseling, steps must be taken to determine whether the client is at risk for iron and/or zinc deficiency since the bioavailability of iron and zinc varies depending upon the dietary source. The frequency of use of iron and zinc supplements and of foods fortified with these minerals may significantly influence the iron/zinc nutritional status of a person. It is important to increase awareness about the daily requirements for iron and zinc, and when necessary discuss the problems associated with iron and zinc deficiency. It would be prudent to pay attention to meal composition as well as to utilize food preparation methods to achieve optimal iron and zinc status.

— by Srimathi Kannan, PhD

Srimathi Kannan, PhD is Visiting Assistant Professor of Nutrition, School of Public Health, University of Michigan, Ann Arbor.

Section 8.3

Getting Enough Protein

Excerpted from Messina, Ginny, MPH, RD, "Eating Right: Getting Enough Protein," http://vegan.com/issues/1999/apr99/messina.htm, April 1999. Reprinted with permission.

"I have been a vegetarian for about a 1½ years now. I think I am eating too much pasta and breads. I have noticed some muscle loss and gained a little weight. I want to lose the spare tire and get some of the muscle mass back. Exercise is good but what are the vegetarian foods I should be eating to get more protein?"

"I'm 18 and I have been a vegetarian for about 2 years now, and recently for about 3 months have gradually eliminated all animal products in my diet. My problem is I have very low calcium and protein, I eat a lot of beans but is there any suggestions on things I could eat. I'm constantly feeling light headed and fainted a few times."

"Eight days ago I decided to change my lifestyle completely. I decided to enjoy the vegan style of eating. Not an easy decision. I was trained that you need protein with every meal, 20–30 grams. HELP!! Every Vegetarian book tells me that is too much protein and you can get enough from plant sources. My biggest problem is breakfast. I need help in what to eat other than oatmeal that is a protein source."

Protein is, of course, the nutrient that new vegetarians worry about the most. First, let's clear up some misconceptions: plant foods are actually very good sources of protein and most vegetarians have no trouble getting enough of this nutrient. The rules for getting adequate protein:

1.   Eat enough calories to maintain ideal weight.

2.   Eat a variety of foods.

That variety should include—on a daily basis—foods like legumes (all kinds of cooked, dried beans like pintos, kidney beans, lentils, etc., and soyfoods like tofu, soymilk, and tempeh) and a serving or two every day of nuts or seeds or nut or seed butters (peanut butter, almond butter, tahini, etc.).

These are the plant foods that are highest in protein. But other foods like bread, pasta, grains, and vegetables also contribute small amounts of protein to the diet. For example, if your diet included 6 servings of some kind of grain food every day like bread, cereals, pasta, etc. (and six servings is pretty the much the minimum amount you should have for good health), this alone would provide between 12 and 18 grams of protein, depending on the types of foods you choose. That's about 30% of your daily need just from foods that we don't think of as being especially protein rich.

It is true that vegetarians have slightly higher protein needs than nonvegetarians and also that plant foods tend to be lower in protein than most animal foods. While it's good to be aware of this, it's not anything to worry about especially. As long as you follow the two rules above—a variety of plant foods and enough calories—it's extremely unlikely that you won't meet protein needs. The only time this may not be true is for women who have low calorie intakes. If women are dieting or just normally eat a low-calorie diet to maintain their weight, they may find that their protein intake is marginal. In this case, it's a good idea to make sure you are including at least 2–3 servings every day of the high protein foods like soyfoods, beans, or nuts. (A vitamin and mineral supplement is also a good idea when calorie intake is low, and this is true for everyone, not just vegans).

It's also extremely unlikely that one will suffer a loss of muscle along with a gain in fat because they are eating too little protein on their vegetarian diet. Loss of muscle occurs when you don't eat enough calories and when you don't exercise. It takes very little extra protein to gain muscle mass. The key to maintaining muscle mass and to losing fat is exercise—a combination of aerobic and muscle-building exercise (like weight lifting) is best. However, if you are really gaining a lot of fat on your new vegetarian diet, it's a good idea to meet with someone (a registered dietitian) who can help to determine an ideal calorie intake for you.

As far as breakfasts that provide enough protein, there are many choices. I had a bean burrito for breakfast this morning and my usual breakfast is a veggie burger cooked in olive oil with bread and a couple of kiwi fruit. Other choices are any kind of cereal with soymilk; scrambled tofu; peanut butter on a bagel; baked beans on toast; or a baked potato with steamed veggies. Don't let yourself be constrained by ideas about what is appropriate for breakfast. Any healthful food that you enjoy eating in the morning is appropriate!

One final note about calcium in the diet. It's true that many vegan women don't get enough calcium. But you wouldn't know this from the way you feel. The body maintains normal blood calcium levels all the time, no matter how low your diet is in this nutrient. This is because we would die if the calcium levels of the blood get too high or too low. The body does this by taking calcium out of the bones, so a calcium deficiency affects us over many years with a gradual decrease in bone health. Fainting spells would not be due to too little calcium or protein. However, it's a good idea—especially for women—to give your calcium intake a boost by using supplements or fortified foods like fortified soymilk or orange juice.

Make sure you get at least 1,000 mg of calcium every day. And if you do have frequent dizzy or fainting spells, do see a doctor about this to rule out other problems.

Section 8.4

Calcium

Excerpted from "Information Sheet: Calcium," Vegetarian Society UK, http://www.vegsoc.org/info/calcium.html, copyright 2001, reprinted with permission. Some words have been changed to conform to American spelling conventions. Material may be viewed in its original format on the Vegetarian Society of the UK website: http://www.vegsoc.org.

Calcium is the most abundant mineral in the human body. Of the body's total calcium, about 99% is in the bones and teeth where it plays a structural role. The remaining 1% is present in body tissues and fluids where it is essential for cell metabolism, muscle contraction, and nerve impulse transmission.

Functions

The main function of calcium is structural. The skeleton of a young adult male contains about 1.2 kg of calcium. There is continuous movement of calcium between the skeleton and blood and other parts of the body. This is finely controlled by hormones. Metabolites of Vitamin D are important in this, increasing reabsorption of calcium by bones.

Calcium also plays a role in cell biology. Calcium can bind to a wide range of proteins altering their biological activity. This is important in nerve impulse transmission and muscle contraction. Calcium is also needed for blood clotting, activating clotting factors.

Vitamin D is needed for absorption of dietary calcium and so calcium deficiency may be linked with rickets in children. In adults, calcium deficiency may lead to osteomalacia (softening of bones). This may be related to repeated pregnancy with lengthy breast feeding.

Osteoporosis can be due to calcium deficiency. This involves loss of calcium from the bones and reduced bone density. This causes bones to be brittle and liable to fracture. Bone loss occurs with age in all individuals. This usually occurs after 35–40 years and involves the shrinking of the skeleton. Bone loss is greatest in women following the menopause. This is due to reduced levels of the hormone, oestrogen. Postmenopausal women are particularly at risk from osteoporosis.

Some research has indicated vegetarian women are at less risk of osteoporosis than omnivorous women. This is thought to be due to animal protein increasing calcium loss from bones. However, other research has found no difference between vegetarians and omnivores.

The risk of osteoporosis may be altered by factors other than diet. Lack of exercise, being underweight, smoking, and alcohol can all increase the risk.

A low level of calcium in the blood and tissues can cause hypocalcemia. This involves sensations of tingling and numbness and muscle twitches. In severe cases muscle spasms may occur. This is called tetany. It is more likely to be due to a hormonal imbalance in the regulation of calcium rather than a dietary deficiency.

Excess calcium in the blood can cause nausea, vomiting and calcium deposition in the heart and kidneys. This usually results from excessive doses of vitamin D and can be fatal in infants.

Dietary Sources

Calcium is present in a wide range of foods. Dairy products, leafy green vegetables, nuts, and seeds (almonds, brazils, sesame seeds), tofu, and dried fruit are all good sources of calcium for vegetarians. Most flour is fortified with calcium carbonate so cereals can also be a good source. Hard water may also provide calcium. Meat is a very poor source of calcium.

Calcium balance can be affected by a range of other factors. Vitamin D is essential for absorption of calcium from the gut. This is because calcium is transported into the body by a special carrier protein which requires vitamin D for its synthesis.

A number of substances can inhibit the absorption of calcium. Phytic acid, found in bran, whole cereals, and raw vegetables is one of these. Uronic acid, a component of dietary fiber, and oxalic acid, found in certain fruits and vegetables can also bind calcium. However, diets habitually high in these acids are not thought to have a major effect on calcium absorption. Saturated fats can also lessen calcium absorption.

Calcium is lost in the feces, urine, and sweat. Calcium loss is roughly equal to dietary calcium in adults. Calcium loss is reduced if dietary calcium is low. Adaptation to both high and low calcium intakes occur. Reduced intake leads to increased efficiency of absorption. In infants and children calcium is retained for new bone growth. Calcium is also lost during lactation in breast milk.

Required Intakes

- During pregnancy, calcium absorption from the gut increases and no additional calcium is generally needed. Pregnant adolescents

Table 8.3. Sources of Calcium (single servings).

Good Sources		Fair Sources		Poor sources	
Tofu (60g or 2oz)	304 mg	Brown bread (2 slices)	70 mg	Spaghetti, boiled (100g or 3½ oz)	7 mg
Cheddar cheese (slice, 40g)	288 mg	Brazil nuts (9 nuts, 30g)	54 mg	Brown rice (190g or 8oz)	7 mg
Cows milk (0.3 pint)	234 mg	Dried apricots (8 apricots)	46 mg		
Spinach, boiled (130g or 5oz)	208 mg	French beans, boiled (100g)	41 mg		
Dried figs (4 figs)	168 mg	Cottage cheese (45g or 1½ oz)	33 mg		
Soya cheese (slice, 40g)	180 mg	Sesame seeds (15g or ½ oz)	20 mg		
Chick peas boiled (200g or 8oz)	92 mg				
Baked beans (200g or 8 oz)	90 mg				
Broccoli, boiled (95g or 3½ oz)	72 mg				

are an exception to this, having particularly high calcium needs.

- Breast feeding women need an extra 550 mg of calcium. A lactating women can lose up to 300 mg a calcium/day in breast milk.

- Calcium absorption decreases with age so it is important the elderly have adequate dietary calcium.

Section 8.5

Eating Soy May Lower Osteoporosis Risk for Vegans

Excerpted from Anderson, John J. B., PhD, "Dietary Phytoestrogens and Bone Health." This article is reprinted with permission from *Vegetarian Nutrition Update*, the official newsletter of the Vegetarian Nutrition Dietetic Practice Group of the American Dietetic Association. © 1999. The full text of this article including references can be found at www.andrews.edu/NUFS/ Dietary%20phytoestrogens%20and%20bone%20health.html.

Introduction

The importance of soy foods in the diet to the health of populations throughout the world has only recently been recognized, primarily because these legumes contain phytoestrogens, i.e., plant molecules that have estrogenic properties. Only in Asian nations have soy products historically been used to any great extent for human consumption. In the US, the use of these products has had a slight upswing, but estimates of human intake remain very low—of the order of about 5 g per person per day. Therefore, information on the benefits of soy and foods derived from soy to human health is based almost totally on experimental results using animal models rather than on human investigations.

Observations of populations such as the high soy-consuming Japanese, including epidemiologic data, provide limited but nevertheless important suggestions about the benefits of soy consumption in reducing the adverse effects of chronic diseases in these populations.

Investigations of experimental animal models and isolated cells have been most useful in advancing our knowledge of the beneficial molecules, such as genistein and daidzein, found in soy foods. The phytoestrogens in soy foods are known as isoflavones because of their unique organic structures.

The focus of this text is on the effects of genistein and other isoflavones on bone tissue. This review covers several topics related to the phytoestrogens found in soy products: food sources; structures of the major molecules of the isoflavone class; and the digestion, absorption, and utilization of genistein and related isoflavones. In addition, the current thinking about the functions of the phytoestrogens in bone tissue and the mechanisms of action of these molecules at the cellular level are explored. Some comments about the potential of soy products in the prevention of osteoporosis are given. Reviews on this topic have recently been published.

Food Sources of Isoflavones

Of the diverse plants that constitute the legume family, only soy and its derivative foods provide significant amounts of the isoflavones, genistein, daidzein, and others, in the human diet. Table 8.4 lists the content of isoflavones in selected soy foods. Other legumes, such as various beans, also contain phytoestrogens, but at much lower amounts—typically 10 to 100-fold lower. The average amount of soy consumed by a person in the U.S. was estimated to be approximately 5 g a day in the mid-1990s. Most of this amount is from the use of soy meal in small amounts in breads and other baked goods. Americans have very low intakes of phytoestrogens, and an increase in the

Table 8.4. Isoflavone Content of Soy Foods on a Per Dry Weight Basis

Soy Food	Daidzein (mg/100g)	Genistein (mg/100g)
Soybeans	84	11
Soybeans (roasted)	56	87
Soy flour	23	81
Tempeh	27	32
Tofu	15	16

consumption of soy products over the next decade or longer will be desirable if they hope to get into the range of isoflavone dosages that have even greater health benefits.

Table 8.5 lists the contents of isoflavones in other legumes. Note that the amounts in other legumes are considerably lower than in soy and its products. The data in Tables 8.4 and 8.5 are based on the reports of several different research groups.

Structures of Isoflavones

The major isoflavones found in soy are genistein (~ 60%), daidzein (approximately 25%), and glycitein (~15%). In addition, several derivative molecules are made by the gut bacteria, including equol and para-ethylphenol. The structures of the isoflavones have some similarity

Table 8.5. Phytoestrogen Content of Legumes. Legumes were analyzed for daidzein (D), genistein (G), coumestrol (C), formononetin (F), and biochanin A (B). Legumes that were found to have no detectable phytoestrogrens include green peas, fava beans, lentils, barley, sesame seeds, and radish sprouts.

Legume	Phytoestrogens (mg/kg)	Phytoestrogen Molecules
Seeds:		
Green beans-fresh, raw	2	F
Lima beans-dry, raw	15	C
Garbanzo beans	15	B
Kidney beans-cooked	4	B
Pinto beans-dry	42	C, B
Great northern beans	6	B
Black eyed beans-dry	17	B
Green split beans dry	73	D
Mung beans-dry	6	F
Sprouts:		
Clover sprouts	311	G, C, F, B
Alfalfa sprouts	47	C

to estradiol. Genistein and daidzein differ by one hydroxyl group (-OH) on the A ring of the isoflavone structure.

The isoflavones provided in the diet from soy products, which exist primarily as glycones, undergo metabolic transformations in the gut to the functional molecules, such as genistein and daidzein. Major metabolic changes include the conversion of genistin to genistein and daidzin to daidzein. The former molecules are called glycones because they have a glucose molecule attached to them, whereas the latter molecules are referred to as aglycones because the glucose molecules are enzymatically removed.

The aglycones function in plants as antioxidants and as repellants of animals (phytoalexins). The glycones apparently serve only as storage molecules.

After the isoflavones and their metabolites are taken up by cells throughout the body, they may exert their actions—whether it be to lower blood lipids, improve vascular epithelial cell proliferation, impede the proliferation of cells that might become malignant (cancers), or enhance the bone forming activities of bone cells known as osteoblasts. This last topic is explored in more detail in the next section.

Functions of Isoflavones on Osteoblast-Like Cells in Culture

Once in the cells of the different tissues of the body, the isoflavones act as weak agonists or antagonists of estrogens, using estradiol as the model estrogen molecule. Studies of bone-forming osteoblast-like cells in culture have shown that an optimal dose range of pure genistein exists for maximal responses, e.g., enzyme synthesis and release, but doses that are too high can produce cell death by a genetically controlled process called apoptosis, also known as programmed death of cells, generally a healthy process. Doses that are too low have little or no effect on the endpoints of these bone-forming cells. It is generally accepted that doses of isoflavones (mixture of them) in the range of 50–100 mg per day provide optimal effects, but the intake within this dose range must occur approximately every day and indefinitely.

Human Skeletal Benefits of Phytoestrogens

Selected skeletal benefits have been identified for isoflavones and their derivative molecules in human subjects and animal models, though more research is needed to arrive at firm conclusions. The potential of soy products for the prevention of osteoporosis has given the isoflavones in soy an entirely new meaning—far afield from their role as antioxidants in plants. Researchers are undertaking investigations around the world on the effects of phytoestrogens on human functions. Unfortunately, at this time an insufficient number of human trials on the effects of isoflavones on bone, especially utilizing the measurement of bone mineral density (BMD), has been published, although several studies are currently in progress.

One of the enigmas of the human studies and of one primate study is the dose-response issue. It is entirely possible that, despite encouraging results from studies of rodent models, humans may require a higher dose of isoflavones before an improvement of BMD can be observed. For example, in the report of Potter et al., two doses were used in the study of BMD changes in elderly women, but only the high dose (~ 90 mg per day) yielded a positive effect on lumbar vertebral BMD (but not on BMD at any other site). The problem with the primate study was that only one dose (~ 28 mg per day) was employed, and this dose may not have been high enough to exert a skeletal effect even though it was sufficient to exert lowering effects on blood lipids. These findings, taken in their totality, suggest that a threshold dose (~50–90 mg per day) must be reached before a benefit to humans is observed. (A side issue of this dosing confusion may relate to the current impossibility of studying the effects of pure isoflavone preparations, such as genistein alone, because the preparations available today all contain significant amounts of soy protein and other soy constituents.

Another issue related to the effects of isoflavones on human bone is that the duration of the treatment at a sufficiently high dose, i.e., threshold dose, may be longer than previously thought to obtain a relative improvement in BMD compared to a control group. The study by Potter et al. found an effect at the high dose of isoflavones (~90 mg per day) after only six months of treatment of elderly postmenopausal women. The primate study lasted for one year. Other human studies have been of too short a duration to find an increase in BMD, but one study reported improvements in bone biochemical markers of postmenopausal Italian women after several months of treatment.

Animal Studies of the Effects of Phytoestrogens on Bone

Experimental animal models, especially rats, have been employed to establish dose-response effects and general changes in tissues after sufficient periods of treatment with isoflavones. In the few published reports, using ovariectomized (OVX) rat models of osteoporosis, the addition of isoflavones in the animal feed contributes to improved bone mass in comparison to animals fed on diets that do not contain the isoflavones.

In three different studies using rats as the experimental animal, the conclusion of each experiment is the same, although each study had a different design: animals fed soy-containing isoflavones or purified isoflavones (primarily genistein and daidzein) from soy had significant gains in bone mass when compared to control animals. These studies demonstrated that soy protein which contains the bulk of the isoflavones in the natural minimally modified soy resulted in greater amounts of bone mass and that either isolated, partially purified protein containing the isoflavones, or chemically purified genistein (~95 % purity) also improved bone mass. Another important aspect of these three studies is that the dose (amount) of the isoflavones employed must achieve a critical threshold before a significant gain in bone mass is accumulated. Therefore, the dose of isoflavone administered on a daily basis as well as the duration of treatment is critical for obtaining a benefit of these bone-conserving molecules.

Conclusions

Phytoestrogens, represented by soy-derived isoflavones and other molecules, such as coumestans and lignans, are receiving considerable attention because of their potential health benefits to human populations. The positive effects of isoflavone-rich preparations and of soy containing these phytoestrogens on bone tissue in rodent models holds promise for similar benefits in humans. Animal model experiments have been so encouraging as to suggest that human adults will receive similar improvements, either absolute gain in BMD or retention of BMD relative to loss of BMD in the untreated group (placebo).

Vegetarians, especially vegans, may obtain significant benefits from the consumption of soy products because they may be otherwise at a disadvantage of lower lifetime exposure to estrogens as a result of other nutrients or non-nutrient factors in their typical diets. They are, however, at a lower risk of breast and other reproductive cancers—as a trade-off for the low estrogen exposure. Too few human investigations have been undertaken and published at this time to make broad conclusions about the health benefits of these molecules. Nevertheless, based on a limited number of human studies, a dose between

50 and 90 mg per day seems to be needed to show a skeletal benefit. The amount of soy needed to provide 50–90 mg of isoflavones depends on the types of soy foods consumed; in the U.S., however, isoflavone supplements would typically be required to achieve these intakes (amounts). The issue of safety from excessive intakes has not yet been addressed in toxicity studies of human subjects, but the National Cancer Institute (NCI) is supporting such studies that are just getting underway.

Section 8.6

Getting Enough Vitamin B$_{12}$

Excerpted from "Information Sheet: Vitamin B$_{12}$," Vegetarian Society UK, http://www.vegsoc.org/info/b12.html, copyright 2001, reprinted with permission. Some words have been changed to conform to American spelling conventions. Material may be viewed in its original format on the Vegetarian Society of the UK website: http://www.vegsoc.org.

Introduction

Vitamin B$_{12}$ is a member of the vitamin B complex. It contains cobalt, and so is also known as cobalamin. It is exclusively synthesized by bacteria and is found primarily in meat, eggs and dairy products. There has been considerable research into proposed plant sources of vitamin B$_{12}$. Fermented soya products, seaweeds, and algae such as spirulina have all been suggested as containing significant B$_{12}$. However, the present consensus is that any B$_{12}$ present in plant foods is likely to be unavailable to humans and so these foods should not be relied upon as safe sources. Many vegan foods are supplemented with B$_{12}$. Vitamin B$_{12}$ is necessary for the synthesis of red blood cells, the maintenance of the nervous system, and growth and development in children. Deficiency can cause anemia. Vitamin B$_{12}$ neuropathy, involving the degeneration of nerve fibers and irreversible neurological damage, can also occur.

87

Functions

Vitamin B_{12}'s primary functions are in the formation of red blood cells and the maintenance of a healthy nervous system. B_{12} is necessary for the rapid synthesis of DNA during cell division. This is especially important in tissues where cells are dividing rapidly, particularly the bone marrow tissues responsible for red blood cell formation. If B_{12} deficiency occurs, DNA production is disrupted and abnormal cells called megaloblasts occur. This results in anemia. Symptoms include excessive tiredness, breathlessness, listlessness, pallor, and poor resistance to infection. Other symptoms can include a smooth, sore tongue, and menstrual disorders. Anemia may also be due to folic acid deficiency, folic acid also being necessary for DNA synthesis.

B_{12} is also important in maintaining the nervous system. Nerves are surrounded by an insulating fatty sheath comprised of a complex protein called myelin. B_{12} plays a vital role in the metabolism of fatty acids essential for the maintenance of myelin. Prolonged B_{12} deficiency can lead to nerve degeneration and irreversible neurological damage.

When deficiency occurs, it is more commonly linked to a failure to effectively absorb B_{12} from the intestine rather than a dietary deficiency. Absorption of B_{12} requires the secretion from the cells lining the stomach of a glycoprotein, known as intrinsic factor. The B_{12}-intrinsic factor complex is then absorbed in the ileum (part of the small intestine) in the presence of calcium. Certain people are unable to produce intrinsic factor and the subsequent pernicious anemia is treated with injections of B_{12}.

Vitamin B_{12} can be stored in small amounts by the body. Total body store is 2–5mg in adults. Around 80% of this is stored in the liver.

Vitamin B_{12} is excreted in the bile and is effectively reabsorbed. This is known as enterohepatic circulation. The amount of B_{12} excreted in the bile can vary from 1 to 10 μg (micrograms) a day. People on diets low in B_{12}, including vegans and some vegetarians, may be obtaining more B_{12} from reabsorption than from dietary sources. Reabsorption is the reason it can take over 20 years for deficiency disease to develop in people changing to diets absent in B_{12}. In comparison, if B_{12} deficiency is due to a failure in absorption it can take only 3 years for deficiency disease to occur.

Dietary Sources

The only reliable unfortified sources of vitamin B_{12} are meat, dairy products, and eggs. There has been considerable research into possible plant food sources of B_{12}. Fermented soya products, seaweeds, and algae have all been proposed as possible sources of B_{12}. However, analysis of fermented soya products, including tempeh, miso, shoyu and tamari, found no significant B_{12}.

Spirulina, an algae available as a dietary supplement in tablet form, and nori, a seaweed, have both appeared to contain significant amounts of B_{12} after analysis. However, it is thought that this is due to the presence of compounds structurally similar to B_{12}, known as B_{12} analogues. These cannot be utilized to satisfy dietary needs. Assay methods used to detect B_{12} are unable to differentiate between B_{12} and its analogues. Analysis of possible B_{12} sources may give false positive results due to the presence of these analogues.

Researchers have suggested that supposed B_{12} supplements such as spirulina may in fact increase the risk of B_{12} deficiency disease, as the B_{12} analogues can compete with B_{12} and inhibit metabolism.

The current nutritional consensus is that no plant foods can be relied on as a safe source of vitamin B_{12}.

Bacteria present in the large intestine are able to synthesize B_{12}. In the past, it has been thought that the B_{12} produced by these colonic bacteria could be absorbed and utilized by humans. However, the bacteria produce B_{12} too far down the intestine for absorption to occur, B_{12} not being absorbed through the colon lining.

Human feces can contain significant B_{12}. A study has shown that a group of Iranian vegans obtained adequate B_{12} from unwashed vegetables which had been fertilized with human manure. Fecal contamination of vegetables and other plant foods can make a significant contribution to dietary needs, particularly in areas where hygiene standards may be low. This may be responsible for the lack of anemia due to B_{12} deficiency in vegan communities in developing countries.

Good sources of vitamin B_{12} for vegetarians are dairy products or free-range eggs. One half pint of milk (full fat or semi skimmed) contains 1.2 μg. A slice of vegetarian cheddar cheese (40 g) contains 0.5 μg. A boiled egg contains 0.7μg. Fermentation in the manufacture of yoghurt destroys much of the B_{12} present. Boiling milk can also destroy much of the B_{12}.

Vegans are recommended to ensure their diet includes foods fortified with vitamin B_{12}. A range of B_{12} fortified foods are available. These include yeast extracts, Vecon vegetable stock, veggieburger mixes, textured vegetable protein, soya milks, vegetable and sunflower margarines, and breakfast cereals.

Required Intakes (RNI)

Reference nutrient intakes (RNI) for Vitamin B_{12}, μg/day (1000 μg = 1 mg). The RNI is the amount of nutrient which is enough for at least 97% of the population.

- 0 to 6 months: 0.3 μg
- 7 to 12 months: 0.4 μg
- 1 to 3 yrs: 0.5 μg
- 4 to 6 yrs: 0.8 μg
- 7 to 10 yrs: 1.0 μg
- 11 to 14 yrs: 1.2 μg
- 15 + yrs: 1.5 μg
- breast feeding women: 2.0 μg

Pregnant women are not thought to require any extra B_{12}, though little is known about this. Lactating women need extra B_{12} to ensure an adequate supply in breast milk. B_{12} has very low toxicity and high intakes are not thought to be dangerous.

Section 8.7

Getting Enough Vitamin D

Excerpted from "Vitamin D," The Vegan Society,
http://www.vegansociety.com/html/info/info17.html, copyright 1997,
reprinted with permission.

Introduction

Vitamin D is a fat-soluble vitamin which acts like a hormone, regulating the formation of bone and the absorption of calcium and phosphorus from the intestine. It helps to control the movement of calcium between bone and blood, and vice versa. In infancy and childhood, deficiency of vitamin D causes the deformed bones characteristic of rickets, while in adults a lack of the vitamin causes a softening of the bones known as osteomalacia. Deficiency is seen more often in northern countries, or where tradition dictates that the body is well covered by clothes, such as in parts of the Islamic world. An excess of the vitamin can cause loss of appetite, weight loss, nausea, headache, depression, and deposits of calcium in the kidneys.

Vegans and Vitamin D

Vegans usually obtain vitamin D from the action of sunlight on the skin or by taking fortified foods such as soya milk, margarine, breakfast cereals, and vitamin supplements which are made from yeast or other fungi. Fortified vegan products contain D_2 (ergocalciferol). Foods with naturally occurring vitamin D are, however, usually animal derived containing the vitamin D_3 (cholecalciferol).

The most significant supply of vitamin D (for omnivores as well as vegans) comes from the action of ultra-violet B light on sterols in the skin. Most people, including infants, require little or no extra from food when regularly exposed to sunlight when the sun is high in the sky. Bright sunlight is not necessary; even the sky shine on a cloudy summer day will stimulate formation of some D in the skin, while a short summer holiday in the open air will increase blood levels of the vitamin by two or three times the amount.

Northern Latitudes

The effective light wavelength—ultra-violet B (UVB, 290–315 nanometers in wavelength)—is not present in winter sunlight between October and March in countries above latitude 52 degrees north. Winter time supplies of vitamin D depend on the previous summers exposure creating adequate stores in the liver, or on dietary sources.

Requirements for Vitamin D

It has been found that bone loss in post menopause women occurs mostly in the winter due to falling levels of vitamin D products in the blood. A winter intake from fortified foods or supplements is strongly recommended to promote bone health. Winter intakes of about 15 μg (micrograms) per day appear to be appropriate to prevent bone loss.

There is growing evidence that low vitamin D levels contribute to cancer and auto immune disease. If we lived as we evolved—in the open nearer the equator—we would synthesize vitamin D from sunlight equivalent to 100 μg or more per day and dietary intake would be irrelevant.

Conclusions

Adult vegans obtain adequate vitamin D if they regularly spend time outdoors in spring, summer, and autumn. A dietary intake of the vitamin in the winter can be ensured by taking fortified products or supplements. In northern latitudes vegan women who are breast feeding should ensure their intake during winter by using fortified foods or taking supplements. Parents are advised to include vitamin D fortified foods or supplements if they wean their infants during the winter months, especially if they are dark skinned.

Table 8.6. Vegan Sources of Vitamin D

Type of Food	Amount of D
Plamil Concentrated sugar free (undiluted)	1.5 µg per l00ml
Vitaquell Extra Margarine	7.5 µg per l00g
Freeda Vitamins	
Vitamin D2 supplement	10 µg (ACCIU)
Multivitamin and mineral supplements	(typically 5 µg)

Section 8.8

Essential Fatty Acids

Excerpted from Davis, Brenda, RD, "Essential Fatty Acids in Vegetarian Nutrition." This article is reprinted with permission from *Vegetarian Nutrition Update*, the official newsletter of the Vegetarian Nutrition Dietetic Practice Group of the American Dietetic Association. © 1998. The original document, including references, can be found at http://www.andrews.edu/NUFS/essentialfat.htm.

Mahatma Gandhi once said, "Wherever flaxseeds become a regular food item among the people, there will be better health." While this prediction was based on simple observation, scientific evidence would suggest there is more than a grain of truth to his words. Flaxseeds are an exceptional source of lignans, a potent anticarcinogen and the richest known source of the essential omega-3 fatty acid, alpha-linolenic acid.

It is generally assumed that North Americans need not worry about getting enough fat of any kind, but as research unfolds, a fatal flaw in this thinking is revealed. Not all fats are damaging to health. Some fats are protective, and two in particular are essential to life—they are the essential fatty acids (EFA), linoleic acid (omega-6) and alpha-linolenic acid (omega-3).

Changes in our food supply since the industrial revolution have jeopardized both the quantity and balance of these nutrients. Our current dietary pattern provides excessive amounts of omega-6 fatty acids in relation to omega-3 fatty acid content. This imbalance of essential fatty acids affects vegetarians at least as much as omnivores. In addition, the trend towards very low fat vegetarian diets (10% or less of calories from fat) may further compromise essential fatty acid intake.

Function of EFAs

Essential fatty acids are necessary for the formation of healthy cell membranes, the proper development and functioning of the brain and nervous system, and for the production of hormone-like substances called eicosanoids (thromboxanes, leukotrienes, prostaglandins). These chemicals regulate numerous body functions including blood pressure, blood viscosity, vasoconstriction, and immune and inflammatory responses. Humans have the ability to convert the linoleic and alpha-linolenic acid to longer chain fatty acids, which serve as precursors for eicosanoids.

Eicosanoids formed from arachidonic acid (AA) (omega-6 family) have the potential to increase blood pressure, inflammation, platelet aggregation, thrombosis, vasospasm, allergic reactions, and cell proliferation. Those formed from eicosapentaenoic acid (EPA) (omega-3 family) have opposing affects. Omega-6 and omega-3 fatty acids are not interchangeable; we must consume both.

These two families of essential fatty acids compete for enzymes involved in their desaturation, thus the excessive consumption of foods rich in omega-6 fatty acids may compromise the conversion of alpha-linolenic acid to EPA, with adverse affects for health and disease. Current research suggests that the levels of essential fatty acids and the balance between them may play a critical role not only in growth and development, but also in the prevention and treatment of chronic diseases including coronary artery disease, hypertension, type II diabetes, arthritis and other immune/inflammatory disorders, and cancer.

The primary sources of essential fatty acids are plants on land and in the sea. Linoleic acid is found primarily in seeds, nuts, grains, and legumes. Alpha-linolenic acid is found in the green leaves of plants, including phytoplankton and algae, and in selected seeds, nuts, and legumes (flax, canola, walnuts and soy). Arachidonic acid (AA) and docosahexaenoic (DHA) acid are obtained directly from animal foods— AA from meat and poultry and DHA and EPA from fish.

When addressing the issue of essential fatty acids in vegetarian diets, three key questions arise:

1. How much omega-6 and omega-3 fatty acids do vegetarians need?

2. Do vegetarians convert alpha-linolenic acid to EPA and DHA in sufficient quantity?

3. How can vegetarians insure an adequate intake of omega-3 fatty acids?

How Much Omega-6 and Omega-3 Do Vegetarians Need?

There are two primary considerations when assessing the adequacy of these essential fatty acids: quantity and balance. The World Health

Organization recommends that polyunsaturated fats make up 3–7% of the energy in the diet, without any specification as to the amount needed from each family of fats. However, experts advise that one should consume a minimum of 3% of energy from omega-6 fatty acids and 0.5% from omega-3 fatty acids. Many now suggest that infants, and others who do not consume preformed EPA and DHA, should consume 1% of their energy needs as omega-3. This would include vegetarians and others who do not eat fish. While no definitive recommendations are in place for pregnant and lactating vegetarians, it may be appropriate to increase the intake of alpha-linolenic acid to 2% of calories due to the importance of long chain omega-3 fatty acids in the developing fetus and infant.

An adult consuming 2000 calories could achieve the recommended minimum 3% omega-6 fatty acids and 1% omega-3 fatty acids with 60 calories of linoleic acid (6.7 g) and 20 calories of alpha-linolenic acid. Obtaining 6.6 g of linoleic acid is easy on almost any diet, even those that are very low fat (10–15% fat). Omega-3 fatty acids are not as plentiful in our food supply, and the primary source for most North Americans is fish. Vegetarians and others not eating fish are well advised to include omega-3-rich plants in their diet on a regular basis.

Scientists use the ratio of omega-6 fatty acids to omega-3 fatty acids to assess the balance between essential fatty acids in the diet. Research scientists from around the world recommend ratios varying from 5:1 to 10:1, while some experts suggest a ratio of between 1:1 and 4:1 as being optimal. The current ratio in our diet is estimated to be 14:1 to 20:1 with some studies indicating higher ratios in vegetarian populations compared to omnivorous populations.

Are Plant Sources of Omega-3 Sufficient for Human Needs?

Vegetarians and vegans have no direct sources of eicosapentaenoic acid (EPA) and docosahexaenoic acid (DHA) (long chain omega-3 fatty acids) in the diet, hence they must convert alpha-linolenic acid to EPA and DHA in the body. Researchers have questioned whether this conversion is adequate to meet human needs for long chain omega-3 fatty acids. Scientific studies suggest that although the conversion is slow and incomplete (perhaps only 10% of alpha-linolenic acid is converted), and although vegetarians tend to have lower blood levels of long chain omega-3 fatty acids, it is sufficient to meet the needs of most people.

It is important to note, however, that certain factors can depress the enzymes responsible for the desaturation of alpha-linolenic acid, thus adversely affecting this important conversion process. These factors include high intakes of saturated fat, trans fatty acids, cholesterol, and alcohol, an inadequate intake of energy or protein, or a deficiency of certain nutrients, such as zinc or copper. There may also be conversion problems for people with diabetes or other metabolic disorders and for those who inherit a limited ability to produce conversion enzymes (possibly where fish has been a major component of the diet for centuries).

In addition, infants convert alpha-linolenic acid to DHA and EPA more slowly than adults. Studies have provided evidence that preterm infants do not have the capacity to form sufficient DHA, resulting in reduced visual acuity and brain function. Thus DHA must be considered an essential nutrient for these babies.

Breastfed infants generally receive ample DHA from their mother's milk, although amounts vary considerably depending on maternal intake of omega-3 fatty acids. Vegetarian and vegan mothers have lower concentrations of DHA in their milk, although infant levels of DHA appear to be only slightly less than that of infants of omnivorous mothers. A DHA supplement based on cultured microalgae (under the trademark Neuromins) is now available from natural food stores nationwide.

How Can Vegetarians Insure an Adequate Intake of Omega-3?

The following four guidelines will help to insure an appropriate quantity and balance of essential fatty acids in vegetarian and vegan diets:

Limit intake of saturated fats and trans fatty acids. In vegetarian diets the primary sources of saturated fats are dairy products and eggs, while vegan diets are low in saturated fats, unless there is a heavy reliance on tropical oils. Trans fatty acids come primarily from hydrogenated vegetable oils. These fats have the potential to interfere with the conversion of alpha-linolenic acid to DHA, in addition to increasing risk for degenerative diseases. Trans fatty acids are plentiful in shortening, hydrogenated margarines, processed foods containing hydrogenated and partially hydrogenated vegetable oils (crackers, cookies, cakes, pastries, frozen convenience foods, snack foods) and fast foods (hydrogenated oils are used for deep frying).

Make monounsaturated fats the principal fat in the diet. Monounsaturated fats should make up the largest portion of fat in the diet, as they have proven to have neutral or positive affects on health. In addition, emphasizing monounsaturated fats will help to keep saturated fats, trans fatty acids and omega-6 fatty acids to a modest level. Olive oil (77% mono-fat) and/or canola oil (58% mono-fat) would be the recommended oils to use. Avocados, olives, hazelnuts, pistachios, almonds, macadamia nuts, peanuts, and pecans are also excellent sources of monounsaturated fats. These foods also provide valuable vitamins, minerals, phytochemicals, and fiber, and when used moderately, make an excellent addition to the vegetarian diet.

Limit the intake of omega-6-rich vegetable oils. Minimizing the use of oils rich in omega-6 fatty acids is the easiest way to keep linoleic acid levels at a reasonable level. Oils that contain predominately omega-6 fatty acids include corn oil, sunflower oil, safflower oil, and cottonseed oil. Commercial products such as margarine, salad dressing, and mayonnaise that are made with these oils should also be limited. Soybean oil and walnut oil are also rich sources of omega-6 fatty acids, but their omega-6 content is partially compensated for by an omega-3 content of 5–8%.

Include a source of omega-3 fatty acids in the daily diet. In order to obtain sufficient omega-3 fatty acids in the vegetarian diet, good plant sources of this nutrient must be incorporated into the daily diet. If we assume an energy intake of 2000 kcal/day, 5% of calories as polyunsaturated fats, and a omega-6: omega-3 ratio of 4:1, one would require 8.9 g of omega-6 and 2.2 g of omega-3 fatty acids. It would not be a challenge to consume the 9 grams of omega-6 fatty acids, even on a very low-fat vegetarian diet. The Reversal Diet (the Dean Ornish program that allows for no oils, nuts, or seeds) provides an average 6 grams of linoleic acid primarily from whole grains and soy products. On the other hand, it would require considerable effort for vegetarians to get 2.2 grams of omega-3 fatty acids, by carefully selecting excellent plant sources of omega-3.

The best source of alpha-linolenic acid is flaxseed oil (57% omega-3 and 17% omega-6 fatty acids). Other omega-3-rich plant foods are much less concentrated sources of this nutrient, often coming packaged with much higher amounts of linoleic acid. Table 8.7 lists good plant sources of alpha-linolenic acid.

Practical Pointers for Using Flaxseeds and Flaxseed Oil

The oil from flaxseeds is highly unsaturated, thus will be easily damaged upon exposure to light, heat, or air. Flaxseed oil can be purchased in the refrigerator section of natural food stores. It is packaged in black plastic bottles or dark brown glass bottles to protect it from light. The oil must be kept refrigerated and will stay fresh for up to 8 weeks after it is opened. One should check the expiration date. Flax oil that will not be used within this time should be frozen. It normally lasts for a year or more in the freezer. Rancid flax oil will smell "skunky" and should be discarded.

Flax oil should never be exposed to direct heat, thus it should not be used in cooking. It works well as a salad dressing base or as a tasty

Table 8.7. Plant Sources of Omega-3 Fatty Acids

Food (serving size)	Omega-3 (g)	Omega-6 (g)
Oils		
Flax seed oil, 1 Tbsp.	6.6	1.6
Canola oil, 1 Tbsp.	1.6	3.2
Walnut oil, 1 Tbsp.	1.4	7.6
Soy oil, 1 Tbsp.	1.0	7.0
Nuts and Seeds		
Flax seeds, ground, 2 Tbsp.	3.2	0.8
Walnuts (English), 2 Tbsp.	1.0	5.4
Vegetables, Fruits, and Legumes		
Soybeans, cooked, 1 cup	1.1	7.8
Tofu, firm, one-half cup	0.7	5.0
Tofu, medium, one-half cup	0.4	2.9
Soy milk, 1 cup	0.4	2.9
Berries, 1 cup	0.2	0.2
Peas, one-half cup	0.2	0.2
Legumes, one-half cup	0.05	0.05
Green leafy vegetables (broccoli, kale, Chinese greens, salad greens), 1 c. raw or ½ c. cooked	0.1	0.03
Grains		
Oat germ, 2 Tbsp.	0.2	1.6
Wheat germ, 2 Tbsp.	0.1	0.8

topping for pasta, potatoes, rice, or vegetables (garlic/chili flavored flaxseed oil is a great choice). It can also be added to hot cereal, soup, sauces, dips, or blender drinks. Mix flax oil with butter or a non-hydrogenated margarine for an omega-3-rich spread. The oil can also be taken as a supplement (1–2 tsp./day or in pill form for those who don't like the taste).

Whole flaxseeds are protected by a hard outer coat and will last for many months in your pantry. Unfortunately, because the seeds are so small, they generally enter the gastrointestinal system intact, and exit intact also. To enhance the digestibility of flaxseeds, simply grind them in a blender or a coffee grinder. Flaxseeds can be purchased in the bulk section of natural food stores and in most large grocery stores. Once flaxseeds are ground they go rancid quickly, thus should be stored in the refrigerator or freezer.

Ground flaxseeds can be sprinkled on salad or cereal. The soluble fiber in the seeds will make the liquid in your cereal very thick if it sits for too long. Ground flaxseed also makes an excellent egg replacer. One tablespoon of ground flax mixed with 3 tablespoons of liquid replaces one egg in baking. This works especially well in muffins, pancakes, cookies, and cakes.

Flaxseed Cautions

Flaxseeds absorb 5 to 6 times their weight in water, so it is important to drink plenty of fluids when consuming ground seeds.

Raw flaxseeds, but not the flaxseed oil, contain cyanogenic glucosides, which are converted in the body to thiocyanates. These chemicals may interfere with iodine uptake by the thyroid gland and may increase the risk of goiter (especially when dietary iodine is limited). It has been suggested that intake of raw flaxseed should be restricted to 3–4 tablespoons a day. Cooking inactivates the cyanogenic glucosides, so there is less concern with flaxseed used in baking.

Chapter 9

Are Vegetarian Diets Healthier?

Many people choose a vegetarian diet because they believe that vegetarianism is associated with good health. A substantial body of scientific literature supports this belief. Several large epidemiologic studies have indicated that vegetarians (primarily lacto- or lacto-ovovegetarians) have lower mortality rates and lower rates of chronic diseases than do meat eaters. This doesn't mean, however, that meatless diets are uniquely advantageous.

Vegetarian diets often come closer to meeting official dietary guidelines than do typical omnivorous diets because vegetarian diets contain less fat, less saturated fat, and fewer calories while including more whole grains, more fruits, and more vegetables. It is not necessary to become a vegetarian, however, to conform to official guidelines. Eliminating meat from the diet can be one way to reduce saturated fat and increase the consumption of plant foods, but it is not the only way. People can also reduce their risks of chronic diseases by adopting omnivorous diets that meet current dietary recommendations. This means limiting quantities of high-fat foods; choosing lean red meat, skinless poultry, and low-fat or non-fat dairy products; and eating generous amounts of grains, fruits, and vegetables.

Excerpted from Meister, Kathleen, M.S., "Vegetarianism," American Council on Science and Health, http://www.acsh.org/publications/booklets/vegetarian.pdf, July 1997. Reprinted with permission of American Council on Science and Health (ACSH), 1995 Broadway, 2nd Floor, New York, NY 10023-5800. To learn more about ACSH, visit www.acsh.org. Despite the age of this document, readers seeking information about the healthfulness of vegetarian diets will find this information useful.

Diet Versus Lifestyle

Vegetarians may also be healthy for reasons not related to their dietary choices. Many vegetarians are health conscious; they exercise regularly, maintain a desirable body weight, don't smoke, don't abuse illegal drugs, and don't abuse alcohol. These lifestyle choices contribute to reducing health risks. Although most epidemiologists have attempted to take these factors into account in their analyses, it is possible that they did not control adequately for the effects of some or all nondietary factors.

People who choose vegetarianism may also differ from the rest of the population in other ways that influence health. For example, Western vegetarians tend to be of relatively high socioeconomic status. As a rule, affluent people are healthier than those living in poverty simply because of their better living conditions and greater access to medical care.

An authoritative review of vegetarianism and chronic diseases classified the evidence for various alleged health benefits of vegetarianism as either "strong," "good," "fair," or "poor." The evidence that vegetarians are at lower risk for obesity, constipation, lung cancer, and alcoholism was found to be "strong." The evidence that risks of hypertension (high blood pressure), coronary artery disease, type II (adult-onset) diabetes mellitus, and gallstones are lower among vegetarians was regarded as "good." The data supporting a link between vegetarianism and reduced risks of breast and colon cancers, diverticular disease, osteoporosis, kidney stones, dental erosion, and dental caries were classified as "fair to poor."

For some of these diseases it is likely that the vegetarian diet itself is the key protective factor. For example, the low incidence of constipation in vegetarians is almost certainly due to their high intake of foods rich in dietary fiber. For other diseases, however, lifestyle factors other than diet may be more relevant. For example, the low rate of lung cancer in vegetarians is attributable primarily to their extremely low rate of cigarette smoking. There are many risk factors for most chronic diseases; diet is only one of them.

Choosing a Healthful Vegetarian Diet

The mere fact that a diet is vegetarian does not guarantee that it is healthful. The keys to any healthy eating plan, vegetarian or otherwise, are moderation and variety. For a healthful diet, vegetarians like everyone else should eat a variety of different types of nutritious foods; should limit their intake of high-calorie foods that make little positive nutritional contribution to the diet; should use the information given in the Nutrition Facts labels on food products; and should limit their overall intake of fat and calories.

Although vegetarian diets are usually low in total fat and saturated fat, this is not always the case. Lacto-ovo-vegetarians, in particular, need to realize that their diets are not automatically low in saturated fat and cholesterol. Like omnivores, lacto-ovo-vegetarians need to choose foods carefully to conform to current dietary recommendations.

Vegetarians who eat large amounts of fried foods, full-fat cheeses, whole milk, nuts, and/or commercial meat substitutes may consume more total fat and saturated fat than do some omnivores. Vegetarians eating large quantities of eggs may exceed current recommendations for cholesterol intake. A healthful lacto-ovo-vegetarian diet should emphasize low-fat rather than full-fat dairy products; should include eggs and nuts only in moderation; and should balance high-fat or high-cholesterol foods with lower-fat, lower-cholesterol choices.

Chapter 10

More Benefits of Fiber Are Discovered

Because it causes gas, bloating, and other uncomfortable side effects, fiber may be the Rodney Dangerfield of food constituents. But with more and more research showing that a high-fiber diet may help prevent cancer, heart disease, and other serious ailments, roughage has started to get some respect.

The problem is that most Americans don't get enough fiber to realize its potential benefits. The typical American eats only about 11 grams of fiber a day, according to the American Dietetic Association. Health experts recommend a minimum of 20 to 30 grams of fiber a day for most people.

The Food and Drug Administration (FDA) has recognized fiber's importance by requiring it to be listed on the Nutrition Facts panel of food labels along with other key nutrients and calories. And, based on scientific evidence, the agency has approved four claims related to fiber intake and lowered risk of heart disease and cancer.

One claim states that dietary soluble fiber, when part of a diet low in saturated fat and cholesterol, may reduce the risk of coronary heart disease. In 1997, FDA approved this claim for certain foods containing whole oats and in 1998, for certain foods containing psyllium seed husk. The other three claims, allowed since 1993, are:

- Diets low in fat and rich in fiber-containing grain products, fruits, and vegetables may reduce the risk of some types of cancer.

"Bulking up Fiber's Healthful Reputation," *FDA Consumer*, July-August 1997, Revised September 1998, U. S. Food and Drug Administration (FDA) Pub. No. 98-2313, http://www.fda.gov/fdac/features/1997/597_fiber.html.

- Diets low in saturated fat and cholesterol and rich in fruits, vegetables, and grain products that contain fiber, particularly soluble fiber, may reduce the risk of coronary heart disease.

- Diets low in fat and rich in fruits and vegetables, which are low-fat foods and may contain fiber or vitamin A (as beta-carotene) and vitamin C, may reduce the risk of some cancers.

Found only in plant foods, such as whole grains, fruits, vegetables, beans, nuts, and seeds, fiber is composed of complex carbohydrates. Some fibers are soluble in water and others are insoluble. Most plant foods contain some of each kind.

Some foods containing high levels of soluble fiber are dried beans, oats, barley, and some fruits, notably apples and citrus, and vegetables, such as potatoes. Foods high in insoluble fiber are wheat bran, whole grains, cereals, seeds, and the skins of many fruits and vegetables.

Fiber's Health Benefits

What can fiber do for you? Numerous epidemiologic (population-based) studies have found that diets low in saturated fat and cholesterol and high in fiber are associated with a reduced risk of certain cancers, diabetes, digestive disorders, and heart disease. However, since high-fiber foods may also contain antioxidant vitamins, phyto-chemicals, and other substances that may offer protection against these diseases, researchers can't say for certain that fiber alone is responsible for the reduced health risks they observe, notes Joyce Saltsman, a nutritionist with FDA's Office of Food Labeling. "Moreover, no one knows whether one specific type of fiber is more beneficial than another since fiber-rich foods tend to contain various types," she adds.

Recent findings on the health effects of fiber show it may play a role in:

Cancer. Epidemiologic studies have consistently noted an association between low total fat and high fiber intakes and reduced incidence of colon cancer. A 1992 study by researchers at Harvard Medical School found that men who consumed 12 grams of fiber a day were twice as likely to develop precancerous colon changes as men whose daily fiber intake was about 30 grams. The exact mechanism for reducing the risk is not known, but scientists theorize that insoluble fiber adds bulk to stool, which in turn dilutes carcinogens and speeds their transit through the lower intestines and out of the body.

The evidence that a high-fiber diet can protect against breast cancer is equivocal. Researchers analyzing data from the Nurses' Health Study, which tracked 89,494 women for eight years, concluded in 1992 that fiber intake has no influence on breast cancer risk in middle-aged women. Previously, a review and analysis of 12 studies found a link between high fiber intake and reduced risk.

In the early stages, some breast tumors are stimulated by excess amounts of estrogen circulating in the bloodstream. Some scientists believe that fiber may hamper the growth of such tumors by binding with estrogen in the intestine. This prevents the excess estrogen from being reabsorbed into the bloodstream.

Digestive disorders. Because insoluble fiber aids digestion and adds bulk to stool, it hastens passage of fecal material through the gut, thus helping to prevent or alleviate constipation. Fiber also may help reduce the risk of diverticulosis, a condition in which small pouches form in the colon wall (usually from the pressure of straining during bowel movements). People who already have diverticulosis often find that increased fiber consumption can alleviate symptoms, which include constipation and/or diarrhea, abdominal pain, flatulence, and mucus or blood in the stool.

Diabetes. As with cholesterol, soluble fiber traps carbohydrates to slow their digestion and absorption. In theory, this may help prevent wide swings in blood sugar level throughout the day. Additionally, a study from the Harvard School of Public Health, published in the 2/12/97 issue of the *Journal of the American Medical Association*, suggests that a high-sugar, low-fiber diet more than doubles women's risk of Type II (non-insulin-dependent) diabetes. In the study, cereal fiber was associated with a 28 percent decreased risk, with fiber from fruits and vegetables having no effect. In comparison, cola beverages, white bread, white rice, and french fries increased the risk.

Heart disease. Clinical studies show that a heart-healthy diet (low in saturated fat and cholesterol, and high in fruits, vegetables and grain products that contain soluble fiber) can lower blood cholesterol. In these studies, cholesterol levels dropped between 0.5 percent and 2 percent for every gram of soluble fiber eaten per day.

As it passes through the gastrointestinal tract, soluble fiber binds to dietary cholesterol, helping the body to eliminate it. This reduces blood cholesterol levels, which, in turn, reduces cholesterol deposits on arterial walls that eventually choke off the vessel. There also is some evidence that soluble fiber can slow the liver's manufacture of cholesterol, as well as alter low-density lipoprotein (LDL) particles to make them larger and less dense. Researchers believe that small, dense LDL particles pose a bigger health threat.

Recent findings from two long-term large-scale studies of men suggest that high fiber intake can significantly lower the risk of heart attack. Men who ate the most fiber-rich foods (35 grams a day, on average) suffered one-third fewer heart attacks than those who had the lowest fiber intake (15 grams a day), according to a Finnish study of 21,903 male smokers aged 50 to 69, published in the December 1996 issue of *Circulation*. Earlier in the year, findings from an ongoing U.S. study of 43,757 male health professionals (some of whom were sedentary, overweight or smokers) suggest that those who ate more than 25 grams of fiber per day had a 36 percent lower risk of developing heart disease than those who consumed less than 15 grams daily. In the Finnish study, each 10 grams of fiber added to the diet decreased the risk of dying from heart disease by 17 percent; in the U.S. study, risk was decreased by 29 percent.

These results indicate that high-fiber diets may help blunt the effects of smoking and other risk factors for heart disease.

Obesity. Because insoluble fiber is indigestible and passes through the body virtually intact, it provides few calories. And since the digestive tract can handle only so much bulk at a time, fiber-rich foods are more filling than other foods—so people tend to eat less. Insoluble fiber also may hamper the absorption of calorie-dense dietary fat. So, reaching for an apple instead of a bag of chips is a smart choice for someone trying to lose weight.

But be leery of using fiber supplements for weight loss. In August 1991, FDA banned methylcellulose, along with 110 other ingredients, in over-the-counter diet aids because there was no evidence these ingredients were safe and effective. The agency also recalled one product that contained guar gum after receiving reports of gastric or esophageal obstructions. The manufacturer had claimed the product promoted a feeling of fullness when it expanded in the stomach.

An Apple a Day and More

Recent research suggests that as much as 35 grams of fiber a day is needed to help reduce the risk of chronic disease, including heart disease. A fiber supplement can help make up the shortfall, but should not be a substitute for fiber-rich foods. "Foods that are high in fiber also contain nutrients that may help reduce the risk of chronic disease," Saltsman notes. In addition, eating a variety of such foods provides several types of fiber, whereas some fiber supplements contain only a single type of fiber, such as methylcellulose or psyllium.

To fit more fiber into your day:

- Read food labels. The labels of almost all foods will tell you the amount of dietary fiber in each serving, as well as the Percent Daily Value (DV) based on a 2,000-calorie diet. For instance, if a half cup serving of a food provides 10 grams of dietary fiber, one serving provides 40 percent of the recommended DV. The food label can state that a product is "a good source" of fiber if it contributes 10 percent of the DV—2.5 grams of fiber per serving. The package can claim "high in," "rich in" or "excellent source of" fiber if the product provides 20 percent of the DV—5 grams per serving.

- Use the U.S. Department of Agriculture's food pyramid as a guide. If you eat 2 to 4 servings of fruit, 3 to 5 servings of vegetables, and 6 to 11 servings of cereal and grain foods, as recommended by the pyramid, you should have no trouble getting 25 to 30 grams of fiber a day.

- Start the day with a whole-grain cereal that contains at least 5 grams of fiber per serving. Top with wheat germ, raisins, bananas, or berries, all of which are good sources of fiber.

- When appropriate, eat vegetables raw. Cooking vegetables may reduce fiber content by breaking down some fiber into its carbohydrate components. When you do cook vegetables, microwave or steam only until they are al dente—tender, but still firm to the bite.

- Avoid peeling fruits and vegetables; eating the skin and membranes ensures that you get every bit of fiber. But rinse with warm water to remove surface dirt and bacteria before eating. Also, keep in mind that whole fruits and vegetables contain more fiber than juice, which lacks the skin and membranes.

- Eat liberal amounts of foods that contain unprocessed grains in your diet: whole-wheat products such as bulgur, couscous or kasha and whole-grain breads, cereals and pasta.

- Add beans to soups, stews and salads; a couple of times a week, substitute legume-based dishes (such as lentil soup, bean burritos, or rice and beans) for those made with meat.

- Keep fresh and dried fruit on hand for snacks.

"So many foods contain fiber that it's really not that hard to get your intake up where it should be," Saltsman says.

Slow Going

A word of caution: When increasing the fiber content of your diet, it's best to take it slow. Add just a few grams at a time to allow the intestinal tract to adjust; otherwise, abdominal cramps, gas, bloating, and diarrhea or constipation may result. Other ways to help minimize these effects:

- Drink at least 2 liters (8 cups) of fluid daily.

- Don't cook dried beans in the same water you soaked them in.

- Use enzyme products, such as Beano or Say Yes To Beans, that help digest fiber.

— by Ruth Papazian

Ruth Papazian is a writer in Bronx, NY, specializing in health and safety issues.

Chapter 11

Cancer, Heart Disease, and Vegetarian Diets

Chapter Contents

Section 11.1

Vegetarian Diets, Cholesterol, and Fat

"Information Sheet: Fats and Cholesterol," Vegetarian Society UK, http://
www.vegsoc.org/info/fats.html, copyright 2001, reprinted with permission.
Some words have been changed to conform to American spelling conventions.
Material may be viewed in its original format on the Vegetarian Society of the
UK website: http://www.vegsoc.org.

Introduction

Fats provide a concentrated source of energy in the diet. The building blocks of fats are called fatty acids. These can be either saturated,
monounsaturated, or poly-unsaturated. Foods rich in saturated fats
are usually of animal origin. Vegetable fats are generally unsaturated.

Saturated fat raises the level of cholesterol in the blood. Cholesterol is present in animal foods but not plant foods. It is essential for
metabolism but is not needed in the diet as our bodies can produce
all that is needed. Raised blood cholesterol is associated with an increased risk of heart disease.

Fats and oils are essentially the same. Fats tend to be solid at room
temperature while oils are liquid. The term lipids include both fats
and oils.

Structure and Functions

Fats consist of fatty acids and glycerol. Nearly all the fats in our
bodies and in foods are triglycerides, being made up of three fatty acid
molecules to one glycerol molecule. There are about 16 different fatty
acids commonly present in foods. The nature of fat depends on its
constituent fatty acids.

Fats can be classed as either saturated, monounsaturated or polyunsaturated. This depends on the type of chemical bonds present in
the fatty acid. If a fatty acid has all the hydrogen atoms it can hold it
is termed saturated. However, if some of the hydrogen atoms are absent and the usual single bond between carbon atoms has been replaced by a double bond, then it is unsaturated. If there is just one
double bond then it is monounsaturated. If there is more than one

112

then it is polyunsaturated. Most fats contain a proportion of each of these three basic types of fatty acid but are generally described according to which type predominates.

Saturated fats tend to be animal fats and are solid at room temperature. Butter, lard, suet and meat fat are saturated fats. Unsaturated fats are liquid at room temperature. They are usually of plant origin, though fish oils may also be high in polyunsaturated fatty acids. Plant oils may be hardened by the addition of hydrogen atoms, converting double bonds to single bonds. This process is known as hydrogenation. Hydrogenated vegetable oils are often present in margarine and other processed foods.

Fats have a number of important functions in the body. As well as being a concentrated source of energy, fats act as carriers for fat-soluble vitamins A, D, E and K. Fats are also essential for the structure of cell membranes and are precursors of many hormones.

Essential Fatty Acids

Two fatty acids are termed essential fatty acids. These are linoleic acid and a-linolenic acid. These must be present in the diet as the body is unable to make them itself. They are widely present in plant oils such as sunflower, rapeseed, and soybean oils.

Linoleic acid is converted into the body to arachidonic acid from which prostaglandins and other vital compounds are made. Because of this conversion, arachidonic acid is not an essential fatty acid as was once believed. A-linolenic acid is converted to eicosapentaenoic acid (EPA) which is important in proper nerve function. EPA is present in fish oils and is claimed to be beneficial in reducing the symptoms of arthritis and the risk of heart disease. For this reason, fish oils are sometimes used therapeutically. Plant oils containing large amounts of a-linolenic acid can be used as an alternative by vegetarians. Linseeds and linseed oil are particularly rich sources of a-linolenic acid.

Cholesterol

Cholesterol belongs to the sterol group of fats. It is present in all animal tissues but is absent from plants. Cholesterol is essential as a component of cell membranes and a precursor of bile acids and certain hormones. The body can make its own cholesterol and so a dietary source is not required.

Cholesterol is transported in to various proteins. These complex molecules are called lipoproteins. There are four main types of lipoprotein involved in cholesterol transport. The most commonly referred to are low density lipoprotein (LDL) and high density lipoprotein (HDL).

Cholesterol may form plaques on artery walls if levels in the blood are too high. This can lead to atherosclerosis. Because of this high blood cholesterol is linked with heart disease. It is the LDL cholesterol which has been linked to heart disease. HDL cholesterol may help protect against the risk of heart disease.

The amount of dietary cholesterol is not clearly linked to levels of cholesterol in the blood. Blood cholesterol is more closely related to the amount of saturated fat in the diet, saturated fat raising blood cholesterol. Unsaturated fats are not thought to raise blood cholesterol and may indeed lower levels.

Trans Fatty Acids

Unsaturated fatty acids can exist in two different geometric forms. These are called the cis and trans forms. Unsaturated fatty acids exist naturally in the cis form. During food manufacturing processes these cis fatty acids may be changed to trans fatty acids. Hydrogenation of margarine causes this to occur. It has been suggested that trans fatty acids can increase the risk of heart disease.

Free Radicals

Free radicals are highly reactive molecules which have been linked to both heart disease and cancer. A number of factors, including alcohol, stress and environmental pollutants can increase the generation of free radicals in the body. Polyunsaturated fats can also generate free radicals, especially when exposed to heat or sunlight. Because of this it is suggested that vegetable oils should be stored out of direct sunlight. Mono-unsaturated olive oil is less vulnerable to free radical generation and so is a better choice for frying.

Anti-oxidants such as vitamins A, C, and E offer protection against free radicals. Fresh fruit and vegetables are rich in these anti-oxidants.

Dietary Sources

Saturated fats are nearly always from animal foods. Meat, eggs, and dairy products all contain saturated fats. Lard and suet are saturated fats. Coconut oil and palm oil are vegetable sources of saturated fats. Olive oil is a monounsaturated fat. Polyunsaturated fats are usually from plant sources.

The ratio of polyunsaturated to saturated fats in the diet is often called the P:S ratio.

Cholesterol is present in all animal foods but not plant foods. Egg yolks and high-fat dairy products are high in cholesterol.

Required Intakes

Currently it is believed that around 42% of energy in the typical British diet is from fat. Dietary advice is to reduce this. The COMA (Committee on Medical Aspects of Food Policy) report advocated that no more than 35% of daily energy requirement should come from fat whilst the NACNE (National Advisory Committee on Nutritional Education) paper recommends a reduction to no more than 30%. Special emphasis is placed on reducing the amount of saturated fat in the diet.

Vegetarian diets tend to be lower in fat than omnivore diets. However, vegetarians consuming dairy products and processed foods high in fat may still be consuming too much. Advice to vegetarians is to keep fat intake to a minimum, avoid high fat dairy products and processed foods containing dairy fats and hydrogenated vegetable fats, and to use olive oil for cooking purposes.

Section 11.2

Vegetable-Based Diets and Cancer Prevention

This section contains text from Farley, Dixie, "Vegetarian Diets—The Pluses and the Pitfalls," *FDA Consumer*, May 1994, FDA (Food and Drug Administration) Pub. No. 93-2258, http://www.pueblo.gsa.gov/cic_text/food/veg-diet/veg-diet.txt. Updated in April, 2001 by Dr. David A. Cooke, MD, Diplomate, American Board of Internal Medicine.

Can Veggies Prevent Cancer?

The National Cancer Institute states in its booklet *Diet, Nutrition and Cancer Prevention: The Good News* that a third of cancer deaths may be related to diet. The booklet's "Good News" is: Vegetables from the cabbage family (cruciferous vegetables) may reduce cancer risk, diets low in fat and high in fiber-rich foods may reduce the risk of cancers of the colon and rectum, and diets rich in foods containing vitamin A, vitamin C, and beta-carotene may reduce the risk of certain cancers.

Despite studies showing lower rates of cancers in people who consume diets high in fruits in vegetables, it has been very difficult to determine exactly what accounts for this benefit. It does not appear to be as simple as more vitamins or fiber. Studies which added specific vitamins or vitamin combinations to participants' diets have not shown reduced risks of cancer. Perhaps there are as yet unidentified substances present in these foods which are responsible for their benefits.

As for increasing fiber in the diet, Joanne Slavin, PhD, RD, of the University of Minnesota, gives this advice: "Animal studies show that soluble fibers are associated with the highest levels of cell proliferation, a precancerous event. The current interest in dietary fiber has allowed recommendations for fiber supplementation to outdistance the scientific research base. Until we have a better understanding of how fiber works its magic, we should recommend to American consumers only a gradual increase in dietary fiber from a variety of sources."

Unfortunately, despite ten years and multiple research trials, the effect of fiber on cancer has not been settled. Several studies looking specifically at the effect of increasing dietary fiber on colon cancer have shown no real benefit of the extra fiber. However, it is possible that these studies did not last long enough, or that a high-fiber diet may need to be followed for decades in order to help. Therefore, the jury is still out on this question.

FDA (Food and Drug Administration) acknowledges that high intakes of fruits and vegetables rich in beta-carotene or in vitamin C have been associated with reduced cancer risk. But the agency believes the data are not sufficiently convincing that either nutrient by itself is responsible for this association.

Pointing out that plant foods' low fat content also confers health benefits, FDA states in its proposed rule that diets low in fat give protection against coronary heart disease and that it has tentatively determined, "Diets low in fat are associated with the reduced risk of cancer."

FDA notes that diets high in saturated fats and cholesterol increase levels of both total and LDL (low density lipoprotein) cholesterol, and thus the risk for coronary heart disease, and that high-fat foods contribute to obesity, a further risk factor for heart disease. (The National Cholesterol Education Program recommends a diet with no more than 30 percent fat, of which no more than 10 percent comes from saturated fat.)

For those reasons, the agency would allow some foods to be labeled with health claims relating diets low in saturated fat and cholesterol to decreased risk of coronary heart disease and relating diets low in fat to reduced risk of breast, colon, and prostate cancer. "Examples of foods qualifying for a health claim include most fruits and vegetables; skim milk products; sherbets; most flours, grains, meals, and pastas (except for egg pastas); and many breakfast cereals," the proposed rule states.

Johanna Dwyer, DSc, RD of Tufts University Medical School and the New England Medical Center Hospital, Boston summarizes these plant food benefits:

> "Data are strong that vegetarians are at lesser risk for obesity, atonic [reduced muscle tone] constipation, lung cancer, and alcoholism. Evidence is good that risks for hypertension, coronary artery disease, type II diabetes, and gallstones are lower. Data are only fair to poor that risks of breast cancer, diverticular disease of the colon, colonic cancer, calcium kidney stones, osteoporosis, dental erosion, and dental caries are lower among vegetarians."

Death rates for vegetarians are similar or lower than for non-vegetarians, Dwyer reports, but are influenced in Western countries by vegetarians' "adoption of many healthy lifestyle habits in addition to diet, such as not smoking, abstinence, or moderation in the use of alcohol, being physically active, resting adequately, seeking ongoing health surveillance, and seeking guidance when health problems arise."

Section 11.3

Not All Vegetarians Avoid Cancer and Heart Disease

Excerpted from Bronfman, David E., "Not All Vegetarians Avoid Cancer and Heart Disease," Toronto Vegetarian Association, *Lifelines*, January-February 1996, http://www.veg.ca/newsletr/janfeb96/janfeb96.html. Reviewed in April, 2002 by Dr. David A. Cooke, MD, Diplomate, American Board of Internal Medicine.

The kind of foods you eat can make a huge difference when it comes to preventing disease and achieving optimum health. Given that there can be vast differences in eating styles among vegetarians, it's worth considering which kinds of vegetarians do best.

In a 12-year study published in the *British Medical Journal*, "non-meat" eaters were said to have 20% less heart disease and 40% less cancer. Great news for vegetarians? Well, yes and no. The study does not differentiate between vegetarians, semi-vegetarians, and total vegetarians (vegans). The study merely divides subjects into two groups: omnivores (not vegetarian) and "non-meat" eaters—broadly defined as those who eat meat or fish less than once a week, those who eat no meat or fish whatsoever, and those who follow a totally dairy-free and egg-free "vegan" vegetarian diet. A 20–40% reduction in disease may sound impressive, but it pales in comparison to results from a similar study in China.

According to T. Colin Campbell, Ph.D, professor of nutritional biochemistry at Cornell University and director of the "China Health Project" of 6,500 "primarily vegetarian" persons in rural China—possibly the most comprehensive study ever undertaken on diet and disease—the Chinese experience rates of cancer "that are probably in the neighborhood of only about 5 to 10 percent, at most, of what you would tend to see in Britain or the United States. So there you're talking about a 90 to 95 percent reduction." Heart disease in some areas of China is virtually a negligible disease. It's almost not seen. It's a tremendous rate reduction compared to what we see in the west. Again, I would say at least a 90 to 95 percent reduction."

Campbell suggests that the British study does not look at serious vegetarians and that it fails to recognize that 90% of vegetarians tend to eat dairy products and eggs: "It turns out that their nutrient intakes are really not that different from the non-vegetarians." A chief reason for the Chinese advantage, he explains, is that dairy consumption in China "is unheard of. It's just not used." Egg consumption in China is also very low: between 0–15 grams per day, compared with 15–128 grams per day in the U.S.

Another British research team reflects this same theme—that there are big differences between a vegetarian diet rich in saturated fat (from eggs and dairy) and a vegetarian diet moderate in these foods. James Bell, Ph.D, of London's Hammersmith Hospital, has looked at the issue: "We found the [lacto-ovo] vegetarians consumed as much saturated fat as the meat-eaters," said Bell in a recent interview. "The [lacto-ovo] vegetarians tended to substitute dairy products for meat, which is simply substituting one type of saturated fat for another," he is quoted assaying in the January 1994 issue of *Vegetarian Times*.

One of the world's top heart researchers—Dr. William Castelli, medical director of the Framingham Heart Study—repeats this same point. In a recent interview, he explained: "The [lacto-ovo] vegetarians tended to substitute one type of saturated fat for another" "There are all kinds of vegetarians. In fact, in the most famous study by [Dr. R.L.] Phillips, of the Seventh-Day Adventist, he split them up into the really true vegetarians and the lacto-ovo's. The true vegetarians did better than the lacto-ovo's." And according to vegetarian dietitian Suzanne Havala—principal author of the American Dietetic Association's position paper on vegetarian diets—"some of the [Seventh-Day] Adventists that have been looked at have pretty hefty intakes of cholesterol and saturated fat from dairy products."

In an address given in Toronto, Havala depicted how someone consuming very small amounts of meat, fish, and fowl—and hardly any eggs or dairy—could be eating less saturated-fat than a vegetarian consuming copious amounts of eggs and dairy products. For Havala, more important than group data is the eating habits of individual vegetarians: "Personally, my lacto-ovo vegetarian diet looks more like a vegan diet in nutrient composition than it does a rich lacto-ovo diet.

You have to look at the individual diet because vegetarian diets are on a continuum."

Clearly, as many experts conclude, optimum protection from your vegetarian diet means eating foods that are low in fats.

Chapter 12

Food-Borne Illness from Produce

The Food and Drug Administration is advising consumers to be aware of safe handling and preparation practices for fresh fruits and vegetables.

Food-borne illness can cause serious and sometimes fatal infections in young children, frail or elderly people, and others with weakened immune systems. Healthy persons with foodborne illness can experience fever, diarrhea, nausea, vomiting, and abdominal pain.

Following are some steps that consumers can take to reduce the risk of foodborne illness from fresh produce:

- At the store, purchase produce that is not bruised or damaged. If buying fresh cut produce, be sure it is refrigerated or surrounded by ice.

- At home, chill and refrigerate foods. After purchase, put produce that needs refrigeration away promptly (fresh whole produce such as bananas and potatoes do not need refrigeration). Fresh produce should be refrigerated within two hours of peeling or cutting. Leftover cut produce should be discarded if left at room temperature for more than two hours.

- Wash hands often. Hands should be washed with hot soapy water before and after handling fresh produce, or raw meat, poultry,

Excerpted from "FDA Advises Consumers about Fresh Produce Safety," Food and Drug Administration (FDA) Talk Paper T00-24, http://vm.cfsan.fda.gov/~lrd/tpproduc.html, May 26, 2000.

or seafood, as well as after using the bathroom, changing diapers, or handling pets.

- Wash all fresh fruits and vegetables with cool tap water immediately before eating. Don't use soap or detergents. Scrub firm produce, such as melons and cucumbers, with a clean produce brush. Cut away any bruised or damaged areas before eating.

- Wash surfaces often. Cutting boards, dishes, utensils, and counter tops should be washed with hot soapy water and sanitized after coming in contact with fresh produce, or raw meat, poultry, or seafood. Sanitize after use with a solution of 1 teaspoon of chlorine bleach in 1 quart of water.

- Don't cross contaminate. Use clean cutting boards and utensils when handling fresh produce. If possible, use one clean cutting board for fresh produce and a separate one for raw meat, poultry, and seafood. During food preparation, wash cutting boards, utensils or dishes that have come into contact with fresh produce, raw meat, poultry, or seafood. Do not consume ice that has come in contact with fresh produce or other raw products.

- Use a cooler with ice or use ice gel packs when transporting or storing perishable food outdoors, including cut fresh fruits and vegetables.

Following these steps will help reduce the risk of foodborne illness from fresh produce.

Chapter 13

Storing Fruits and Vegetables

The extraordinary diversity of common fruits and vegetables may become baffling when one must decide how to store them. Poor storage conditions may cause spoilage and/or loss of nutrients and/or disappointing flavor, but different foods crave different conditions! Just throwing everything into the refrigerator in paper bags isn't the best strategy.

Always remember that, in general, fruits (and tomatoes) do not ripen under refrigeration! Putting fruits in cold storage before they are fully ripe will backfire.

Although 32° F (0° C) is a favorable spoilage-slowing temperature for most fruits and vegetables, some items don't do so well at 32° F (0° C), and keep much better at 45° or 50° F (7–10° C). For example:

- avocados, honeydews and tomatoes (best to keep these away from vegetables in storage since while ripening they release gases which can harm the latter)

- fresh beans, cucumbers, okra, potatoes, and summer squash (these are especially vulnerable to gas damage)

LeRoy, Bob, MS, EdM, RD, Nutrition Advisor, North American Vegetarian Society, "Fruits and Vegetables: How to Store Them, What to Do with Them," European Vegetarian Union (EVU), *European Vegetarian*, http://www.european-vegetarian.org/evu/english/news/news964/fruits.html, 1996. Updated in April 2002 by Dr. David A. Cooke, MD, Diplomate, American Board of Internal Medicine.

- eggplants, California oranges, peppers, pineapples and water-melons

Once these items get cut, bruised, or frost-damaged, though, they are of course on a fast track toward rotting, so refrigeration then is a means for delaying the inevitable.

Warmer-still 55–60° F (13–15° C) temperatures are desired by (gas-producer) bananas; (gas-vulnerable) sweet potatoes; grapefruits and various tropical fruits; and ginger, pumpkins and winter squash, which are almost unique among vegetables in preferring dry, not humid, storage. Garlic (cold-lover) and onions (not fussy) go the dry route as well.

For most vegetables, preventing dehydration is crucial. It is helpful to set stem bases in cool water for a while before storage, and mist and sprinkle water on greens while they are air-exposed. You can combat the drying of foods that will be refrigerated by storing them in water-tight refrigerator compartments or plastic bags.

A potato peculiarity: Potatoes need dark storage, or else the skins and outermost flesh turn green. These green areas, like areas around sprouting eyes, are mildly toxic and taste horrible.

It has been a nutritional and economic blessing throughout human history that certain fruits and vegetables, when provided with their individually suitable storage conditions, will keep without spoiling for many months after harvest. Thus even in short-growing-season areas, a supply of some varieties of locally grown produce can be maintained all winter.

Long-storable vegetables emerged as staple foods in some cultures, as with potatoes in Ireland and parts of South America, sweet potatoes in some tropical areas, and many kinds of starchy tubers in the Caribbean. Other examples of long-storage crops include: carrots, beets, turnips, rutabagas, parsnips, daikon radish, onions and root vegetables in general; winter squashes; and apples and most pears. Foods among these which contain orange-to-deep-yellow flesh are important winter vitamin A sources. Generally speaking, the root vegetables are useful sources of vitamin C unless seriously overcooked.

Preparation pointers are simpler than storage pointers! When fruit vegetables are prepared for raw use, always minimize the amount of time that cut surfaces are exposed to the air, to the light, and to warm temperatures. Protective cell walls have been broken, so nutrients are easily lost through dehydration or oxidation, and little defense remains against rotting or molding. Prepare what will be used when it will be used, rather than create a stockpile for leftover use.

The heat of cooking causes dramatic loss of some vitamins, and other nutritional compromises. When cooking, use the minimum cooking temperature and time required to reach the texture and palatability you're looking for (modest excess of either can also turn the texture to a repulsive mush).

Don't add acidic-pH ingredients (e.g. lemon, vinegar) before cooking because that prolongs texture-softening time, thus destroying more nutrients in the process.

Don't discard the cooking water, as large amounts of nutrients seep out into it! Use the least cooking water feasible, or else use no more liquid than you are willing to drink down in addition to the vegetables (whether used along with the cooked item, or creatively used for something else, such as a separate broth or sauce, etc.)

Baking root vegetables or winter squashes whole avoids water-related losses altogether. Frying or sauteeing vegetables in oil raises other nutritional issues: The majority of calories coming out of the pan is from refined oil products, not from fresh vegetables. Thus a dish presumably chosen to add greater prominence to vegetables in the diet will actually add greater prominence to fat, to high-heat-refined and chemical-solvent-refined foods, and to fibre-free foods. One should consider this when deciding how much to fry.

Preparation hints could actually be summed up as: THINK FRESH! For greatest nutritional reward, eat fruits or vegetables in the freshest, closest-to-natural state possible.

Chapter 14

Gluten Allergies in Vegans

In recent years, food allergies have taken on the magnitude of a modern epidemic. "We are what we eat" is being held as gospel, ignoring the fact that some people follow extremely healthy diets and yet are ill, while others live on junk food and are irritatingly well.

Diet is much more than eating, and most vegans have selected their food with a view not simply to health but also motivated by wider moral concerns. Attitudes towards food undoubtedly influence our health and this exclusive search for 'culprit' foods which make us ill ignore a range of other contributory causes of disease.

Nonetheless, we cannot ignore the fact that certain food, no matter how nutritious to the majority, is poison to the unfortunate few. These food intolerance can cause skin conditions, respiratory problems, migraines, hyperactivity, and digestive disorders among other things. Common foods are dairy products and gluten, and it is the latter that can be devastating news to the vegan.

Picture the scene. You have made a decision to eschew all animal products such as meat, fish, eggs, and dairy products and are living predominantly on cereals, grains, fruit, and vegetables. Instead of feeling well, you start suffering from migraines and stomach pains, and discover to your horror that you are allergic to gluten, the protein

Excerpted from Hollwey, Sara, "Being a Gluten Free Vegan: More than Just Survival!" The Vegan Society, http://www.vegansociety.com/html/info/info48.html, 1997. Reprinted with permission. Despite the age of this document, readers seeking an understanding on gluten allergies in vegans will find this information useful.

127

in wheat, rye, barley, and oats. In children, gluten intolerance is known as celiac disease and prevents the proper digestion of food, leading to weight loss, diarrhea, and vitamin deficiencies. However, it is now suspected that many other illnesses, such as irritable bowel syndrome and myalgic encephalopathy (ME) may also be related to gluten, such that even small amounts can exacerbate problems.

So what can you do? It need not rule out being a vegan, but you will have to take more care to ensure a nutritionally adequate diet, seeking medical supervision if possible. Systematically go through the steps in setting up a special diet as outlined below; it prevents unnecessary hardships later on in the process.

The Setting-Up Stages

- Keep a food diary, noting what you eat, when, and assess the severity of the symptoms on a scale of 1 to 10. Even if you are sure that you are allergic to gluten, you need to check if any other foods are involved.

- Stay off the suspect foods for three weeks and an improvement should come about in your health if these are indeed responsible. Gradually reintroduce each product one by one and note the effects.

- Be careful to test each flour on its own. Some people cannot take wheat but can tolerate oats, barley and rye which have lower gluten contents.

Coping

Having clearly identified the food to which you are allergic, it now remains to stock your larder with a range of alternatives. There are several gluten-free flours which can replace wheat, oats, and other forbidden ingredients:

- Brown rice and brown rice flour: Preferable to white rice products because of its higher fiber, vitamin, and mineral content. Rice flour biscuits and cakes turn out rather crumbly due to its poor binding properties but grated apple can help to bind the mixture.

- Maize flour: A yellow flour made from ground corn-on-the-cob kernels. Traditionally used to make polenta and tortillas, it can also be mixed with other flours to make biscuits and cakes.

- Soya flour: Another yellow flour made from the soya bean and best blended with other flours because of its distinctive flavor. It is an excellent source of protein and vitamins.

- Potato flour: A fine white flour without much taste and a good source of protein.

- Millet flakes and millet flour: Good for making biscuits and as a base for muesli.

- Carob flour: A useful binder in baking because of its pectin content. It is ideal as an alternative to chocolate.

Baking Powder

- 4 oz (115 g) rice flour
- 2 oz (55 g) bicarbonate of soda
- 2 oz (55 g) tartaric acid

Mix the ingredients together and sift several times. Store in a screw top jar.

Put your baking ingredients on a special shelf so that they are readily available. You may also need to buy gluten-free tomato sauce, tamari, and mustard and these are readily available in many stores. A simple recipe is provided below for those feeling more adventurous. All of the fruits, vegetables, pulses, oils, and nuts are gluten-free so you can use ordinary vegan recipe books for those foods.

Useful Additions

Salad Dressing

- 1 level tablespoon soya flour
- 2 tablespoons vinegar
- 4 tablespoons oil
- 2 level tablespoons brown sugar
- ½ level teaspoon salt
- ¼ teaspoon mustard

Mix well together and store in the refrigerator. Shake well before using.

Tomato Sauce

- 1 oz (30 g) vegan margarine
- 1 oz (30 g) brown rice flour
- 1 pint (600 ml) tomato juice
- ¼ pint (150 ml) water
- Tabasco Sauce (optional)
- salt and pepper

Melt the margarine in a saucepan, add the rice flour and stir over a low heat for 2 to 3 minutes. Add tomato juice and water. Whisk as liquid comes to the boil and thickens very slightly. Add seasoning and a few drops of Tabasco Sauce to taste.

Tahini

- 4 oz (115 g) sesame seeds
- 2 tablespoons sunflower oil
- salt

Toast the seeds for 15 minutes. Blend with the oil until smooth. Variations: substitute sunflower seeds, peanuts, almonds, walnuts or cashews for the seeds.

Once you get used to the new diet you will begin to wonder why you dreaded it so much. To get you started, here are a few specific recipes that traditionally use many of the gluten flours and cereals. The substitutes are just as tasty and often more so.

Breakfast

Rice Porridge

- 2 heaped tablespoons rice flakes
- ½ pint (300 ml) water or soya milk
- salt or sugar to taste
- ½ oz (15 g) ground almonds (optional)

Stir the rice flakes and the water together and simmer for 5 minutes until the porridge thickens.

Gluten-Free Muesli

- 4 oz (115 g) brown rice flakes
- 2 oz (55 g) millet flakes
- 1 oz (30 g) sunflower seeds
- 4 oz (115 g) mixed dried fruit or chopped fresh fruit
- 1 oz (30 g) nuts (almonds, hazelnut, coconut)

Mix together and store in an air-tight container.

Baking

If you have mastered breakfast, baking is the next step to ensure that you don't miss out on breads, pastries, and biscuits.

Short-Crust Pastry

- 7 oz (200 g) cornflour or sago flour
- 3 ½ oz (100 g) hard vegan margarine
- pinch salt

Sift together the flour and salt. Rub in the fat until the mixture resembles fine breadcrumbs. Add sufficient water to mix it until a firm dough is formed. Chill for at least 20 minutes before rolling out and use as required.

For a sweet short-crust pastry add 3 oz (85 g) finely grated apple and one teaspoon of sugar before mixing in the water.

Soda Bread

- 2 oz (55 g) soya flour
- 10 oz (280 g) brown rice flakes
- ½ teaspoon salt
- 3/4 teaspoon cream of tartar
- 3/4 teaspoon bicarbonate of soda
- 1 tablespoon sunflower oil
- 9 fl oz (275 ml) soya milk

Put the dry ingredients in a bowl and mix in the oil and soya milk to form a soft dough. Form into a round shape and place on a greased tray. Bake for 40–45 minutes.

Soya & Rice Bread

- ¼ oz (8 g) dried yeast
- 1 teaspoon raw cane sugar
- 5 fl oz (150 ml) tepid water
- 10 oz (280 g) brown rice flour
- 2 oz (55 g) soya flour
- ½ teaspoon salt

Preheat the oven to 200° C/400° F.

Mix the yeast, sugar, and water together and leave to froth in a warm place. Sift the rice flours, soya flour and salt together, adding the yeast mixture when ready. Stir to make a smooth stiff batter, adding extra water as needed. Pour into a greased 1 lb (455 g) loaf tin and leave to rise in a warm place. Bake for 30–40 minutes.

Millet Flapjacks

- 4 oz (115 g) vegan margarine
- 2 oz (55 g) light brown sugar
- 2 tablespoons golden syrup
- 8 oz (225 g) millet flakes

Preheat the oven to 180° C/350° F. Heat the margarine, sugar and syrup over a gentle heat until melted. Add the millet flakes, mixing thoroughly. Grease an 8" (20 cm) square sandwich tin. Spoon in the millet mixture and spread flat with a palette knife. Bake for 30 minutes or until evenly golden brown. Mark out into portions and allow to cool before removing from the tin. Store in an airtight tin.

Carob Crunch Crisps

- 4 oz (115 g) vegan margarine
- 2 tablespoons golden syrup
- 1oz (30 g) carob powder
- 8 oz (225 g) Jordans or Quaker 'Rice Puffs'
- 4 oz (115 g) raisins

Place the margarine in a saucepan and melt with the golden syrup. Add a little of the mixture to the carob powder to form a smooth paste and then return the paste to the saucepan, blending in well. Add the 'Rice Puffs' and stir in evenly until coated. Divide between 20 paper sweet cases. Chill until set.

Rice Custard

- 1 pint (600 ml) soya milk or water
- 1 vanilla pod
- 2 oz (55 g) pudding rice
- 1½ oz (45 g) vegan margarine
- Raw cane sugar to taste

Heat the soya milk with the vanilla pod and allow to cool. Remove the pod and add the rice to the milk, bring to a boil and reduce the heat to simmer. Stir frequently and add extra soya milk or water if necessary. Sweeten to taste with raw cane sugar, add the margarine and blend until smooth. Serve hot or cold.

Creamy Topping

- 1 oz (30 g) cornflour
- ½ pint (300 ml) soya milk
- 2 oz (55 g) vegan margarine
- 1 oz (30 g) icing sugar

Blend the cornflour with a little of the milk. Heat the remaining soya milk in a saucepan and pour on to the blended cornflour. Mix well and return to the pan. Bring to the boil and simmer for one minute. Allow to cool, stirring occasionally. Blend the margarine until soft and gradually work in the icing sugar. Add the milk, a little at a time, beating vigorously to produce a smooth consistency.

As you can see, the possibilities are endless, once you are familiar with the basic ingredients. Indeed, you will probably find yourself cooking for the whole family, as gluten-free vegan dishes are as tasty as they are nutritious, and as easy to prepare as their nongluten-free counterparts. Bon appetit!

For further information about gluten allergies: http:// www.coeliac. co.uk

Chapter 15

How Vegetarians Can Gain Necessary Weight after an Illness

Introduction

If you have lost a lot of weight due to illness, your doctor or dietitian may advise you to increase your intake of energy and protein. They may try to persuade you that your vegetarian diet is unsuitable. This chapter is to enable you to choose vegetarian foods which will help you to gain weight and recover from illness.*

The energy density of foods is important when trying to gain weight. Energy density refers to the amount of energy or calories compared to the weight of the food. Vegetable foods tend to be less energy dense and so it is particularly important for vegetarians to be aware of suitable foods.

When you are ill, modern healthy eating advice to reduce fat, reduce sugar and increase fiber is peripheral to your immediate needs. If you know you must increase your energy and protein intake, you can do so by increasing your fat and sugar intake, and also try to avoid large amounts of fiber.

Excerpted from "Information Sheet: Increase Food Intake," Vegetarian Society UK, http://www.vegsoc.org/info/increase.html, copyright 2001, reprinted with permission. Some words have been changed to conform to American spelling conventions. Material may be viewed in its original format on the Vegetarian Society of the UK website: http://www.vegsoc.org.

* **Editor's Note:** Omnigraphics and the *Health Reference Series'* editorial staff encourage all people to make health care decisions in consultation with an appropriate health care provider.

If You Are Underweight but Healthy

If you are not ill but feel you are underweight and need to gain then not all the advice here is suitable for you. You should try and increase your food intake without consuming too much fat and sugar— although a little with the right type of food is fine. For example, you can use olive oil on baked or boiled potatoes and sugar in a nutritious wholemeal fruit cake.

Regular meals, especially breakfast, are important if you find it difficult to gain weight. Taking your time with meals and making sure you are relaxed is also important to ensure that your digestive system functions properly. A glass of wine with an evening meal is beneficial to relax you as well as stimulating your digestive juices.

Some people are just naturally thin no matter how much they eat, and the envy of those who gain weight easily. As long as you are in good health and do not drop below the recommended range of weights for your height you should not worry. Exercise can help build up your muscles and make you feel better about your body shape.

Lack of Appetite

If your appetite is poor, you must not forget to eat. Try to have small but frequent meals, and if you can manage, snacks in between. You may like to try nutritious drinks between meals.

If you feel nauseous, try to avoid strong cooking smells and have a short walk or perhaps just sit in the fresh air before a meal.

Protein

Protein is essential to the body, for repair, to enable the immune system to function, and for recovery from illness. If you are recovering from illness, it is important to include adequate protein in your diet. Good vegetarian sources of protein include: cereals, nuts and seeds, soya products (soya milk, tofu, tempeh, etc.) and legumes. Milk, yogurt, cheese, and free range eggs are also excellent protein sources for the non-vegan.

You must ensure that you include a protein source at each meal. Try to choose the energy dense sources of protein that are relatively soft and which do not contain to much fiber, for example, the soya or dairy sources of protein.

Try nut butters. There are many more available other than peanut butter, try others such as hazel nut or cashew nut butter.

Soya products are excellent and easily digested sources of protein. Choose the nutritional supplemented soya milks with added calcium and sugar.

If you use dairy products, make good use of soft milky puddings, such as custard and rice pudding. Vegans can also get a variety of soya pudding, including soya rice pudding. If you like, add jam, honey, ground nuts or cream to your pudding. Porridge with a couple of tablespoons of added vegetable oil, perhaps with some nuts and/or dried fruit, can be very nutritious.

If you prefer to have white bread, white pasta, and refined rice, then do so. But remember that the whole grain varieties are very good sources of the B vitamins.

Make good use of cereal products (wheat, barley, rye, oats, etc.), although avoid too much fiber. Complement cereals with other sources of proteins, such as nuts, seeds, legumes, milk and cheese.

Seeds, such as sesame seeds (tahini) or sunflower seeds, when ground as a paste, can also provide an energy dense source of protein in the diet. Tahini is particularly good when combined with a mashed legume, such as chick peas, to make hummus.

Legumes are more easily digested, if well cooked and mashed. Try mashed lentils or pureed black eye beans.

Energy

In order to gain weight it is essential to increase the energy content of your diet. Also, in order for your body to make proper use of protein, you must ensure sufficient energy. The most concentrated form of energy in the diet is from fat. If you can tolerate fat then try and increase the fat content of your diet.

Alcohol is also a concentrated form of energy and can be taken in moderation, perhaps before meals, as it may help improve your appetite. Only take alcohol with your doctors permission.

If you can tolerate oils, try adding some vegetable oil or vegetable margarine to your food, particularly to mashed legumes, salads, and potatoes. If you like fried foods, then have fried foods.

Use cream if you can tolerate fats. A good vegan alternative to cream is cashew nut cream, made from ground cashew nuts and water.

Do not restrict your sugar intake, although always have sweet foods after the savory part of your meal. Glucose is a less sweet and more concentrated form of sugar. Glucose can be added to foods and drinks, such as porridge and cocoa drinks, to increase your energy intake. Check with your dietitian about using glucose. She may suggest that your doctor prescribes you a special type of non-sweet, high calorie supplement, which can be added to foods and drinks.

If you like to have soup, make sure the soup is as nutritious as possible. Add pureed lentils, vegetable oil, butter, whole milk, cream, or cheese.

Make good use of the wide range of vegetable pates and spreads available.

General Advice

- You may prefer to eat puddings half an hour to one hour after your first course, this will enable time for the first course to settle.

- You may find ice-cream, soya or dairy, refreshing after meals.

- Make good use of a food blender, if you have one, to blend fruit, vegetable, and legumes.

- Have meals with a good sauce, made with pureed fried onions, perhaps with tomatoes or mushrooms. To increase the energy density of sauces use butter or vegan margarine and add soya milk, silken tofu, cow's milk, or cream.

- Make sure you include a source of vitamin C in your diet, perhaps fresh fruit juice, black-currant cordial, or rosehip syrup.

- Try and eat some fresh fruit and vegetables or salad each day, especially green vegetables, to ensure you get your full compliment of vitamins and minerals. If you cannot tolerate whole fruit or crunchy vegetables, take them as fruit juice or a pureed soup made with fresh vegetables.

- High energy drinks can be made using whole cow's milk, sweetened soya milk, or silken tofu, with glucose, honey, or sugar and a flavoring of your choice such as chocolate or vanilla.

- You can buy products from the drug store, to have as meal replacements, when your appetite is particularly poor. Check on their suitability for vegetarians.

- Ask your doctor or dietitian about including a vitamin or mineral supplement in your diet. If you choose to take a supplement, inform your doctor and dietitian. Multi-vitamin and mineral tablets should not do you any harm, as long as you stick to the recommended dose.

If You Still Need Extra Protein and Energy

Your doctor can prescribe for you special supplements which can help you to gain weight. You would usually be referred to a dietitian, who can nutritionally assess you and recommend the correct type of supplement.

Part Three

Vegetarian Food Choices

Chapter 16

Common Foods That Make up Vegetarian and Vegan Diets

Chapter Contents

Section 16.1

Nuts and Seeds

Introduction

Nuts are seeds that are covered with a hard shell. Most are the seeds of trees, but the seeds of a few other plants that are not strictly nuts will also be considered here as they can be conveniently classified with nuts for culinary purposes.

Nuts can be used in many ways. Whole, flaked and ground nuts and nut butters are widely available. A classic vegetarian savory is nut roast and many vegetarian cook books give a recipe for one, which can be endlessly varied with different herbs and flavorings and different combinations of nuts and cereals. Nuts can be added to sweet dishes, cakes, and biscuits, and nut butters can be added to soups and stews to thicken them.

Nutrition

Nuts in general are very nutritious, providing protein and many essential vitamins, such as A and E, minerals, such as phosphorous and potassium, and fiber. Nuts are also high in carbohydrate and oils, so shouldn't be eaten in excess.

Whereas pulses all belong to the legume group of plants, nuts come from a variety of different plant groups, so the nutritional content is more varied too. A brief description of individual varieties is given below, together with the main nutrients they contain.

Storage

Nuts should be stored in cool, dry conditions in airtight containers away from the light. Because of their high fat content, many of them benefit from storage in the fridge or freezer to deter rancidity.

Nuts

Almonds

Probably originated in the Near East but now grows in Southern Europe, Western Asia, California, South Australia and South Africa. Almond oil is used for flavoring and for skin care preparations and is extracted from the kernel of the Bitter Almond. The Sweet Almond is grown for nuts for eating and have the largest share of the nut trade world-wide. Almond flour is available and it is possible to make a nutritious nut milk from almonds. Almonds are particularly nutritious, 100 g contain 16.9 g protein, 4.2 mg iron, 250 mg calcium, 20 mg vitamin E, 3.1 mg zinc and 0.92 mg vitamin B_2.

Brazils

A native of South America. The nuts grow inside a hard, woody fruit rather like a coconut shell which has to be broken open to expose the 12–24 nuts inside. Brazils are high in fat, which causes them to go rancid very quickly, and protein. 100 g of brazils contain 12 g protein, 61 g fat, 2.8 mg iron, 180 mg calcium, 4.2 mg zinc.

Cashews

Native to America but now grown extensively in India and East Africa. It will withstand rather drier conditions than most other nuts. The nut grows in a curious way on the tree, hanging below a fleshy, apple-like fruit. It is related to the mango, pistachio, and poison ivy. High in protein and carbohydrate, 100 g cashews contain 17.2 g protein, 60 micrograms vitamin A, 3.8 mg iron.

Chestnuts

The sweet chestnut is a native of South Europe but is planted elsewhere extensively for both nuts and timber. The nuts can be used in soups, fritters, porridges, stuffings, and stews, as well as being roasted or boiled whole. Available fresh (in autumn), dried, canned—whole or pureed, or ground into flour. Dried chestnuts need soaking for at least 1–2 hours and boiling for 45–60 minutes, fresh need boiling for 40 minutes before being peeled. Preserved in syrup they become the famous delicacy, Marron-glace. High in starch, but low in protein and fat, 100 g chestnuts contain 36.6 g carbohydrate, only 2 g protein (the lowest of all nuts) and 2.7 g fat.

Coconuts

The coconut palm is common in tropical regions all over the world. The nut is covered in a fibrous outer coating on the tree and all parts of the tree are useful, the trunks for timber, the leaves for thatch, the fibrous husk produces coir—the starting material for ropes and coconut matting—and the nuts are used for food. Unripe nuts contain coconut milk. The nutmeat can be eaten fresh or dried (desiccated or flaked coconut) and is also available in blocks of creamed coconut. A valuable oil is also extracted from the nut meat and used for cooking (although it is very high in saturated fat), margarines, soaps, and detergents. 100 g fresh coconut contain 3.2 g protein and 36 g fat, desiccated contain 5.6 g protein and 62 g fat.

Hazels

Hazel, also called Cob, is a common wild tree in Europe and Asia and its nuts have been eaten by humans since earliest times. The cultivated varieties are bigger and the filbert is a similar but bigger species from South East Europe. Used in sweet and savory dishes, they are available whole, ground, and flaked, or made into oil and nut butter. 100 g hazel nuts contain 7.6 g protein, and they are lower in fat than most other nuts.

Macadamia Nuts

A native of North East Australia, now also grown commercially in Hawaii. Notoriously difficult to extract from their shells, they are expensive but have a delicious creamy flavor and crunchy texture. Low in carbohydrate, but quite high in fat, 100 g Macadamia nuts contain 7 g protein and 40 mg calcium.

Peanuts

Also known as groundnuts or monkey nuts, peanuts are actually legumes. Of South American origin, it's now an important crop all over the tropics and southern USA. It gets its name groundnut because as the pods ripen, they are actually forced underground. Peanuts are high in protein and contain 40–50% oil. The oil is used in cooking, as salad oil, in margarines and the residue is fed to animals. Whole peanuts can be eaten raw or roasted or made into peanut butter (look out for brands which do not contain hydrogenated oils, which are highly saturated). As they are usually inexpensive, they can be mixed with other kinds of nuts to bring down the cost, while still maintaining flavor and good nutrition. 100 g peanuts contain 24.3 g protein, 2 mg iron and 3 mg zinc.

Pecans

A native of North America where it is used extensively in ice cream, cakes, nut bread and confectionery. The flavor is rather like a mild, sweet walnut. 100 g pecans contain 9.2 g protein, a very high fat content of 71.2 g, 130 micrograms vitamin A (also very high), 2.4 mg iron and 73 mg calcium.

Pine Nuts

These are the seeds of the Stone Pine, a native of the Mediterranean region, but the seeds of various other pines are eaten in various parts of the world including the seeds of the Korean Pine or North American pinon tree. They are very difficult to harvest, hence their cost. They are vital for pesto sauce, and are delicious lightly toasted. They become rancid very easily and should be stored in the fridge or freezer. 100 g pine nuts contain 31 g protein, the highest of the nuts and seeds.

Pistachios

Native to the Near East and Central Asia but has long been cultivated in the Mediterranean region and more recently in the Southern U.S. The kernels are green and are prized as much for their ornamental color as for their flavor. Also sold roasted and salted in their shells. They are more expensive than most other nuts. 100 g pistachios contain 19.3 g protein, 14 mg iron, 140 mg calcium.

Walnuts

The walnut is native to South East Europe and West and Central Asia but is now grown in the United Kingdom, California, and China as well. It is grown for timber as well as its nuts. Walnut oil has been used for centuries in the preparation of artists paints. The black walnut is a native of North America, introduced into Britain in the 17th century. The butternut is also from North America. These two have much thicker shells than European walnuts. High in fat, they go rancid very quickly and should be stored in the fridge or freezer. 100 g walnuts contain 10.6 g protein and 2.4 mg iron.

Seeds

Pumpkin

Can be eaten raw or cooked in both sweet or savory dishes. Delicious toasted, sprinkled with soya sauce while hot, and served on salads. They are rich in protein, iron, zinc, and phosphorous. 100 g pumpkin seeds contain 29 g protein, 11.2 mg iron and 1144 mg phosphorous.

Sesame

Of African origin but now common in tropical and sub-tropical Asia. An oil is extracted from the seed and used for cooking, salad oil, and margarines. It is also available as toasted sesame oil for oriental cooking. The whole seeds can also be eaten and are most often seen as a decoration on cakes, confectionery, etc. Sesame seed paste, tahini, is used in many dishes e.g. hummus. Halva, a sweet made from sesame seeds, is often found in health food shops. A good source of protein and calcium, 100 g sesame seeds contain 26.4 g protein, 12.6 mg vitamin B_3, 7.8 mg iron, 131 mg calcium and 10.3 mg zinc.

Sunflower

An annual plant belonging to the daisy family, it probably originated in North America or Mexico. North American Indians cultivated sunflowers as long as 2,000 years ago. The oil extracted from its seeds is used in margarine, varnishes, and soaps but the seeds can be eaten whole, raw, or cooked. They can be added to breads and cakes or sprinkled over salad or breakfast cereals. A good source of potassium and phosphorous, 100 g sunflower seeds also contain 24 g protein and 7.1 mg iron and 120 mg calcium.

Section 16.2

Legumes (Pulses)

Excerpted from "Information Sheet: Pulses," Vegetarian Society UK, www.vegsoc.org/info/pulses.html, copyright 2001, reprinted with permission. Some words have been changed to conform to American spelling conventions. Material may be viewed in its original format on the Vegetarian Society of the UK website: http://www.vegsoc.org.

Introduction

Peas, beans and lentils are known as pulses. They are the seeds of plants belonging to the family *Leguminosae*, which gets its name from the characteristic pod or legume that protects the seeds while they are forming and ripening. With approximately 13,000 species, the family *Leguminosae* is the second largest in the plant kingdom and it is very important economically.

Different kinds of legumes provide us with food, medicines, oils, chemicals, timber, dyes and ornamental garden plants. Legume products include carob, senna, gum arabic, balsam, indigo and licorice. Pulses are valuable because they contain a higher percentage of protein than most other plant foods.

Origins

Pulses have been used as food for thousands of years. The lentil was probably one of the first plants ever to be domesticated by humans. Most pulses prefer warm climates but there are varieties which grow in temperate regions. They can be eaten fresh or dried and come in a great number of varieties with a range of colors, flavors, and textures. In spite of its common name, the peanut or groundnut is also a legume rather than a nut.

Nutrition

All pulses, except for soya beans, are very similar in nutritional content. They are rich in protein, carbohydrate, and fiber, and low in fat which is mostly of the unsaturated kind. They are also important sources of some B vitamins. Fresh pulses contain vitamin C, but this declines after harvesting and virtually all is lost from dried pulses. Canned pulses however, retain about half their vitamin C except for canned, processed peas which have been dried before canning. Canning doesn't affect the protein content, eliminates the need for soaking and considerably reduces the cooking time compared with dried pulses. Frozen peas will have also lost about a quarter of their vitamin C content.

Pulses are usually eaten for their high protein content. A typical nutritional breakdown is that for haricot beans which are used to make baked beans, contain, per 100 g dried beans: 21.4 g protein, 1.6 g fat, 45.5 g carbohydrate, 25.4 g fiber, 6.7 mg iron and 180 mg calcium.

The nutritional quality of the soya bean is superior to that of other pulses. It contains more protein and is also a good source of iron and calcium. The nutritional breakdown of soya is per 100 g of dried beans: 34.1 g protein, 17.7 g fat, 28.6 g carbohydrate, 8.4 mg iron and 226 mg calcium. Dried soya beans are lengthy to prepare because they need at least 12 hours soaking and 4 hours cooking time, boiling for the first hour, but nowadays a large number of soya based foods including tofu, tempeh and textured vegetable protein (TVP) are available.

Storage and Cooking

One advantage of dried pulses is that they will store very well for long periods if kept in a dry, airtight container away from the light. However it is best to eat them as fresh as possible. Pulses toughen on storage and older ones will take longer to cook. Allow about 55 g dried weight per person, once soaked and cooked they will at least double in weight. Most dried pulses need soaking for several hours before they can be cooked, exceptions are all lentils, green and yellow split peas, blackeye, and mung beans. Soaking times vary from 4–12 hours; it is usually most convenient to soak pulses overnight. Always discard the soaking water, rinse and cook in fresh water without any salt, which toughens the skins and makes for longer cooking. Changing the water will help to reduce the flatulence some people suffer when eating pulses, also reputed to help is the addition of a pinch of aniseeds, caraway, dill, or fennel seeds.

Toxins in Pulses

Consumers should be aware that it is not safe to eat raw or undercooked kidney and soya beans. There is no need to avoid them as long as they are thoroughly cooked.

Red kidney beans. Incidents of food poisoning have been reported associated with the consumption of raw or undercooked red kidney beans. Symptoms may develop after eating only four raw beans and include nausea, vomiting, and abdominal pain followed by diarrhea. A naturally occurring hemagglutinin is responsible for the illness, but can be destroyed by high temperature cooking, making the beans completely safe to eat. For this reason, kidney beans must not be sprouted. Kidney beans should be soaked for at least 8 hours in enough cold water to keep them covered. After soaking, drain and rinse the beans, discarding the soaking water. Put them into a pan with cold water to cover and bring to the boil. The beans must now boil for 10 minutes to destroy the toxin. After this the beans should be simmered until cooked (approximately 45–60 minutes) and they should have an even creamy texture throughout—if the center is still hard and white, they require longer cooking.

Soya beans. Contain an anti-trypsin factor (or trypsin inhibitor) which prevents the assimilation of the amino acid methionine. Soya beans also require careful cooking to ensure destruction of this factor. They should be soaked for at least 12 hours, drained and rinsed then covered with fresh water and brought to a boil. Soya beans should be boiled for the first hour of cooking. They can then be simmered for the remaining 2–3 hours that it takes to cook them.

Soya flour should state heat treated on its packaging. Other soya products (e.g. tofu, tempeh, soya milk, soya sauces and miso) are quite safe to use. Soya beans can be sprouted, but the sprouts should be quickly blanched in boiling water to inactivate the trypsin inhibitor.

Pressure cooking. The temperatures achieved in pressure cooking are adequate to destroy both hemagglutinins and the trypsin inhibitor. Pressure cooking also considerably reduces cooking times—kidney beans 10–20 minutes, soya beans 1 hour.

Canning. The temperature achieved in the canning process also renders pulses quite safe.

Slow cookers. Pulses must be soaked and boiled for 10 minutes before being added to a slow cooker, as they do not reach sufficiently high temperatures to destroy the toxins.

As beans and peas are all very similar nutritionally, with the exception of soya, they can be interchanged in most recipes if you want to experiment or have run out of one kind, as long as you take into account the different cooking times. If the beans are likely to need a lot longer to cook than the other ingredients, try pre-cooking them in a separate pan before adding to the other ingredients or using canned beans.

Sprouting

Many whole pulses (e.g. aduki, chickpeas, whole lentils, marrow-fat peas, mung, and soya beans) can be sprouted which increases their nutritional value.

Section 16.3

Grains (Cereals)

Excerpted from "Information Sheet: Cereals," Vegetarian Society UK, http://www.vegsoc.org/info/cereals.html, copyright 2001, reprinted with permission. Some words have been changed to conform to American spelling conventions. Material may be viewed in its original format on the Vegetarian Society of the UK website: http://www.vegsoc.org.

Introduction

All too often, cereal products are thought of as nothing more than starchy fillers, and indeed, when you consider how some commercial products like cakes and biscuits and breakfast cereals are made from over-refined grains with nearly all the nutrients except the starch extracted, and then loaded with fat, sugar, artificial flavorings etc., you might be forgiven for thinking that's true. But go back to the original, unrefined grains and you have a wealth of nutrients in a small package. Grains have been the staple foods of many civilizations for thousands of years. Wheat, barley, oats, and rye in Europe, maize in America, quinoa in South America, rice in the East, and millet in Africa.

Nutrition

Cereals are seeds of plants, usually members of the grass family but there are a few exceptions. They are annuals, that is they have to be planted every year and at the end of the summer, when they have produced ripe seeds, they die down. Like all seeds, cereals are very nutritious because they contain all the nutrients the embryo plant needs to start growing. Unrefined cereals are valuable sources of proteins, carbohydrates, B vitamins; and also contain some fat, iron, vitamin E, and trace minerals, and are a very good source of fiber in the diet. Some cereals (wheat, barley, rye and oats) contain the protein gluten, which is essential for leavened bread-making. Without sufficient gluten, bread will not rise. People suffering from gluten intolerance or coeliac disease must avoid any cereal containing gluten. In some parts of the world unleavened (unrisen) bread is eaten or the staple cereal is made into noodles or pasta. They are usually cheap to buy and are a valuable source of variety in the vegetarian diet.

Storage

Keep in airtight containers in a cool, dark, dry place. Whole grains can be stored for up to 2 years; flaked, cracked grains and flours should be used within 2–3 months of purchase.

Sprouting

Whole grains can be sprouted, which greatly enhances their nutritional value, e.g. wheat grains, raw buckwheat and barley.

Cooking

Cereals can be used in other ways, besides being ground into flour for bread, cakes etc. Whole grains can be added to stews and casseroles, or cooked until soft. Cracked or kibbled grains are cut or broken pieces of whole grains e.g. kibbled wheat and bulgur wheat. Meal, a coarse kind of flour, can be used to make porridge, thicken soups or mixed with wheat flour to add interesting flavors and textures to ordinary breads, biscuits, muffins etc.

Whole grains should be washed thoroughly. Boil the required amount of water, add the washed grain, stir once, put a tight-fitting lid on the pan and simmer for the required cooking time or until the liquid is absorbed. Turn off the heat and leave to stand for 5 minutes before removing the lid.

Barley

Barley grows in a wider variety of climatic conditions than any other cereal. It used to be a very important source of direct human food, but its use has diminished over the last 250 years, replaced by wheat, and it is now used almost exclusively as animal feed or for making beer and whisky. It contains gluten, so barley flour can be made into bread. More usually found in the shops as whole or pot barley, or polished pearl barley, it is also possible to buy barley flakes or kernels. The whole barley is more nutritious with 100 g providing 10.5 g protein, 2.1 g fat, 69.3 g carbohydrate, 4 g fiber, 50 mg folic acid, 6 mg iron and 50 mg calcium. It can be cooked on its own (1:3 parts water for 45–60 minutes) as a pleasant alternative to rice, pasta or potatoes, or added to stews. Malt extract is made from sprouted barley grains.

Buckwheat (Gluten Free)

Buckwheat is not a true cereal as it is not a member of the grass family, instead being related to sorrels and docks. If you look at docks closely, you can see that the seeds, though smaller, have the same distinctive triangular shape. Buckwheat, a native of central Asia, is now grown in Europe, North America, and the former USSR countries, but it is still not widely used in Britain. 100 g of buckwheat provides 11.7 g protein, 3.9 mg iron and it is very high in calcium with 114 mg per 100 g. Available raw, the seeds are greenish-pink, or roasted (known as kasha) the seeds are darker reddish-brown. It can be cooked (1:2 parts water for 6 minutes, leave to stand for 6 minutes) and served like rice or you can add it to stews and casseroles. Buckwheat flour can be added to cakes, muffins, pancakes etc. where it imparts a distinctive flavor. Look out too for buckwheat spaghetti, soba.

Corn or Maize (Gluten Free)

Maize is the principal food plant of America and was unknown in other parts of the world until Columbus reached America in 1492. It was grown by the Maya, Inca, and Aztec civilizations, and by various North American Indian tribes, and now has spread to Canada, USSR, Italy, Spain, Egypt, India, and South Africa. It is used for human food, animal feed, and as a source of raw materials for industry. 100 g maize gives 9 g protein. Fresh maize is often available (sweet corn, corn on the cob) but remember that nutritional values will be lower because less concentrated. We most often see maize as cornflakes or popcorn, but cornmeal or polenta is available and can be added to soup, pancakes, muffins etc. Tortillas are made from maize meal, as are quite a lot of snack foods. Do not confuse cornmeal with highly refined corn starch/flour, used for thickening.

Millet (Gluten Free)

Millet is the name applied to a variety of grasses first cultivated in Asia or Africa. It is a staple crop in Africa because it is drought resistant and keeps well. 100 g millet provides 9.9 g protein, and 6.8 mg iron (higher than other cereals). Millet makes a delicious alternative to rice but the tiny seeds need to be cracked before they will absorb water easily, so they should be first sauteed with a little vegetable oil for 2–3 minutes until some are seen to crack, then add water with care (1:3 parts), bring to the boil and simmer for 15–20 minutes until fluffy. Millet flakes can be made into porridge or added to muesli and millet flour is available, sometimes also made into pasta.

Oats

Oats are thought to have originated in Western Europe and may originally have appeared as a weed in barley and so got spread with the barley. They're now grown in many parts of the world including North West Europe, the former USSR countries, North America, Canada, Australia, and China. Used mostly as animal feed, they are very nutritious. In fact, as they are usually inexpensive to buy, they can be a real boon to people trying to get a good diet on a low budget. 100 g oats gives 13 g protein, 55 mg calcium (more than any other cereal except buckwheat), and 4.6 mg iron. Available as groats (whole grains with the husks removed) but more usually as various grades of oatmeal, rolled oats, or jumbo oat flakes. Oat groats need cooking for 45 minutes in 1:3 parts water. All forms can be used to make porridge, combined with ground nuts to make a roast or added to stews. Oatmeal is low in gluten so can't be used to make a loaf, but can be mixed with wheat flour to add flavor and texture to bread, muffins, pancakes etc.

Quinoa (Gluten Free)

Quinoa is an ancient crop which fed the South American Aztec Indians for thousands of years, and which has recently been cultivated in Britain. Unlike most grains, it does not belong to the grass family, but is a relative of the garden weed called Fat Hen. It is very nutritious, containing between 13–14% protein with a good amino acid composition but has no gluten so it cannot be used for breadmaking. Instead, it is cooked for 15 minutes in 1:3 parts water and served as a side dish or may be used in risotto, pilaf, vegetable stuffings, etc.

Rice (Gluten-Free)

Rice is one of the world's most important crops. It originated in Asia but is now grown throughout the humid, sub-tropical regions. It differs from most other cereals in requiring land that is submerged in water to grow, though some varieties do grow in upland areas. Rice is a good source of carbohydrate but doesn't have quite as much protein as some other cereals (6.5 g per 100 g). Unpolished rice (i.e. whole grain/brown rice) is a good source of B vitamins too. There are three basic kinds in culinary terms: long, medium and short grain. Long used traditionally in savory dishes, short in dessert cooking, although this varies across the globe and it is really a matter of personal preference. Long whole grain rice needs to cook in 1:2 parts water for 35–40 minutes. Rice flour is available but because of the lack of gluten, it cannot be used to make a yeasted loaf but can be used for cakes, biscuits, and pancakes. Rice flakes (brown and white) can be added to muesli or made into a milk pudding or porridge.

Wild Rice

Wild rice is not a rice at all but an American grass used as an important food by the Indians and early settlers. Difficulty in harvesting makes it expensive, but the color, a purplish black and its subtly nutty flavor make it a good base for a special dish and it can be economically mixed with other rices, but may need pre-cooking as it takes 45–50 minutes to cook in 1:3 parts of water.

Rye

Rye is the least important cereal crop and is usually only grown where conditions are relatively unfavorable and other cereals don't do well. It probably originated in South West Asia, but the name occurs in Northern European languages, which suggest early cultivation in that area. It is very hardy and so grows in temperate and cool regions and at high altitudes, and is very tolerant of poor soil fertility. It is the only cereal apart from wheat and barley that has enough gluten to make a yeasted loaf, but it has less gluten than wheat, so rye bread is denser. It is more usual to mix rye flour with wheat flour.

Rye grains should be cooked in 1:3 parts water for 45–60 minutes. Kibbled rye is often added to granary-type loaves. You can also add rye to stews and rye flakes are available, which can be used in muesli. 100 g of rye gives 9.4 g protein.

Spelt

Spelt is closely related to common wheat, originating in the Middle East, and has been popular for decades in Eastern Europe. Higher in protein than wheat, it appears to have a different molecular structure, appearing to cause less problems than wheat for some sufferers of grain allergies. It has an intense nutty, wheaty flavor. The flour is excellent for breadmaking and spelt pasta is becoming more widely available.

Wheat

This is the most familiar cereal used in Britain today, it is used for bread, cakes, biscuits, pastry, breakfast cereals, and pasta. All the present varieties of wheat seem to be derived from a hybrid wild wheat that grew in the Middle East 10,000 years ago. Over 30,000 varieties are said to be in cultivation. Wheat can be grown in a very wide range of climatic conditions but is most successful in temperate zones including the UK, North America, Southern Russia and South West Australia.

Nutritionally, 100 g whole wheat provide 14 g protein, 2.2 g fat, 69.1 g carbohydrate, 2.3 g fiber, 3.1 mg iron, 36 mg calcium. Wheat grains, also called wheat berries, can be eaten whole, cooked in 1:3 parts of water for 40–60 minutes; they have a satisfying, chewy texture. Cracked or kibbled wheat is the dried whole grains cut by steel blades. Bulgur wheat, made from the whole grains steamed before cracking, only needs rehydrating by soaking in boiling water or stock. Couscous is the steamed, dried and cracked grains of durum wheat and is more refined than bulgur. Soak in 2 parts of water/stock to rehydrate, traditionally it is steamed after soaking. Strong wheat flour (high gluten content) is required for yeasted breadmaking and puff pastry. Plain flour is used for general cooking including cakes and short crust pastry. Wheat flakes are used for porridge, muesli and flapjacks. Wheat germ is an excellent source of nutrients, especially vitamin E.

Section 16.4

Cheese

Introduction

Cheese is made by coagulating milk to give curds which are then separated from the liquid, whey, after which they can be processed and matured to produce a wide variety of cheeses. Milk is coagulated by the addition of rennet. The active ingredient of rennet is the enzyme, chymosin (also known as rennin). The usual source of rennet is the stomach of slaughtered newly-born calves. Vegetarian cheeses are manufactured using rennet from either fungal or bacterial sources. Advances in genetic engineering processes means they may now also be made using chymosin produced by genetically altered micro-organisms.

Manufacture

The exact processes in the making of cheese varies between different varieties. However, all cheeses are made by essentially the same method. Initially, the milk is usually pasteurized by heating at 72° C for 15 seconds to destroy potentially harmful bacteria. The milk is then cooled to around 30° C and a starter culture of lactic acid bacteria is added to help souring. These convert lactose into lactic acid and help in the coagulation process. In addition, they also have a beneficial effect on the eventual quality, taste, and consistency of the cheese. Some cheeses are coagulated entirely by lactic acid bacteria and are known as lactic-curd or acid-curd cheeses. However, some cheeses sold as lactic-curd cheese may have had rennet added.

The next stage is the addition of rennet, containing the enzyme chymosin. Rennet is usually sourced from the abomasum (fourth stomach) of newly-born calves. Here, chymosin aids the digestion and absorption of milk. Adult cows do not have this enzyme. Chymosin is extracted by washing and drying the stomach lining, which is then cut into small pieces and macerated in a solution of boric acid or brine at 30° C for 4–5 days. Pepsin may sometimes be used instead of chymosin. This is usually derived from the abomasum of grown calves or heifers, or less commonly pigs. Pepsin may be mixed with calf rennin. Rennet coagulates the milk, separating it into curds and whey. This is called curdling.

Chymosin breaks down the milk protein casein to paracasein which combines with calcium to form calcium paracaseinate, which separates out. Milk fat and some water also becomes incorporated into this mass, forming curds. The remaining liquid is the whey. The strength of different rennets can vary, though usual strength varies between 1:10,000 and 1:15,000 i.e. one part rennin can coagulate 10–15,000 parts milk.

Other substances may also be added during the cheese making process. Calcium chloride is added to improve the curdling process, and potassium nitrate is added to inhibit contaminating bacteria. Dyes (e.g. annatto, beta-carotene), *Penicillium roquefortii* mold spores to promote blue veining, or propionic acid bacteria to encourage hole formation may be added.

Following curdling, the curds are cut and drained. The size of the cut and the methods used vary for different cheese varieties. For soft cheeses, the curds are sparingly cut and allowed to drain naturally. For hard cheeses, the curds are heated and more whey is drained off. The curds are then cut into small pieces, placed in vats and pressed.

After pressing, the curds may be treated in a number of ways. They may be moulded into different shapes, soaked in a saltwater solution, be sprayed with mould forming spores or bacteria, washed in alcohol, or covered in herbs.

The final stage is ripening, or maturation. This can vary in length from 4 weeks to 2–3 years, depending on the type of cheese. During ripening flavors develop, the cheese becomes firmer and drier, and special characteristics such as holes, blue veining and crust formation occurs.

Vegetarian Cheeses

Vegetarian cheeses are made with rennets of non-animal origin. In the past, fig leaves, melon, wild thistle, and safflower have all supplied plant rennets for cheese making. However, most widely available vegetarian cheeses are made using rennet produced by fermentation of the fungus *Mucor miehei*. Vegetarian cheese may also be made using a rennet from the bacteria *Bacillus subtilis* or *Bacillus prodigiosum*.

Advances in genetic engineering techniques mean that some vegetarian cheeses may now be made using chymosin produced by genetically engineered micro-organisms. The genetic material (DNA) which encodes for chymosin is introduced into a micro-organism which can then be cultured to produce commercial quantities of chymosin. This is done by extracting genetic material from calf stomach cells which acts as a template for producing the chymosin encoding DNA. This can then be introduced into the micro-organism. Once the genetic material is introduced there is no further need for calf cells. Alternatively, the chymosin encoding DNA can be bio-synthesized in the laboratory without the use of calf cells.

The chymosin produced is identical to that produced by calf stomach cells. The development of genetically engineered chymosin has been encouraged by shortages and fluctuations in cost of rennet from calves. It's manufacturers claim that genetically engineered chymosin will end the cheese making industry's reliance on the slaughter of calves.

Chymosin encoding DNA has been introduced into three different micro-organisms. These are the yeast *Kluyveromyces lactis*, the fungus *Aspergillus niger var. awamori*, and a strain of the bacteria *Escherichia coli*. All of these have now been approved and cleared for use by the Ministry of Agriculture, Fisheries, and Food [in the UK]. There is no legal requirement for manufacturers to state whether a genetically engineered rennet has been used in the cheese making process.

Vegetarian cheeses are widely available in supermarkets and health food stores. A wide variety of cheeses are now made with non-animal rennet and labeled as suitable for vegetarians. No particular type of cheese is exclusively vegetarian. Soft cheeses are as likely to be non-vegetarian as hard cheese.

Types of Cheese

The type of cheese produced depends on the milk used and the cheese making process. The milk used may be full fat, semi-skimmed or fully skimmed, this affecting the fat content of the cheese. It may be pasteurized or unpasteurized. Milk from different animals and different breeds is important in determining the final flavor. As well as cow's milk, cheese may be made from sheep or goat's milk.

Soft cheeses may be fresh or ripened. Fresh cheeses include quark, cottage cheese, and cream cheese. Ripened soft cheeses include Brie and Camembert. Semi-soft cheeses include Stilton, Wensleydale and Gorgonzola. Hard cheeses include Cheddar, Cheshire, and Gruyere. Parmesan is a strongly pressed, very hard, dry cheese ripened for 2–3 years and then grated. Whey cheeses such as Ricotta are made as a by-product of other cheeses from the whey removed during pressing. Processed cheeses are either made with trimmings that are left over from the manufacture of other cheeses, or from dried milk powder. Flavorings, colorings and other additives are used.

Nutritional Aspects

Cheese is a good source of protein, calcium, zinc, and vitamin B_{12}. However, full fat cheese is a major source of saturated fat which can lead to raised serum cholesterol levels. Also, it contains no carbohydrate or fiber, and is a very poor source of iron. Vegetarians, particularly new vegetarians, should be wary of too high a consumption of cheese.

Section 16.5

Soy

Excerpted from Henkel, John, "Soy: Health Claims for Soy Protein, Questions about Other Components," *FDA Consumer*, May-June 2000, http://www.fda.gov/fdac/features/2000/300_soy.html.

Soy Benefits

Soy protein products can be good substitutes for animal products because, unlike some other beans, soy offers a "complete" protein profile. Soybeans contain all the amino acids essential to human nutrition, which must be supplied in the diet because they cannot be synthesized by the human body. Soy protein products can replace animal-based foods—which also have complete proteins but tend to contain more fat, especially saturated fat—without requiring major adjustments elsewhere in the diet.

While foreign cultures, especially Asians, have used soy extensively for centuries, mainstream America has been slow to move dietary soy beyond a niche market status. In the United States, soybean is a huge cash crop, but the product is used largely as livestock feed.

With the increased emphasis on healthy diets, that may be changing. Sales of soy products are up and are projected to increase, due in part, say industry officials, to the FDA-approved health claim. (U.S. retail sales of soyfoods were $.852 billion in 1992 and are projected to rise to $3.714 billion in 2002.) "We've seen this before with other claims FDA has approved," says Brian Sansoni, senior manager for public policy at the Grocery Manufacturers of America. "It brings attention to products; there are newspaper and TV stories and information on the Internet."

To qualify for the health claim, foods must contain at least 6.25 grams of soy protein per serving and fit other criteria, such as being low in fat, cholesterol, and sodium. The claim is similar to others the agency has approved in recent years to indicate heart benefits, including claims for the cholesterol-lowering effects of soluble fiber in oat bran and psyllium seeds.

FDA determined that diets with four daily soy servings can reduce levels of low-density lipoproteins (LDLs), the so-called "bad cholesterol" that builds up in blood vessels, by as much as 10 percent. This number is significant because heart experts generally agree that a 1 percent drop in total cholesterol can equal a 2 percent drop in heart disease risk. Heart disease kills more Americans than any other illness. Disorders of the heart and blood vessels, including stroke, cause nearly 1 million deaths yearly.

FDA allowed the health claim for soy protein in response to a petition by Protein Technologies International Inc., a leading soy producer that tracks its origins to soybean studies sponsored by Henry Ford in the early 1930s. The company was acquired by E.I. du Pont de Nemours and Company (DuPont) in 1997. In considering the petition, FDA reviewed data from 27 clinical studies submitted in the petition, as well as comments submitted to the public record and studies identified by FDA. The available research consistently showed that regular soy protein consumption lowered cholesterol to varying degrees.

One of the studies, conducted over nine weeks at Wake Forest University Baptist Medical Center and reported in the Archives of Internal Medicine in 1999, found that soy protein can reduce plasma concentrations of total and LDL cholesterol but does not adversely affect levels of HDL, or "good" cholesterol, which at high levels has been associated with a reduction in heart disease risk. Another often-quoted study, published in the *New England Journal of Medicine* in 1995, examined 38 separate studies and concluded that soy protein can prompt "significant reductions" not only in total and LDL cholesterol, but also in triglycerides, another fat linked to health problems when present at elevated levels.

Other studies hint that soy may have benefits beyond fostering a healthy heart. At the Third International Symposium on the Role of Soy in Preventing and Treating Chronic Disease, held in late 1999, researchers presented data linking soy consumption to a reduced risk of several illnesses. Disorders as diverse as osteoporosis, prostate cancer, and colon cancer are under investigation.

Soy's Many Faces

Though soy may seem like a new and different kind of food for many Americans, it actually is found in a number of products already widely consumed. For example, soybean oil accounts for 79 percent of the edible fats used annually in the United States, according to the United Soybean Board. A glance at the ingredients for commercial mayonnaises, margarines, salad dressings, or vegetable shortenings often reveals soybean oil high on the list.

But the health claim only covers the form that includes soy protein. This form can be incorporated into the diet in a variety of ways to help reach the daily intake of 25 grams of soy protein considered beneficial.

While not every form of the following foods will qualify for the health claim, these are some of the most common sources of soy protein:

Tofu is made from cooked pureed soybeans processed into a custard-like cake. It has a neutral flavor and can be stir-fried, mixed into "smoothies," or blended into a cream cheese texture for use in dips or as a cheese substitute. It comes in firm, soft, and silken textures.

"Soymilk," the name some marketers use for a soy beverage, is produced by grinding dehulled soybeans and mixing them with water to form a milk-like liquid. It can be consumed as a beverage or used in recipes as a substitute for cow's milk. Soymilk, sometimes fortified with calcium, comes plain or in flavors such as vanilla, chocolate, and coffee. For lactose-intolerant individuals, it can be a good replacement for dairy products.

Soy flour is created by grinding roasted soybeans into a fine powder. The flour adds protein to baked goods, and, because it adds moisture, it can be used as an egg substitute in these products. It also can be found in cereals, pancake mixes, frozen desserts, and other common foods.

Textured soy protein is made from defatted soy flour, which is compressed and dehydrated. It can be used as a meat substitute or as filler in dishes such as meatloaf.

Tempeh is made from whole, cooked soybeans formed into a chewy cake and used as a meat substitute.

Miso is a fermented soybean paste used for seasoning and in soup stock.

Soy protein also is found in many "meat analog" products, such as soy sausages, burgers, franks, and cold cuts, as well as soy yogurts and cheese, all of which are intended as substitutes for their animal-based counterparts.

Make sure the products contain enough soy protein to make a meaningful contribution to the total daily diet without being high in saturated fat and other unhealthy substances.

Adding Soy Protein to the Diet

For consumers interested in increasing soy protein consumption to help reduce their risk of heart disease, health experts say they need not completely eliminate animal-based products such as meat, poultry, and dairy foods to reap soy's benefits. While soy protein's direct effects on cholesterol levels are well documented, replacing some animal protein with soy protein is a valuable way to lower fat intake. "If individuals begin to substitute soy products, for example, soy burgers, for foods high in saturated fat, such as hamburgers, there would be the added advantage of replacing saturated fat and cholesterol [in] the diet," says Alice Lichtenstein, D.Sc., professor of nutrition at Tufts University. Whole soy foods also are a good source of fiber, B vitamins, calcium, and omega-3 essential fatty acids, all important food components.

The American Heart Association recommends that soy products be used in a diet that includes fruits, vegetables, whole grains, low-fat dairy products, poultry, fish, and lean meats. The AHA also emphasizes that a diet to effectively lower cholesterol should consist of no more than 30 percent of total daily calories from fat and no more than 10 percent of calories from saturated fat.

Nowadays, a huge variety of soy foods is on shelves not only in health food stores, but increasingly in mainstream grocery stores. As the number of soy-based products grows, it becomes increasingly easy for consumers to add enough soy to their daily diets to meet the 25-gram amount that FDA says is beneficial to heart health. According to soybean industry figures, the numbers add up quickly when you look at the protein contained in typical soy foods. For example:

- Four ounces of firm tofu contains 13 grams of soy protein.

- One soy "sausage" link provides 6 grams of protein.

- One soy "burger" includes 10 to 12 grams of protein.

- An 8-ounce glass of plain soymilk contains 10 grams of protein.

- One soy protein bar delivers 14 grams of protein.

- One-half cup of tempeh provides 19.5 grams of protein.

- A quarter cup of roasted soy nuts contains 19 grams of soy protein.

Chapter 17

High Energy Vegetarian Foods for Growing Kids and Active Teens

Book store shelves are stocked with nutrition books on how to lose weight but very little has been written on healthy ways to increase your caloric intake. Vegetarian menu planning, particularly vegan meals, can often be low in calories due to the low fat, high fiber content of whole grains, beans, fruits, and vegetables which is the main components of the diet. So what about all those folks who require high octane foods to meet their energy needs?

If you are looking to boost your caloric intake with healthy nutrient packed fuel, here are some menu planning suggestions that won't leave you hungry.

Breakfast Suggestions

- granola or muesli cereal topped with chopped dates, figs, extra nuts, seeds, and banana slices

- multi-grain cooked cereal topped with dried fruit, nuts, seeds, with nut butters blended

- smoothie blender drinks with banana, ground nuts, seeds, nut butters, or tahini blended in

- nut butter or tahini with banana slices on whole grain bread

From "High Energy Foods for Vegetarians" by Bonnie Kumer, R.D. © Bonnie Kumer. Revised, March 2002. This article originally appeared in the January/February 1997 issue of *Lifelines*, the newsletter of the Toronto Vegetarian Association, Toronto, Canada. Reprinted with permission.

- whole grain pancakes with sliced banana, chopped nuts, soy margarine and maple syrup

- whole grain muffins spread with nut butter or tahini for extra calories

Lunch Suggestions

Sandwiches

- pita stuffed with humus and extra tahini sauce drizzled on top

- pita stuffed with avocado and tofu cheese

- veggie pate and avocado slices on whole grain bun

- veggie burger on whole grain bun with melted tofu cheese or topped with tahini sauce

- nut butter or tahini with banana slices on whole grain bread

- pack leftovers from dinner—see dinner suggestions

Soups

These tend to fill you up without contributing much to calories. To boost the fuel in soups add tofu, rice, pasta, barley, couscous or potato.

Salads

- add tofu, tempeh, and avocado to your salads

- choose more salads made with pasta, rice, potato, or couscous

- sprinkle chopped almonds, cashews, walnuts, pumpkin, or sunflower seeds on top

- add a scoop of humus on top

- be generous with your salad dressing

- tofu, avocado, and tahini based dressing will add extra calories

How to Increase Your Calories at Dinner Entrees

- make more tofu entrees—casseroles, stews, stir-fry, marinades

- explore recipes using tempeh (packed full of nutrient dense calories)

- be more generous with oil when cooking
- drizzle extra oil on your cooked rice, potatoes or pasta, vegetables
- sprinkle ground or chopped nuts and seeds on your pasta, potatoes, or rice
- tofu, tahini, or cashew sauces on your pasta, rice, potatoes, and vegetables

Snack Foods

- trail mix—create you own assorted dried fruits, mixed nuts and seeds
- mashed avocado spread on whole wheat pita wedges
- veggie cheese and avocado on crackers
- nut butter or tahini with sliced banana on whole grain bread
- whole grain muffins, spread with nut butter, or tahini for extra calories
- taco type chips with guacamole or plain mashed avocado, tofu dip, or humus
- smoothie shakes made with banana, soy milk, fruit, (can add soft tofu or tahini for extra calories)
- soy yoghurt topped with granola or chopped nuts and dried fruit

Suggested High Calorie Restaurant Items

- East/Mediterranean—falafel, humus, extra tahini sauce, babghanoush, eggplant moussaka
- Italian—pasta in olive oil, pesto, alfredo or other cream sauces, brushetta
- Chinese—tofu dishes, noodle entrees, fried rice, ask for extra cashews or almonds
- European—potato pierogi
- African—potato/chickpea roti with rice
- Mexican—burritos, tacos, enchiladas, refried beans and tortillas, guacamole, rice

Helpful Hints to Increase Your Weight

- Be aware of your hunger. Eat more often.

- Carry healthy snack foods on you at all times when away from home.

- If you have no chance to make your lunch BUY IT. Avoid skipping meal.

- Plan your meals. Grocery shop more often. Think about your meals a day ahead.

- Cook in double of triple batches and freeze half.

- Have frozen entrees on hand for fast, unplanned dinners.

Recommended Resource Regarding Underweight

Brenda Davis, R.D. & Vesanto Melina, MS, RD, *Becoming Vegan*, Chapter 15 "Underweight," pp. 234–243 (Book Publishing Co. 2000)

Chapter 18

Which Foods Contain Animal Products?

Chapter Contents

Section 18.1

Common Ingredient Pitfalls

Excerpted from "21st Century Vegetarian: Potential Pitfalls," Vegetarian Society UK, http://www.vegsoc.org/news/2000/21cv/pitfalls.html, copyright 2000, reprinted with permission. Some words have been changed to conform to American spelling conventions. Material may be viewed in its original format on the Vegetarian Society of the UK website: http://www.vegsoc.org.

Despite the massive increase in veggie-friendly foods available, even the most apparently innocent of foods may still contain hidden ingredients which are the product of slaughter. But don't worry, for help is at hand! With the knowledge found below you will soon get to know what's what.

Some products carrying vegetarian suitability symbols contain battery-farmed eggs. In the worst of cases, some meals may contain non-vegetarian cheese, as well as other "nasties." Certain products are completely vegetarian, but are not marked as such, so you will have to check the label for ingredients.

Table 18.1. Animal-derived ingredients. (Continued on next page.)

Watch out for...

Albumen	Derived from eggs, probably battery
Anchovies	Little fish
Animal fat	Often found in cakes, biscuits, potentially just about everywhere
Aspic	Savory jelly, meat or fish in origin
Beer (and Wines)	Might have been refined or 'cleared' using Isinglass, made from the swim bladders of fish. Siprits are generally OK for veggies. See the list of veggie friendly beers, spirits and wines [Section 18.2], the good news is there are many available, so if you enjoy a tipple—bottoms up!
Organic	does not necessarily mean veggie.
Bread	A lot of breads now contain vegetable-based emulsifiers, some contain no fats—some do. Certain bakeries will use animal fats to grease tins.

Table 18.1. Animal-derived ingredients. (continued)

Cheese	There is a fine selection of vegetarian cheeses available. Make sure that the rennet does not come from animal sources.
Chips [French Fries]	Fry them in vegetable oil and/or make sure oven chips aren't coated in animal fat. Some fast food outlets use animal fats to cook fries, be sure to ask.
Chocolate	Watch out for whey, animal fat and non-veggie emulsifiers.
Cochineal (E120)	Red food colouring, often found in sweets, cakes and confectionery—made from crushed insects.
Crisps	Often use whey or lactose as flavor carrier.
Eggs	Make sure that they are free-range.
Emulsifiers (and fatty acids)	Sometimes are vegetarian, sometimes not.
Gelatine	A gelling agent, the results of boiling animal hides and bones. Often found in ice cream, sweets, pies and yogurts.
Glycerine	Can be produced from animal fats, but also veggie fermented sugars. Found in many products, from toothpaste to chewing gum.
Ice Cream	May contain battery eggs, animal fats, and gelatine.
Jelly	Made from gelatine, go for a veggie alternative.
Lactose	Produced from milk, often a by-product of cheese making.
Lecithin	Mostly made from soya sources, could come from non-free-range eggs.
Margarine	Watch out for animal-fats, gelatine, and fish oils.
Pasta	May contain battery eggs.
Soup	Take stock and check it's veggie.
Suet	Anyone for an animal's internal organs in your pastry? Thought not. Go for vegetable suet.
Tablets	Make sure capsules are not made from gelatine
Tallow	An animal fat.
Whey	Whey and its powdered version come from cheese making, which could mean making use of animal rennet.
Worcestershire sauce	Leading brands contain anchovies but there are veggie versions available.

Away from the table...

Down	Usually from slaughtered ducks or geese.
Photography	Film uses gelatine, why not go digital?
Silk	Invariably involves killing the silk worm.
Soap	Some soaps include animal fats, and/or glycerine. Get a vegetable-based soap.

Section 18.2

Alcohol

Beers

As a general rule, traditional, cask-conditioned beers ('real ales') are usually clarified (cleared) with isinglass finings. Isinglass is a very pure form of gelatin obtained from the air bladders of some freshwater fishes, especially the sturgeon. The addition of the finings speeds up a process which would otherwise occur naturally. Keg, canned, beer-sphere and some bottled beers are usually filtered without the use of animal substances. Lagers are generally chill-filtered but a few may involve the use of isinglass. The only possibly animal-derived ingredient used in the production of keg beers is E471. Animal-derived finings continue to be used in all Guinness- and Bass-produced beers.

Spirits

The production of spirits does not appear to involve the use of animal substances (Vodka is now filtered using birchwood charcoal).

Wines

Most wines on sale in off-licenses and supermarkets have been fined using one of the following: blood, bone marrow, chitin (organic base of the hard parts of insects and crustacea such as shrimps and crabs), egg albumen (egg white), fish oil, gelatin (jelly obtained by boiling animal tissues such as skin, tendons, ligaments, bones, etc.), isinglass, milk, or milk casein. Non-animal alternatives include limestone, bentonite, kaolin and kieslguhr (clays), plant casein, silica gel, and vegetable plaques.

Vegan Products

Beers/lagers. Whitbread Kaltenberg Pils, Heineken Export Lager, Labatt Blue Lager, Labatt Ice Lager, Scottish Courage Beck's Bier [keg, bottle], Budweiser [keg, can, bottle], Coors Extra Gold [keg, can, bottle], Holsten Pils [keg, can, bottle], Grolsch Grolsch [keg, 450 ml swingtop bottle] (not the 250 ml, 275 ml bottles or 500 ml cans).

Ciders. Merrydown Pulse: White; Shloer: Apple, Peach, Red Grape, Summer Fruits, White Grape; Vintage: Dry, Medium.

Spirits and Aperitifs. International Distillers all Croft Sherries, Cockspur Rum, Cointreau, Croft Vintage Port, Gilbeys Gin, J&B Scotch Whisky, Jack Daniels, Malibu, Metaxa, Popov Vodka, Romana Sambuca, Sapphire Gin, Singleton Whisky, Smirnoff Vodkas, Southern Comfort; Safeways all spirits.

Wines. Most of the larger supermarkets supply some vegan wines. The following companies also sell a comprehensive range.

Section 18.3

Gelling Agents

Excerpted from "Information Sheet: Vegetarian Gelling Agents," Vegetarian Society UK, http://www.vegsoc.org/info/gelling.html, copyright 2001, reprinted with permission. Some words have been changed to conform to American spelling conventions. Material may be viewed in its original format on the Vegetarian Society of the UK website: http://www.vegsoc.org.

Introduction

Gelatin is an unacceptable product to vegetarians as it is a by-product of the slaughterhouse industry, being made of protein derived from animal bones, cartilage, tendons and other tissues such as pig skin. Isinglass, used in fining some alcoholic drinks, is a type of gelatin from the air bladders of certain kinds of fish. Aspic is also unsuitable, as it is made from clarified meat, fish, or vegetable stocks and gelatin.

However, there are various alternatives available, which do not contain any animal products whatsoever. These include agar agar, carrageen and a proprietary product called Gelozone.

Agar Agar (E406)

Probably best known to many as the culture growing medium used in petri dishes in school science laboratories! Also known by its Japanese name Kanten, agar agar is derived from the *Gelidium* genus of red sea vegetables.

For culinary purposes, it is available in different forms: bars, flaked, or powdered, although in this country you are most likely to find it flaked or powdered only. Natural agar agar is unflavored, producing a firm, clear jelly, and is rich in iodine and trace minerals and has mildly laxative properties.

The flakes are produced by a traditional method of cooking and pressing the sea vegetables and then naturally freeze-drying the residue to form bars which are then flaked for easier packing and transport. They are preferable to powdered agar agar which, although cheaper, may be chemically processed using sulfuric acid to dissolve the starches, and inorganic bleaches to neutralize the color and flavor.

Agar agar has stronger setting properties and, unlike gelatin, which requires refrigeration to set, it will set at room temperature after about an hour—although it is advisable to store dishes gelled with agar agar in the fridge as it is a high protein food.

The gelling ability of agar agar is affected by the acidity or alkalinity of the ingredients it is mixed with, also by factors such as the season of the seaweed harvest! More acidic foods, such as citrus fruits and strawberries, may require higher amounts of agar agar. Some ingredients will not set with it at all such as: kiwi fruit (too acidic), pineapple, fresh figs, paw paw /papaya, mango, and peaches, which contain enzymes which break down the gelling ability (although cooked fruit seems to lose this effect), chocolate, and spinach.

Flaked and powdered agar agar need to be used in different proportions, unfortunately many recipes do not specify which is being called for, but here are a few guidelines:

- Powdered agar agar can be substituted for the same quantity of powdered gelatin in a recipe.

- For every teaspoon of agar agar powder, you should substitute a tablespoon of agar agar flakes.

- For a firm jelly you require approximately 2 teaspoons of powder or 2 tablespoons of flakes per 1 pint/600 ml of liquid.

- Agar agar should be soaked in the liquid first for 10–15 minutes, then gently brought to a boil and simmered while stirring until it dissolves completely, this will take about 5 minutes for powder and 10–15 minutes for flakes. Unlike gelatin, agar agar can be boiled and can even be re-melted if necessary. If you are unsure as to the setting ability of your gel, test a small amount on a cold saucer—it should set in 20–30 seconds, if not you may need more agar agar, if too firm—add some more liquid.

Carrageen (or Carragheen)

Also known as Irish Moss, this dense, reddish purple seaweed grows in the temperate North Atlantic coastal waters around the West of Ireland, France and off North America's coastline. It is harvested and sun-dried which bleaches it to a yellowish brown color. Rich in iodine and vitamin A, it produces a softer gel than agar agar.

Carrageen requires thorough rinsing before use. It needs to be soaked and then well cooked with the liquid to be set and does not dissolve completely. Carrageen Mould is a traditional Irish pudding made by soaking ½ oz/10–15 gm carrageen in water, draining and adding it to 1 pint/600 ml of milk, bringing it slowly to the boil and simmering it for 20–30 minutes, straining it and allowing the strained mixture, which can be sweetened, to set on cooling.

Carrageenan (E407) is a by-product of carrageen and is used extensively as an emulsifying, thickening and gelling additive in ice creams, jellies, biscuits, milk shakes, and frozen desserts, even in some cosmetics and medicines!

"Gelozone"

This is a proprietary product made of carrageenan (E407), locust (carob) bean gum (E410), guar gum (E412).

It does not set as firmly as agar agar and has a slightly cloudy appearance. Gelozone is also prepared differently.

1 tsp/5 ml will set 1 pint/600 ml liquid. The powder should be sprinkled onto cold liquid, which is then very gently heated until just steaming, stirring all the time. Do NOT allow the mixture to boil or the Gelozone will not gel. It sets very quickly and requires refrigeration.

Chapter 19

Vegetarian Items at Restaurants and Fast Food Chains

Arby's. Vegetarian items: Baked potato, potato cakes, turnovers (apple, blueberry, cherry), and side salad. Their french fries, which would otherwise be vegan, may be deep-fried in the same oil as non-vegetarian items. Their buns contain eggs or milk derivatives. The milkshakes contain animal gelatin. The cheese contains animal rennet.

Burger King. Vegetarian items: Vegetarian Whopper (regular Whopper with no meat patty: vegans hold cheese and mayo). Buns may contain lard, check with restaurant. The Vegetarian Whopper is not on the menu—just ask for it. Vegan items: French fries, tater tenders, and side salad. Onion rings contain whey. Cherry and apple pies contain casein. Snicker's Ice Cream Bar contains gelatin. Oat bran bun contains dairy products. Bagels contain egg whites.

Hardee's. Vegetarian items: French fries, side salad.

McDonald's. Vegetarian items: Side salad, hash browns, Cheerios, Wheaties, McDonaldland cookies. Red french reduced calorie dressing contains anchovies. All three danishes contain gelatin. Many McDonald's will prepare a Big Mac without meat (buns are vegan, special sauce contains egg yolk) or cheeseburgers without meat if requested. French fries are not vegetarian, they contain beef flavoring.

Excerpted from "Fast Food Information for Vegetarians and Vegans," October 2001, copyright Michael Garnett. Reprinted with permission. The complete document, including contact information for each restaurant can be found at http://nashville.earthsave.org/fastfood.htm.

Subway. Vegetarian items: Most Subway franchises sell the Veggie Max, a no-fat vegan patty. They also sell the Veggie Delite—a sub without meat—cheese is optional. Vegan: foot long sub roll (white and whole wheat), salad. The 4-inch round buns contain egg whites. The cheese Subway uses is made with vegetable rennet.

Taco Bell. Vegetarian items: Most items can be requested without meat or with beans in place of meat. Lacto-Vegetarian: Pintos and cheese, bean burrito, bean tostada, Mexican rice, 7-layer burrito, nacho chips, cheese. Vegan: Bean burrito (without cheese), bean tostada (without cheese), Mexican rice (without cheese), 7-layer burrito (no sour cream, no cheese), hot/mild/fire sauce, fiesta salsa, red sauce.

About their cheese (taken directly from the letter from Taco Bell):

> Historically, enzymes used in the production of cheese were of an animal source. The enzyme, rennet, contains a microorganism called chymosin. Chymosin is the actual agent that causes the state change from liquid to semi-solid (coagulation). Today, due to the need for kosher cheese and the cost of using animal sources, genetically engineered coagulants are used. The genetically engineered chymosin is derived from a modified strain of the dairy yeast *Kluyveromyces lactis*. It is formulated to coagulate the milk so we can make our cheese without the use of animal coagulants. All of the Taco Bell suppliers are kosher plants and are using genetically engineered strains of food yeast.

Taco John's. Vegetarian items: bean burritos, nachos, tortillas (contain dairy). According to the e-mail received from Taco John's: "Based on the most recent information available from our vendors, these products are free of animal products or by-products": refried beans (contains corn oil), corn tortilla, nacho chips, Potato Oles (contains canola/soy oils), Mexican rice, guacamole (contains canola/soy oils), Bunge Pour N Fry shortening (made from soybean oil), and Ventura Chef's Pride shortening (made from soybean oil).

No lard used in food preparation, but the deep-fried items are fried in the same oil as the meat products. Any item on the menu can be made vegetarian by substituting beans for meat. If you are vegan, request no cheese or sour cream. Their cheese does not contain animal rennet.

Wendy's. Vegetarian items: Some baked potato toppings, deluxe garden salad, and side salad. All their cheeses are made with microbial enzymes. You may be able to order a burger without the meat. Vegan: French fries, and baked potato.

Papa John's. As far as I can tell their crust and sauce are both vegan. The garlic dipping sauce appears to be vegetarian.

Pizza Dough: Bleached, enriched wheat flour (niacin, iron (reduced), thiamine mononitrate, riboflavin, folic acid), malted barley flour, clear filtered water, sugar, soybean oil, salt, yeast, soy flour, inactive dried yeast, ascorbic acid, (added as dough conditioner), enzymes.

Pizza Dipping Sauce: Tomato sauce, water, blend of vegetable oils (canola and olive), sugar, salt, oregano, spices (pepper), and citric acid, garlic, basil, soybean oil, pectinase.

Pizza Sauce Mix: Fresh tomatoes, canola oil/extra virgin olive oil blend, salt, oregano, spices (pepper), citric acid, sugar, garlic, basil, soybean oil, pectinase.

Special Garlic Sauce: Liquid margarine [partially hydrogenated soy bean oil, water, salt, mono and diglycerides, lecithin, sodium benzoate (a preservative), calcium disodium EDTA and citric acid (to protect flavor), colored with beta carotene, vitamin A palmitate added], water, garlic powder, salt, lactic acid, natural garlic flavor.

Thin Crust: Flour (wheat, malted barley), water, vegetable shortening (partially hydrogenated soybean oil), yeast, salt, calcium propionate (preservative).

Panera. Our local Panera told us that if the soup does not specifically contain the word "vegetarian" then it is not vegetarian. For instance, the broccoli and cheese soup (which was not listed) uses a chicken stock. I checked back with Panera and they confirmed that the soups listed below use a vegetable base. The following items are vegetarian: vegetarian sandwich, peanut butter and jelly sandwich, vegetarian lentil soup, creamy country asparagus soup, forest mushroom soup, french onion soup, garden vegetable soup, mesa bean and vegetable soup, Santa Fe roasted corn soup, savory vegetable bean soup, tomato mushroom and barley soup, vegetarian black bean soup, portabella and mozzarella panini, and most of their salads.

She also stated they do not use egg in any of their breads, except for their french bread which contains egg whites.

Grocery Stores

Jewel. Vegetarian items: Jewel carries Morningstar Farms and Boca products. They also carry Yves deli slices and soy cheese slices (contain casein) which can be found in the produce section. They also have a large selection of Amy's Kitchen products frozen convenience meals. All can be found in the frozen foods section, and are vegetarian.

Kroger. Vegetarian items: Kroger carries Morningstar Farms and Boca products, which can be found in the frozen foods section. They also have an extensive health food section.

Wal-Mart. Vegetarian items: Wal Mart carries Morningstar Farms and Boca products, which can be found in the frozen foods section. They also carry Yves deli slices and soy cheese slices (contain casein) which can be found in the produce section. They also have a health food section, which contains other meat alternatives, along with soy and rice beverages.

Chapter 20

Vegetarian Cookery Tips

Vegetarian food does not just have to be healthy. There's absolutely no reason at all why it should not look, smell and taste fantastic too—especially when you are cooking in the comfort of your own home. If you're new to vegetarian cuisine, here's a few useful tips to help you cook up a storm in the kitchen.

Always make sure that you use only free-range eggs when cooking and that the cheeses you use are suitable for vegetarians. Be on the look out for hidden animal ingredients, some of the most common of which you might encounter are highlighted in Chapter 18 of this book. With a little knowledge, you will soon learn just what to avoid.

As a general tip, where the option exists, try to grill and steam your food. If you have to fry, always use vegetable oils and use as little as possible. Vary your methods of cooking by using a wok for stir-fries, or why not have a veggie barbecue?

It is always best to have the right tools for the job, but you will not have to invest huge sums of money in a vast array of weird and wonderful utensils or electric gadgetry.

Try and make sure you have a couple of sharp knives, a mixing bowl, two or three saucepans, oven-proof dishes and baking tins for cakes, quiches, and flans. A blender or food processor is a definite advantage in the kitchen and once again need not be too expensive. A lot of the equipment you will require will depend on the recipes you are cooking. Check in advance that you have the necessary things you will need.

Most of your favorite recipes can be adapted to become suitable for vegetarians. Mushrooms, pulses and grains all make excellent substitutes for the bulk and texture of meat.

Should you prefer, there is also an excellent range of meat substitutes now available. These are not expensive or difficult to use and taste quite authentic, if that is what you are after. Add them to casseroles, curries, pasta, and rice dishes instead of the meat or fish.

Did You Know?

Vegetarian food does not have to take a long time to prepare. Why not utilize rice or pasta? While the pasta or rice is cooking, you can quickly whip up a vegetable, tomato, or cheese-based sauce and there are other ingredients you can add to the mix.

Of course you can also use the wide selection of vegetarian ready-made sauces available and it is possible to prepare a simple and delicious meal in no time at all. The beauty of vegetarian cooking is that you make it whatever you want it to be, from the simple, effortless snack right through to meals that offer more of a challenge.

Do not limit yourself in terms of your choice of vegetarian recipes. Be adventurous with your ingredients and explore the full range of spices and herbs. The choice is large, the possibilities endless, so get to know what ingredients create the flavors you like best. Try as many different dishes as you can—there is a great wealth of food out there.

Invest in one or two decent vegetarian cook books. You might be amazed at just how many there now are and they contain some excellent recipes for every occasion, taste, season, and budget with influences coming from all over the world, combining the traditional and the new.

Share your new found cookery skills and knowledge. There are few things more enjoyable than sitting around a table with friends or family enjoying excellent food.

Above all, enjoy your cooking—it should be fun!

Chapter 21

Recipes for the Vegetarian Christmas

Christmas is coming, along with it all those little problems we vegetarians may have to face. Like, you're going to dinner with the family so you tote along your own vegetarian entree and hope that they haven't roasted the potatoes in the same pan as the turkey. You know that at least one person will say, "eat just a little turkey, after all it's only once year and it is Christmas." (Did the turkey care about the season when it faced the chopper?) Or, the family is coming to have dinner with you, brave smiles on their faces, as they thankfully envision the turkey dinner they'll be tucking into the next day. Or, you're just fed up with all the extra work Christmas seems to bring and you've reached the age where it's just for the kids.

Try taking it easy this year. Pre-prepare your main dishes one or two days ahead, then when everyone else is rushing around, relax on the sofa with a good book, take a brisk walk in the crisp December air, or stay in bed all day watching movies (carefully avoiding epics starring Santa Claus and those tiresome reindeers).

Tip: If you yearn for stuffing but can't be bothered to make it from scratch, try a good commercial brand like Paxo. It mixes up in a moment and can be baked in a small casserole dish while you cook the entree.

Dozell, Anne, "Take-It-Easy Christmas," Toronto Vegetarian Association, *Lifelines*, November-December 1998, http://www.veg.ca/lifelines/novdec/christmas.htm. Reprinted with permission.

The Traditional (A Recipe for the Seasonally Addicted)

Tofu Roast

- 1 onion, finely chopped
- 1 cup brown rice (soak in water for at least 2 hours if you have the time)
- 1 cup red lentils
- 2 tsp miso or Marmite
- 1 cup wholewheat breadcrumbs
- 1 cup medium firm to firm tofu
- 1 cup tomato sauce
- 1 tsp oil

Cook the rice and lentils in salted boiling water until tender (about 20 minutes). Cook them together unless you didn't have time to soak the rice, in which case cook them separately as the unsoaked brown rice will take at least 40 minutes to become tender. Meanwhile saute the onion in the oil until lightly browned and add to the cooked rice and lentils, together with the miso or Marmite and the breadcrumbs. Crumble or mash the tofu and add to the rice mixture. Slowly mix in the tomato sauce. The mixture should be moist but firm, add a little more tomato sauce if necessary, but don't make it too sloppy. Press into a baking dish, neaten the top with a fork and bake at 350° F for about 40 minutes. Options: Either refrigerate before cooking, or pre-cook and reheat in a microwave.

The Laid-Back (For Those Who Pretend They're Not Seasonally Addicted, but Really Are)

Barley and Cashew Casserole

- 1 and one-third cups barley
- pinch of salt or 1 Tbsp soy sauce
- 2 cups water
- two-thirds cup soy milk or milk
- 2 medium onions
- 2 cups mushrooms (preferably portabella or cremini)

- 2 fresh or 2 canned tomatoes
- 1–2 tsp olive oil
- 1 cup cashews, crushed
- 1 tsp miso or Marmite

Optional seasonings: black pepper, 1 tsp sage. Soak the barley for 2–4 hours, then cook in the water and soy milk with salt or soy sauce until nearly tender. Chop the onions, tomatoes, and mushrooms and saute in the oil until just tender. Place in the bottom of a casserole dish. Stir the cashews and miso or Marmite into the barley, add optional seasonings to taste. Pour over onion mixture, cover, and place in refrigerator until ready to cook. Bake at 350° F for 20–30 minutes.

The Side Dish (Goes with Most Entrees)

Sweet Potato and Parsnip Casserole

- 3 large onions, thinly sliced
- 3–4 large sweet potatoes peeled and cut into small chunks
- 4–5 parsnips, peeled and cut into one-fourth inch slices
- 2–3 cups vegetable stock
- 1 tsp dried thyme
- salt and black pepper to taste
- one-fourth cup wholewheat breadcrumbs
- 1 Tbsp nutritional yeast (optional)
- 2 tsp olive oil

Saute onions in 1 tsp oil in a large frying pan until a deep golden brown. Add the sweet potatoes and parsnips, vegetable stock, thyme, and a little salt and pepper. (You may not need any salt if you made stock from commercial vegetable cubes. Taste the stock first.) Simmer the mixture for 15 to 30 minutes, until the potatoes are tender and most of the liquid is absorbed. Place mixture in a casserole dish. At this stage, you can refrigerate the dish until ready to cook. Preheat oven to 400° F, mix the breadcrumbs and nutritional yeast with the remaining tsp oil and sprinkle on the top. Bake the casserole for 20–30 minutes or until stock has been absorbed by the potatoes and the top is brown and crusty. Serves 8. Halve the quantities for a smaller number of people.

The Dessert (A New Twist on an Old Favorite)

Ginger Cranberry Mincemeat Pie

Line a pie dish with your favorite pastry recipe, (adding one-fourth tsp cinnamon to the flour) and keep aside any leftovers or trimmings or buy a ready made pastry shell (top and bottom) from the supermarket (read the ingredients, some brands contain lard).

Filling

- 2 cups fresh cranberries or a large can
- Jar of vegetarian mincemeat
- 1 level Tbsp ground ginger
- 2 Tbsp raw cane sugar
- 2 Tbsp water or juice from can

Note: Most supermarkets now sell a vegetarian brand of mincemeat, the real thing contains suet which is animal fat. If you like, add a spoonful of brandy a few hours beforehand.

Put the cranberries in a pan with the sugar and water or juice and cook until softened (if using canned, just heat them through). Cool. Mix in the mincemeat and ginger and pour into the pastry case.

Take the trimmings, or the top piece of the ready made pastry shell, and cut into stars or other seasonal or non-seasonal shapes and arrange around the edge of the filling. Bake for 30 minutes or until pastry is golden, then sprinkle the pastry shapes with a little brown sugar. Eat warm, or refrigerate and pop in the oven to warm up later.

Part Four

Special Groups

Chapter 22

Vegetarianism and Pregnancy

Introduction

Pregnancy is a time of increased nutritional needs, both to support the rapidly growing fetus and to allow for the changes occurring in the pregnant woman's body. Throughout pregnancy, recommended intakes of vitamins and minerals are higher than for the non-pregnant state. For example, the recommendation for folic acid is 50 percent higher and the recommendation for iron is doubled in pregnancy. Vegetarian and vegan diets can easily meet these nutrient needs.

Weight Gain

It is important that all pregnant women have adequate weight gain. Weight gain recommendations vary depending on the pre-pregnancy weight and needs of the woman, therefore energy needs vary as well. A general trend is to have little weight gain (less than 5 pounds) for the first 12 weeks. Then, in the second and third trimesters, a weight gain of a pound or two a week is suggested. Current

Excerpted from Mangles, Reed, "Vegetarian Diets During Pregnancy," Vegetarian Nutrition Dietetic Practice Group, 1998. This article is reprinted with permission from *Vegetarian Nutrition Update*, the official newsletter of the Vegetarian Nutrition Dietetic Practice Group of the American Dietetic Association. © 1999. The full version of this document, including references, can be accessed at http://www.andrews.edu/NUFS/Vegetarian%20Diets%20During%20Pregnancy.html.

weight gain recommendations are applicable to vegetarians. The recommendations for weight gain are listed in Table 22.1.

Table 22.1. Recommended Weight Gain During Pregnancy

Weight status (prior to pregnancy)	Recommended weight gain (lbs.)
Average weight	25–35
Underweight	28–40
Overweight	15–25
Adolescents	30–45
Average weight, twins	35–45

Most pregnant vegetarians, both lacto-ovo and vegan, gain an adequate amount of weight. Birth weights of infants of vegetarian women have frequently been shown to be similar to those of infants of non-vegetarians and to birth weight norms. For example, a small study by King et al found that infants born to vegetarian women had a mean birth weight 200 grams higher than infants born to omnivorous women. A study examining vegan women found that the average birth weight was 3342 grams (about 7 pounds, 5 ounces). Interestingly, for each additional year these women were vegan, birth weight increased by 42 grams.

Some studies done outside the U.S. reported birth weights of infants born to vegetarian women were lower than infants with non-vegetarian mothers. Generally this is found in women following restrictive vegetarian diets, such as macrobiotic diets. These low weights have been attributed to low maternal weight gain and lower maternal intakes of energy, iron, folate, or vitamin B_{12}.

Energy

In order to meet the weight gain recommendations for pregnancy, extra dietary energy is required. The total energy cost of a pregnancy is estimated to be around 55,000 calories over the 280 days of pregnancy. Assuming that caloric intake does not increase during the first month of pregnancy, an additional 200 to 300 calories per day should meet energy needs.

Since caloric needs increase only about 15% and nutrient needs increase up to 50%, a nutritionally dense diet in pregnancy is needed to meet nutrient needs within the caloric recommendations. Vegetarians should be counseled, just like all clients, that excessive intake of low nutrient vegetarian foods such as candy and sweets should be avoided.

Women who were underweight or who are having difficulty gaining weight should be counseled to choose nutritious foods with a higher caloric density. Suggestions include milk shakes (soymilk or cow's milk blended with fruit and tofu or yogurt), nuts and nut butters, dried fruits, soy products, and bean dips. Small, frequent meals and snacks can help increase food intake.

Protein

Protein is needed during pregnancy to support the rapid growth of the fetus and placenta. Protein is also used in the growth of maternal tissue. Current recommendations suggest an increase in protein of 10 grams more than the non-pregnant state for adult women. Ten grams of protein is the amount found in 2 cups of soy milk, 3½ ounces of extra-firm tofu, 3 ounces of tempeh or one large bagel. This amounts to a total of only 60 grams of protein per day; in one study vegan and vegetarian women were consuming that amount even before they were pregnant.

Iron

Iron needs are high during pregnancy because of both the increase in the mother's blood volume and the blood formed for the fetus. Despite compensatory mechanisms such as cessation of menstruation and increased iron absorption, the iron requirement of pregnancy is quite high and the diet needs to be especially rich in iron. Pregnant vegetarians should choose high iron foods like whole grains, legumes, tofu, and green leafy vegetables daily and consume them with foods rich in vitamin C to increase the bioavailability of the iron. Iron supplements of 30 mg daily during the second and third trimester are commonly recommended. Higher dose iron supplements can induce side effects such as constipation, nausea, and heartburn. Supplement doses of 38 to 65 mg of iron per day may reduce zinc absorption.

Researchers are currently studying whether taking iron supplements less frequently than daily is as effective as daily iron supplementation. A study in Indonesia showed that weekly iron supplementation offered similar health effects compared to daily supplementation and the compliance was higher in the group of women supplemented weekly. Therefore an alternative to daily supplementation may be suggested for women experiencing side effects such as constipation that they attribute to iron supplementation.

Iron deficiency anemia is not uncommon during pregnancy, in both vegetarians and non-vegetarians. Several studies of pregnant vegetarians have suggested that dietary iron intakes were close to recommended levels and that rates of anemia were low, although Drake et al. found that dietary supplements were needed to meet iron recommendations in 34 lacto-ovo vegetarians. All pregnant women, including vegetarians, should be checked for iron-deficiency anemia and consider supplementation if they are unable to meet their needs through diet alone.

Calcium

Calcium is needed in pregnancy for synthesis of fetal bones and teeth. Approximately 25 to 30 grams of calcium are transferred to the fetus, primarily in the third trimester. Historically, women have been advised to substantially increase their calcium intake during pregnancy in order to meet the fetus's needs without compromising their own bone density. Current research shows that calcium absorption is increased in pregnancy, resulting in a generally positive calcium balance. The Institute of Medicine has concluded that, as long as calcium intake prior to pregnancy was adequate for maximizing bone accretion, dietary calcium does not need to be increased in pregnancy. The calcium recommendation for pregnant women age 19 and older is 1000 mg a day. Adolescents may have an increased need for calcium to support their own bone development and may benefit from a higher calcium intake. The current recommendation is for 1300 mg of calcium daily for pregnant adolescents.

Calcium intakes of lacto-ovo vegetarian women are often close to levels recommended for pregnancy while calcium intakes of vegan women are generally lower. Pregnant women whose diets do not contain adequate calcium should add calcium-rich foods to their diet or use supplemental calcium. This appears to be especially important in adolescents.

Vegetarians who consume dairy products get calcium from milk and cheese. Many women may be surprised to learn that the many foods thought of as a serving of dairy, such as pudding, hot chocolate and cottage cheese, are not excellent sources of calcium. For example, it would take 3 servings of a ready-to-eat pudding to equal the calcium in one cup of cow's milk. Numerous brands of soy and rice milk, fruit juices, cereals and waffles are fortified with calcium. Plant sources of well-absorbed calcium include soybeans; dark green leafy vegetables like collard greens, kale, and turnip greens; and calcium-precipitated tofu.

Vitamin D

Vitamin D plays an important role in maintenance of maternal calcium absorption. Its role in placental transport of calcium is not clear nor is its role in fetal vitamin D status. Vitamin D status of vegetarians can vary based on sunlight exposure and dietary choices. While it is well known that vitamin D can be made from exposure to the sun, the modern lifestyle of work and leisure spent mostly indoors and the use of sun screens to prevent skin cancer may not guarantee sufficient UV light exposure for adequate vitamin D synthesis. As an illustration: 42% of adults less than 65 years of age, without known risk factors for hypovitaminosis D, admitted to a general medical ward in a Boston hospital were found to be vitamin D deficient. Therefore a dietary source of vitamin D is highly recommended. For lacto-vegetarians vitamin D-fortified cow's milk can used to meet vitamin D requirements. Clients may need to be reminded that other dairy products like cheese are not fortified with this essential nutrient. Some cereals and soy milk are fortified with vitamin D and many multivitamins contain the recommended level of 10 mcg (400 IU) of vitamin D. Many calcium supplements contain vitamin D as well. Supplements of vitamin D_2 (ergocalciferol) and vitamin D_3 (cholecalciferol) are utilized equally well by the mother and fetus.

Folate

The central nervous system develops in the fetus during the first weeks of gestation. By day 23 the neural tube that will become the spinal cord has closed. A lack of folate can keep the neural tube from closing properly, resulting in neural tube defects (NTDs). Since neural tube development is complete before most women are aware that they are pregnant, the current recommendation is that all women of child-bearing years should get at least 400 mcg of folate per day.

Folate derives from the Latin word folium, which means "foliage," and is found in particularly high concentrations in dark green, leafy vegetables. Vegetarian diets tend to be rich in folic acid compared to non-vegetarian diets.

The Food and Nutrition Board suggests an intake of 600 mcg of folic acid during pregnancy. The Food and Drug Administration (FDA) has also mandated the fortification of grain products like bread with folic acid (140 mcg folic acid/100 g of the food item).

Vitamin B_{12}

The recommended level of vitamin B_{12} in pregnancy is 2.6 mcg per day. Vitamin B_{12} is needed during pregnancy for normal cell division and protein synthesis. It appears that maternal stores of vitamin B_{12} may not be available to the fetus, therefore a maternal dietary source should be assured. Vitamin B_{12} is found in animal products such as milk and eggs. Vegans can easily meet vitamin B_{12} needs with the use of foods fortified with vitamin B_{12}, such as breakfast cereals, some soymilks, and Red Star brand T6635 nutritional yeast (also called Vegetarian Support Formula). Foods which have been previously proposed as good sources of vitamin B_{12} such as tempeh, sea vegetables, and algae have been shown to be unreliable and therefore inappropriate sources. In addition these foods may contain vitamin B_{12} analogues (substances which mimic vitamin B_{12} but which actually block vitamin B_{12} absorption).

Zinc

The recommended intake of zinc increases by 50 percent during pregnancy. Mild zinc deficiency has been related to complications of labor and delivery including prolonged or inefficient first stage labor (cervical dilation) and protracted second stage labor (pushing) and premature rupture of the membranes (the sac of fluid that cushions the infant). Many women in the US, both omnivores and vegetarians, do not consume diets that meet the RDA for zinc during pregnancy. Several studies have examined vegetarians' zinc status during pregnancy. One found that although vegetarians' diets were slightly lower in zinc than those of non-vegetarians, their blood and urine zinc levels were similar. In another study, vegetarians' zinc intakes were similar to intakes of non-vegetarians. Since zinc status is difficult to assess and zinc is an essential nutrient for growth and development, pregnant vegetarians should emphasize good food sources of zinc.

Although legumes, nuts and whole grains are good sources of zinc, the availability of the zinc is lower than found in animal products due to the phytic acid content. Zinc availability is increased when grains are sprouted or eaten as yeast-raised bread, as both of these food preparation techniques destroy phytate.

Complications of Pregnancy

Nausea

Nausea and vomiting, also called morning sickness, are a concern of many pregnant women, vegetarians included. Eating low fat, high carbohydrate foods, which are digested fairly quickly, eating often, avoiding foods with strong smells, and eating those healthful foods that are tolerated are some coping mechanisms. The health care provider should be contacted if a pregnant woman is unable to eat or drink adequate amounts of fluids for 24 hours.

Aversions and Cravings

Food aversions are extremely common in pregnancy and are believed to be due to a heightened sense of smell, possibly caused by hormonal changes. Dietetics professionals can offer suggestions for foods to replace those that are no longer attractive to the client. Because many foods served at room temperature or colder have less of an odor than heated foods, some women may tolerate some foods served raw that they will not eat when cooked. For example, broccoli may be tolerated if served raw with a dip and cabbage may be acceptable in cole slaw.

Contrary to popular belief, food cravings are not a sign of a need for a certain nutrient or food. This seems obvious when the most commonly reported foods to be craved are sweets. Interestingly, one of the most common foods that women become averse to eating during pregnancy is meat. Therefore women may become vegetarian or nearly vegetarian during pregnancy simply due to a food aversion.

Constipation

Constipation is a common complaint in pregnancy. The higher fiber diet of vegetarian women may be an asset in avoiding constipation. If a woman feels her constipation is a side effect of iron supplementation, increasing high vitamin C fruits may serve a dual purpose of counteracting the constipating effect and enhancing iron absorption. Assurance of adequate fluid intake is also helpful in preventing and alleviating constipation.

Pre-Eclampsia

Preeclampsia, or pregnancy induced hypertension with proteinuria, is a potentially serious complication of pregnancy. One study has examined the rate of preeclampsia in a community of vegans in Tennessee between 1977 and 1982. Of 775 vegan pregnancies, there was only one case of preeclampsia. This is a much lower rate than that seen in the general population. Since the cause of preeclampsia is still not well understood, it is unclear what factors explain the lower rate of preeclampsia experienced by vegans in this study.

Food Guide

The Vegetarian Nutrition Dietetic Practice Group has produced a food guide for pregnant vegetarians, presented in Table 22.2. These guidelines are an average suggestion and should be adjusted to meet the needs of the individual. Some women will need more calories to support adequate weight gain in pregnancy, especially women expecting twins or triplets, adolescents, and women who entered pregnancy underweight. In this case, additional servings of foods can be added, and fats such as oil and salad dressing used to increase calories. Other

Table 22.2. Meal Planning Guidelines for Pregnant Vegetarians

Food Group	Serving size	No. of Servings	Comments
Grains	1 slice of bread; 1/2 cup cooked cereal, grain or pasta; 3/4 to 1 cup ready-to-eat cereal	7 or more	Choose whole or enriched
Legumes, nuts, seeds, milks	1/2 cup cooked beans, tofu, tempeh; 3 oz of meat analogue; or 2 Tbsp nuts, seeds, nut or seed butter; 1 cup fortified soy milk; 1 cup cow's milk, 1 cup yogurt.	5 or more	Calcium-rich foods such as dried beans, calcium-precipitated tofu, calcium-fortified soymilk, cow's milk, and yogurt should be chosen often. A regular source of vitamin B_{12} should be used.
Vegetables	1/2 cup cooked or 1 cup raw	4 or more	Calcium-rich foods such as kale, collard greens, mustard greens, broccoli, and bok choy, should be chosen often.
Fruits	1/2 cup canned fruit or juice or 1 medium fruit	4 or more	Choose calcium rich figs, and fortified juices often.

women, such as women beginning pregnancy, obese, or women who are very short in stature, may choose lower calorie selections from each of the groups.

Conclusion

A vegetarian diet planned in accord with current dietary recommendations can easily meet the nutritional needs of pregnancy. Potential benefits of a vegetarian diet in pregnancy include adequate folate status at conception and a possible reduced risk of pre-eclampsia.

Chapter 23

Vegetarianism and Lactation

Breast is Best

The earliest food for a vegan baby should ideally be breast milk. For support and information on breast feeding please contact the La Leche League or The National Childbirth Trust. Many benefits are conveyed to the baby by breast feeding, including some enhancement of the immune system, protection against infection, and reduced risk of allergies. In addition, breast milk is designed specifically for babies and quite probably contains substances needed by growing infants which are not even known to be essential and are not included in infant formula.

Formula Milk and Soya Milk

It is important that soya milk should not substituted for soya infant formula as it does not contain the proper ratio of proteins, fats, and carbohydrates, nor the vitamins and minerals required to be used as a sole food. Soya milk should not be fed to babies under 6 months of age because it has levels of protein which are too high and excessive protein intake is thought to be medically undesirable at this stage.

Plamil soya milk is fortified with calcium (to approximately the level of human milk) combined with the necessary vitamin D_2 to enable the

Excerpted from "A Practical Guide to Veganism during Pregnancy and throughout Childhood," The Vegan Society, http://www.vegansociety.com/html/info/info26.html, 1997. Reprinted with permission. Reviewed in April, 2002 by Dr. David A. Cooke, MD, Diplomate, American Board of Internal Medicine.

calcium to be absorbed, plus the essential vitamins B_2 and B_{12}. The sweetened version is suitable for infants during and beyond the weaning stage. Also, where a supplementary feed is required it may be diluted to bring it closer to human milk. Plamil Foods Ltd recommends that no such supplementary feeding takes place without the parent or authorized representative notifying Plamil Foods Ltd in writing at the outset of the name and address of the doctor/medical advisor so the company may provide them with information relating to the product. In such a case, the parent also must undertake to arrange regular medical supervision.

The Best Diet for Breastfeeding

The best diet for breast feeding is similar to that recommended for pregnancy. Calories, protein and vitamin B_{12} are higher while recommendations for iron are lower than during pregnancy. The recommended calorie intake is 500 calories above the usual intake. Breastfeeding women should ensure 2.0 mg per day of B_{12}.

Protein requirements rise to 56 g+ of protein per day for breastfeeding mothers from the birth of the baby until 6 months of age. From the age of 6 months it can be reduced to 53 g+ of protein per day. Portions of some vegan foods providing 10 g of protein:

- peanuts—39 g
- almonds—47 g
- chickpeas, dried and boiled—119 g
- tofu, steamed—124 g
- peas, boiled—159 g
- wholemeal bread—109 g
- brown rice, boiled—109 g
- spinach, boiled—454 g

Weight Loss and Milk Loss

If too little food is eaten while breastfeeding then quantities of milk produced are liable to be lower. However, a loss of weight may be experienced because of a loss of calories in breast milk. It is safe to lose one-half to one lb a week while breastfeeding but more rigorous dieting is not recommended. As with pregnancy, small, frequent meals are best. Since extra fluid is required at this time, use nutritious drinks like fruit and vegetable juices, soya milk (flavored or unflavored), soups and smoothies to provide calories as well.

Chapter 24

Vegetarian Infant Diets and Weaning

Vegetarian Beginnings

Can a Vegetarian Diet Provide the Nutrition an Infant Needs?

A vegetarian eating plan can easily provide the nutrients infants and children need, but because of their high energy needs good planning is essential. Breast milk or formula, soy or milk based, provides all the nutrition infants need for the first four to six months.

Adding solid foods helps meet the needs of the increasingly active child. Iron-fortified cereals, followed by fruits and vegetables, provide the vitamins, minerals and calories a growing child needs. At seven to eight months an infant needs to add protein from yogurt, cheese, tofu or beans. In addition to the protein, these foods increase texture and taste.

For a vegan eating plan, look for B_{12} fortified soy milk or check with a registered dietitian about a supplement. The key to good nutrition, whether vegetarian or not, is variety of choices.

This chapter contains text from "Vegetarian Beginnings," American Dietetic Association (ADA), http://www.eatright.org/erm/erm022098.html, February 1998, © 1998 American Dietetic Association, 216 West Jackson Boulevard Chicago, IL 60606, 800-366-1655, www.eatright.org. Reprinted with permission. Also included in this chapter is, "Information Sheet: Infant Diet," Vegetarian Society UK, http://www.vegsoc.org/info/infant.html, copyright 2001, reprinted with permission. Some words have been changed to conform to American spelling conventions. Material may be viewed in its original format on the Vegetarian Society of the UK website: http://www.vegsoc.org.

Information Sheet: Infant Diet

Weaning Vegetarian Babies

Taking the first steps in bringing your child up as a vegetarian isn't difficult. Remember that the nutritional requirements of a small baby are high, needing more protein, calcium, and most other nutrients than at any other time of life. It is now widely recognized, even by the British Medical Association, that a vegetarian diet can provide all the nutrients needed for growing infants.

Bringing up your child as a vegetarian, you will want to get them used to the vegetarian food groups: cereals, beans, nuts, and seeds, dairy and soya, produce, fruit and vegetables. Your baby may reject stronger-tasting foods, such as broccoli, cauliflower, and cabbage, at six months but may like them several months later.

It is quite safe to bring up your baby as a vegan, with no animal foods at all, as long as you make sure that plenty of nutrient-rich foods are included. Vegan babies need good sources of calcium, vitamin B_{12}, vitamin D, and protein.

Weaning is a gradual process that begins when you start to replace milk with solid foods. Infants should not be given solid foods before the age of four months except on the advise of a health professional. A mixed diet should be offered by the age of six months, at which stage babies need a source of iron in their diet as breast or formula milk can no longer provide enough. Especially if there is a family history of allergies, when you begin weaning your baby, introduce one food at a time and leave a few days between each new food. This way, you will be able to tell if your baby is allergic or sensitive to any particular food.

Stages of Weaning

4–5 Months

Breast or formula milk is still the most important source of nutrition. Start by introducing one teaspoon of baby rice or pureed fruit after a milk feed or in the middle if this works best for your baby. The nutrition of the food is not so important at this stage as milk still supplies all the baby's needs. Just one solid feed a day should be enough for most babies at this stage.

Other foods to try are:

- pureed vegetables, such as potatoes, carrot, or spinach

- pureed fruit, such as apple, banana, or pear

- baby rice, corn meal, sago, or millet can all be given as a thin porridge

- do not give wheat, oats, milk, nuts or eggs

5–6 Months

Milk is still the most important food in your baby's diet, but gradually increase the number of times solid food is given from once to twice and then three times a day.

Try mashed lentils with some added vegetable oil and a wider variety of fruit and vegetables such as avocado and green vegetables. It is still too early to introduce wheat, oats, milk, nuts, or eggs.

6–8 Months

Most babies will by now eat solids although milk is a large part in their diets. Solid foods now provide an important source of iron. Most babies will be having solids three times a day. From six months you can start to introduce wheat and oat-based cereal such as bread and porridge. You can puree or sieve family foods to give variety, as long as they do not contain added salt.

Try introducing tofu, smooth nut butter, and mashed beans. Dairy foods (cow's milk, yogurt and cheese) should not be introduced before six months because of the risk of intolerance. Free-range eggs can be given after six months, as long as they are hard-boiled. Some experts recommend avoiding all dairy products and eggs until 12 months.

8–12 Months

Your baby will gradually be able to cope with lumpier foods. Foods from the family table can be given as long as they do not contain salt. Well cooked and mashed peas and beans can be introduced at around 8 to 12 months. They are difficult to digest and so can cause problems if introduced earlier. Avoid sweet biscuits and rusks. Try introducing pieces of peeled apple, raw carrot, or crusts of bread. When your baby is able to chew pieces of fruit, sandwiches, and toast can become normal everyday foods. By the age of 12 months your baby should be enjoying three meals a day.

Many companies produce baby foods suitable for vegetarians but it's quick and easy to prepare your own food for your baby. If you use shop bought food, always check the ingredients label.

Important Nutrients

Iron

This is an important nutrient during weaning, as milk is a very poor source of iron. Babies are born with their own store of iron but this will be depleted by six months. Although iron is less easily absorbed from non-animal sources, there are plenty of good vegetable sources.

Iron-rich foods suitable for babies after six months include: prune-juice, pureed apricots, molasses, refined lentils, cereals, well mashed beans, and green vegetables. Avoid cereals that are very high in fiber as these may inhibit iron absorption.

Vitamin C aids absorption of iron from plant foods and so it helps to give sources of these nutrients together. Vitamin C is found in frozen, fresh, or juiced fruit and vegetables.

Calcium

Breast or formula milk contains all the calcium your baby needs initially. Good sources of calcium for the later weaning stages include cow's and fortified soya milk, cheese, green vegetables, wholemeal bread, beans, lentils, ground almonds, sesame paste, and tofu.

Protein

Because babies are growing rapidly they require more protein than adults compared to their body weight. Breast or formula milk will provide the major source of protein for the first eight months. Proteins must be balanced in order to get the right balance of amino acids. Combinations of foods such as a cereal with beans or lentils, cereal with nuts or seeds, or milk on its own will provide the right balance of protein.

Energy

Babies between the age of 6 and 12 months require 700 to 1000 calories a day, so they need concentrated sources of energy. Babies and young children do not have the capacity to eat large quantities of food and so they need small and frequent meals. Their diet should not contain too many foods that are bulky or watery. Make sure your baby has some concentrated energy foods like lentils with vegetable oil, avocado, cheese, or smooth nut butter. Sugar is not a good source of energy for babies.

Vitamin B₁₂

Vitamin B_{12} is made by micro-organisms and is found mostly in animal foods. Very young babies will get all the vitamin B_{12} they need from formula or breast milk. Later, vegetarian babies should obtain enough of this vitamin from dairy products and eggs. Vegan babies will need vitamin B_{12} from fortified foods such as some soya milks, low salt yeast extract, or veggie burgers.

Vitamin D

Vitamin D is found in dairy products, eggs, and fortified foods like margarine and some breakfast cereals, and can be made by the action of sunlight on the skin. It is found exclusively in animal foods so vegan babies may need a vitamin D supplement. Breast or formula milk should provide all the vitamin D needed initially.

Fiber

A diet too high in fiber will fill up a child before their nutritional needs have been met and can interfere with absorption of minerals such as zinc, iron, and calcium, so refined bran must not be added to a young child's diet. If you think your baby is constipated give extra fluid such as water or diluted fruit juices.

Milk

Babies under two should not be given semi-skimmed milk and children under five should not be given skimmed milk because skimmed milk lacks the fat soluble vitamins A and D and young children need the energy from fat. Soya milks should be specially formulated for babies if they are used instead of breast milk and should be fortified if used as an alternative to cow's milk for babies and young children.

Salt and Sugar

These should be avoided in the diet of babies and young children. A baby's kidneys are not mature enough to cope with too much salt, and sugary foods and drinks are a prime cause of tooth decay. Sugar gives calories without any associated vitamins or minerals. In addition, a baby who is encouraged to develop a sweet tooth may have problems with obesity in later life.

Nuts

Whole nuts or chopped nuts and seeds are not suitable for children under five because of the danger of choking, but they can be used if finely ground, for example in cooking or smooth nut spread. However many experts suggest avoiding nut products altogether in a small child's diet due to the risk of allergies developing. If there is a history of allergies in a family it is certainly best to avoid any nuts, especially peanuts, until at least three years. The pregnant or breast-feeding mother should also avoid peanuts if there is a history of allergies in the family.

Quorn and TVP

The manufacturers of Quorn recommend that it is not introduced into a child's diet before the age of two years. Textured vegetable protein (TVP) may be difficult for young babies to digest, and its salt content must be watched.

Chapter 25

Is a Vegetarian Diet Healthy for Kids?

Introduction

Childhood nutrition has a significant influence on health and development throughout life. As children grow, their nutritional needs are much greater than those of adults and the consequences of a poor diet will be long lasting. A good diet will protect against everyday illness and ensure the development of strong bones and teeth, firm muscles, and healthy tissues.

Choosing to bring up your child as a vegetarian is a positive step towards a healthy and morally sound diet for your child. Nutritional research has shown that a vegetarian diet can provide all the nutrients necessary for a child's growth and development. Well-informed dietitians, doctors, and other health professionals now accept that vegetarianism is a healthy option for infants and children of all ages.

The Pre-School Child (Age 1–5)

The pre-school child, whether vegetarian or not, is almost totally dependent on others for its food. The eating habits of parents and

Excerpted from "Vegetarian Nutrition for Children, Part I: Introduction—The Pre-School Child (Age 1–5)," http://www.vegsoc.org/info/childre1.html, and "Vegetarian Nutrition for Children, Part II: The School Age Child (Age 5–12)," http://www.vegsoc.org/info/childre2.html, Vegetarian Society UK, copyright 2001, reprinted with permission. Some words have been changed to conform with American spelling conventions. Original version of these documents can be found at the URLs above.

other care givers will be the ones that the child imitates and acquires. Some pre-school children are naturally sensitive to the use of animals for food and occasionally refuse all meats even if their parents aren't vegetarian.

Whether vegetarian or not, it is vital that children have a well balanced diet. This is particularly important during the pre-school years, as this is a time of rapid growth and development. The nutrients to particularly watch are calcium, iron, zinc, protein, vitamin B_{12}, and vitamin D.

Children should be offered a variety of foods which they can enjoy and should not be forced to eat anything if they are determined to resist. Food and eating should not be allowed to become an issue as children can be very fussy at this age.

Good eating habits should begin now, as likes and dislikes will be influenced by what is offered in these early years. High fiber, low fat diets, recommended for adults, are not suitable for children of this age, as explained below. The emphasis should be on family eating habits that are healthy and sensible. Foods containing a lot of sugar and salt should be avoided.

As they are growing very rapidly, young children need a lot of dietary energy (calories) relative to their small size. A diet that is too high in fiber or very low in fat will not provide sufficient concentrated energy or nutrients. Frequent meals containing food of relatively high nutrient and energy density are important, although young children often have marked fluctuations in appetite.

Nutritious snacks between meals will help ensure that enough food is eaten. Try and avoid shop-bought sweets, biscuits and cakes, sweetened fizzy drinks, and salty snacks such as chips. Offer sandwiches, fruit, scone, or malt bread and home-made cake or biscuits instead. Sweets given occasionally as a special treat will not do any harm.

Unless your child is prone to being overweight, you can try to increase the energy density of foods. Vegetable oil can be added to foods like mashed lentils or beans. Include nut and seed purees such as tahini and smooth peanut butter, cheese, yogurt, soya products such as tofu and veggie burgers, and if liked, avocado. Try to include as wide a variety of foods as possible, bearing in mind that children may be fussy or find some foods too strong in taste. Consumption of fresh, frozen, or juiced fruit and vegetables should be encouraged.

Assessment of a child's growth should be made over a period of time, as growth at this age is often very uneven and interspersed with sudden increases in height and weight.

Sugar and Teeth

Children naturally like the taste of sugar and sweet foods. Though sugary foods do provide calories, they have little else of nutritional value and are a major cause of tooth decay. While it may not be practical to ban sugar altogether, it should be limited. It is better to discourage the development of a sweet tooth now. A small amount of sugar with otherwise healthy desserts such as yogurt, soya puddings, and rice pudding is fine and better than using artificial additives for sweetness.

Milk

Children under two should not be given semi-skimmed milk and children under five should not be given skimmed milk because it lacks the fat soluble vitamins A and D. Young children also need the energy from fat. Soya milks should be fortified with calcium, vitamin B_{12} and vitamin D if used as an alternative to cow's milk for young children.

Salt

Salt should be avoided in the diet of young children as their kidneys are not mature enough to cope with large amounts. Many common foods such as cheese, manufactured soup, packet meals, and bread are quite high in added salt. Avoid too many salty snacks, such as chips and other snack foods. Spread yeast extract thinly or use the low salt varieties.

Nuts

Whole nuts and seeds must be avoided until the age of five as young children can easily choke on them. Ground or pureed nuts and seeds are fine and nutritious, for example smooth peanut butter, tahini (sesame seed paste), or ground almonds.

Planning Diets/Menus

Daily Servings: One to Five Years:

- Vegetables: 2 servings, preferably including leafy dark green vegetables each day.

- Fruit: 1–3 servings, with dried fruit every few days or more.

- Grains/cereals: 4–5 servings, including whole grain bread, rice, pasta, breakfast cereals, (and potatoes).

- Pulses, Nuts and Seeds: 1–2 servings, including nut butters, tahini (sesame seed paste), lentils, mashed beans.

- Dairy or Soya: 3 servings, including milk, cheese, hard-boiled free range eggs, yogurt, fortified soya milk, tofu.

A serving will range from half a slice of bread to a few tablespoons of a vegetable. The above should be used as a guide and need not be followed rigidly each day.

The School Age Child (Age 5–12)

By school-age, a child's eating patterns and taste preferences will have been established by the family eating habits. Children are now able to exercise some choice over what they eat and may decide on their own initiative that they don't want to eat meat. They may also be heavily influenced by their peer groups.

Many of the processes that lead to modern adult nutritional diseases, such as heart disease, begin in childhood. Adult healthy eating advice to reduce fat and have enough fiber does apply to school age children. Reports on the diets of British school children show that they tend to eat far too much fat and sugar and not enough dietary fiber, iron, and calcium. Vegetarian children often start with an advantage as their diet is usually lower in fat and higher in fiber.

Numerous studies on the growth of vegetarian children show that they grow just as well and in some cases better than their meat-eating counterparts. In later life vegetarians suffer less of the modern nutritional diseases—particularly heart disease, cancer, and high blood pressure—so you can rest assured that you are giving them the best start in life.

Growing children still need plenty of energy and nutrient dense foods. As they have small stomachs and large energy needs, their meals need to be more frequent and regular than an adult's. The school years before adolescence represent a time of gradual, steady growth, and nutritional risks are lower at this time than during the pre-school years and later during the adolescent growth spurt.

Children need to be encouraged to eat plenty of fresh fruit and vegetables, which provide a rich source of essential vitamins and minerals. Sometimes they prefer raw vegetables, such as carrots and broccoli. It is better not to force a child to eat what they don't like or food can become a battle ground.

Fried, fatty, and sugary foods, such as pies, chips, sweets and chocolate often provide a lot of calories but with few associated nutrients, hence they are often called "junk foods." If your child is eating a varied diet with foods taken from each of the vegetarian food groups, and very little junk food, then it is likely that the nutrient content of the diet will take care of itself, provided they are getting enough energy.

School Meals

Prior to 1980, a school meal was expected to provide one third of a child's daily requirement of protein, energy, and some vitamins and minerals. Now schools are under no obligation to provide nutritionally balanced meals, although many do as a result of campaigns for healthier school meals. The availability of a vegetarian option for children may also vary significantly depending on the area.

Important Nutrients

Protein

Protein is an important nutrient for growth, although it is not difficult for children to get enough, provided a varied diet of sufficient food is eaten. The only foods that are notably low in protein are sugar, fruit, fats, and oils.

Milk, cheese, free-range eggs, yogurt, soya milk, tofu, beans, cereals/grains, nuts, and seeds are all good sources of protein. Proteins must be balanced in order to get the right mixture of amino acids. Normal combinations of foods such as a cereal with beans or lentils, cereal with nuts, seeds or milk provide the right balance of protein.

Energy

Very young children do not have the capacity to eat large quantities of food, and so they need small and frequent meals. Their diet should not contain too many foods that are bulky or watery. Make sure your child has some concentrated energy foods like lentils with vegetable oil, avocado, cheese, or smooth nut butter. High carbohydrate foods are good sources of energy such as bread, rice, pasta, and potatoes. Sugar is not a good source of energy as it lacks essential vitamins and minerals and causes dental decay.

213

Iron

Iron is an important nutrient for growing children and is essential for healthy blood. There are plenty of good vegetable sources although iron is less easily absorbed from non-animal sources. Milk and the other dairy products are very poor sources of iron.

Iron-rich foods suitable for children include: dried fruit, (such as apricots), molasses, beans, lentils, egg yolks, whole grain cereals, and green vegetables. Avoid cereals that are very high in fiber as these may inhibit iron absorption.

Vitamin C aids absorption of iron from plant foods and so it helps to give sources of both these nutrients together. Vitamin C is found in frozen, fresh, or juiced fruit and vegetables.

Calcium

Calcium is an important nutrient for young children, particularly for healthy teeth and bones. Good sources of calcium include cow's milk, yogurt, fortified soya milk, cheese, green vegetables, wholemeal bread, beans, lentils, ground almonds, sesame paste, and tofu.

Zinc

Zinc is essential for growth and cell division. Zinc absorption can be inhibited by too much phytic acid, found in whole grain cereals and other fibrous foods. Vegetarian sources of this vital mineral include cheese, nuts and seeds (particularly pumpkin seeds), pulses, and tofu.

Vitamin B_{12}

Vitamin B_{12} is made by micro-organisms and is found mostly in animal foods. Vegetarian children can usually obtain enough of this vitamin from dairy products and eggs. Vegan children and those who consume few dairy products will need vitamin B_{12} from fortified foods such as some soya milks, low salt yeast extract, or breakfast cereals.

Vitamin D

Vitamin D is essential for the absorption of calcium. It is found in dairy products, eggs, and fortified foods like margarine and some breakfast cereals, and can be made by the action of sunlight on the skin. It is found exclusively in animal foods so vegan children may need a vitamin D supplement, especially during the winter months.

Fiber

A diet too high in fiber will fill up a small child before their nutritional needs have been met and can interfere with absorption of minerals, such as zinc, iron, and calcium. Wholemeal bread is fine but avoid cereals that are very high in fiber. Bran should not be added to a young child's diet.

Chapter 26

In Raising Children as Vegetarians, Planning and Variety Are the Keys

More easily accessible food choices, environmental concerns, social acceptance of lifestyles once considered unusual—all of these factors and more can contribute to a family's decision to raise children following a vegetarian eating style.

And with the subject of meatless, plant-based diets for even very young children cropping up regularly in the news and in public debate, parents may be wondering: Can it be done? Is it possible to raise a child as a vegetarian? Can children's growing bodies meet their needs for nutrition and calories without meat or dairy products?

According to experts with The American Dietetic Association (ADA), the answer is: with careful planning, yes.

"Vegetarian diets can be healthful for people of all ages," says Julie Covington, a Gastonia, North Carolina registered dietitian and chair of ADA's vegetarian nutrition practice group. "The toddler and preschool years particularly are important for developing healthy eating patterns that can establish a **foundation** for a healthful adult diet."

"Research shows a carefully planned vegetarian diet can be nutritionally adequate and healthful for children from infants to teenagers."

Excerpted from "Raising Children as Vegetarians: Planning and Variety Are the Keys, Says the American Dietetic Association," http://www.eatright.org/pr/ press071598.html, July 1998. © 1998 American Dietetic Association, 216 West Jackson Boulevard Chicago, IL 60606; 800-366-1655, www.eatright.org. Reprinted with permission.

That's true, she says, for both the lacto-ovo-vegetarian eating pattern, based on grains, vegetables, fruits, legumes, seeds, nuts, dairy products and eggs; and the vegan pattern, which excludes eggs, dairy, and other animal products.

"With planning, it isn't difficult to provide a child with a healthy, well-balanced vegetarian diet," says Tammy Baker, a Phoenix registered dietitian and spokesperson for ADA.

"You can have meals and snacks that don't include meat products. It can be a balanced diet and it can be fun."

"But planning is the key," Baker says. "Anytime you're excluding food groups, you have to be more careful to make sure you're still getting all the nutrients you need."

Like all children, vegetarians need enough food variety and energy—in the form of calories—to fuel their rapid growth and provide for their high nutrient needs.

"A vegetarian diet, like any other, has the potential to be healthful or unhealthful," Covington says. "You're looking for variety."

ADA's vegetarian nutrition practice group offers parents practical advice for helping vegetarian children meet their nutritional needs in healthful and tasty ways:

- Calories and fat: Vegetarian children's diets sometimes tend to be high in fiber, filling their stomachs but making it difficult for them to consume the levels of energy they need. Avocados, nuts, seeds, dried fruits, and soy products can provide concentrated sources of calories.

- Protein: Protein needs generally can be met by eating a variety of plant foods and having an adequate intake of calories. Foods high in protein include legumes, grains, soy products, nuts, dairy products, and eggs. Grains such as rice, pasta, breads, and cereals provide the same protein.

- Calcium: Good sources of calcium, especially for vegans, include calcium-fortified soy and rice milks and orange juice, tofu, and dark green leafy vegetables.

- Vitamin D: Children regularly exposed to appropriate levels of sunlight—20 to 30 minutes per day on the hands and face, two to three times per week—apparently have no dietary requirement for vitamin D. Children with darker skin or who have limited exposure to sunlight may require vitamin supplements. Dietary sources of vitamin D include fortified cow's milk, some brands of soy or rice milk, and most dry cereals.

- Iron: Iron-deficiency anemia is the most common childhood nutritional problem, but it's no more likely to occur in vegetarian children than non-vegetarians. Good sources of iron include whole or enriched grains, iron-fortified cereals, legumes, green leafy vegetables, and dried fruits.

- Vitamin B_{12}: Vegan children should eat foods fortified with vitamin B_{12}, including fortified soy milk, fortified nutritional yeast, and some breakfast cereals.

- Zinc: Sources include legumes, hard cheeses, whole grain products, wheat germ, nuts, and tofu.

Changing social attitudes and the growing acceptance of vegetarian lifestyles have made it much easier to raise families on plant-based diets, Baker says.

"I am getting more questions lately from parents on how to raise children as vegetarians, particularly Generation X'ers. Their desire seems to be based largely on concerns about the environment."

And as consumers have begun to seek a wider variety of products, grocery stores and supermarkets have responded with greater selections. "Beans and legumes and tofu are much more mainstream than they used to be," Baker says.

Of course, children being children—vegetarian or not—means they can be picky eaters. To try to overcome this natural tendency, ADA offers some recommendations:

- Offer choices of foods: Letting the child make some decisions can increase the acceptance of foods.

- Make foods fun: Make pancakes in different shapes or with faces made from fruit, offer vegetables and dips, hide small pieces of fruit in yogurt.

- Set a good example: Let children see you eating healthy foods.

- Involve the child in food preparation: Young toddlers can tear up lettuce and put pieces of vegetables into a pot. Older preschoolers can wash vegetables, stir a fruit salad and help measure dry ingredients.

- Keep mealtimes pleasant: Don't force a child to eat or use food as a reward. Try to stay calm about food refusals.

Chapter 27

Vegan Children and Social Pressure

Having Friends Around

When dealing with your child's non-vegan friends, it is worth making a note of the types of foods they will be likely to expect at parties, afternoon tea, etc. These foods are likely to be slightly different from those that would be served to fellow vegans who are into the no-sugar whole food type diet. Children are notoriously undiplomatic in expressing their disapproval of food and it can be very upsetting for vegan children to have their food curtly rejected—especially at a birthday party or similar special gathering of friends.

If children are expecting a more conventional approach to meals, try to go along with this expectation. In this way the likelihood is they will think the vegan diet is not so strange after all and be more willing to try more of the same in the future. For example, avoid wholemeal breads if children are used to white bread and avoid wholemeal pastry if they usually have pastry made with white flour. Carob in cakes or sweets is not a good idea if they have never eaten it before because their taste buds are usually anticipating the sweet chocolate taste and are therefore quite disappointed. There are many good quality vegan ice creams on the market which should win over

---

Excerpted from "A Practical Guide to Veganism during Pregnancy and throughout Childhood," The Vegan Society, http://www.vegansociety.com/html/info/info26.html, 1997. Reprinted with permission. Despite the age of this document, readers seeking an understanding of vegan children and social pressure will find this information useful.

any non-vegan child. There are also good quality jellies available now not only in whole food shops but also in supermarkets e.g. the Rowntrees Ready To Eat jellies in small plastic tubs, ideal for little hands to cope with (and the tubs can be re-used again to make jellies, trifles, etc. for kids to take to school for lunch). Add to this sticks of fresh vegetables such as carrots, celery, halves of tomatoes, chips, peanuts, and fruit juices or fizzy drinks. There are plenty of recipes around for good vegan sponge cakes (chocolate is always popular) to round off the meal. If they haven't got any room left for the cake, cut it up into slices and put a couple of portions in their party bag to take home.

Preparing for School

Packed lunches are invariably easier than taking pot luck with school meals. If the school has a good record of providing whole food vegetarian options, there may be no problem requesting a vegan meal. The Vegan Society provides a catering pack which can be passed on to the canteen or catering company dealing with meals for your child's school.

While adults find it difficult to put up with a constant barrage of criticism from relatives and friends, children find it much harder, being more sensitive to criticism and peer pressure. They really just want to fit in with the rest of the kids in the class and not have to constantly defend their food and lifestyle. Other than at lunchtime, veganism is probably not going to be much of an issue at primary school. However, it is wise to prepare children with sound information on veganism so they are able to stand firm against any comments coming their way. Secondary school is likely to be more of a problem depending on the level of awareness in the school. Animal rights as an issue is more and more popular with kids in their teens and vegetarianism (if not veganism) is becoming commonplace. Some schools are making a tremendous effort to provide healthier food in the canteen so things are improving all the time.

There is plenty of literature around from different animal rights organizations that will provide your child with good defense material against peers who question their lifestyle. Animal Aid, for example, has a good Youth Group and plenty of literature and posters aimed at schoolchildren.

Providing vegan parents offer as much support, information, and advice on this subject as they would on any other about which they hold firm convictions then this will give kids a good grounding for the future. Children deserve to have information presented to them in a manner which takes into account of their age, sensitivity, and level of understanding. Honest answers and straight talking will pay rich dividends at a later date. Children who are not fed an assortment of half-truths or deliberate misinformation will have little difficulty in making the connection between live animals and the food on their plate.

Chapter 28

Teenage Vegans

Teenagers who follow a vegan diet have the same nutritional needs as any other teenager. Nutritional requirements are high between the ages of 13 and 19 years and it is generally recommended that they eat a wide variety of whole foods or unrefined foods including fresh fruit and vegetables, bread, pasta, oats and other grains, nuts, seeds, and pulses. Care must be taken to ensure protein, calcium, iron, and B_{12} levels are maintained. In other words teenagers, along with the rest of the population, shouldn't live on coke, chips, and chocolate.

Teenagers or anyone else thinking of becoming vegan shouldn't think they have to weigh everything before they eat or read nutrition charts before every meal. Once a good understanding of nutrition is grasped, it is recommended to chill out and enjoy.

"I'm the Only Vegan in the Family"

If you are the only vegan in your family it's not the end of the world. There are many common foods that everyone can share so you won't feel like a nerd. For example most people eat bread, pasta, baked beans, peas, rice, fruit, vegetables, breakfast cereals, biscuits, peanuts, peanut butter, jam, noodles, soup, vegetable curries, Marmite, porridge, etc.

Excerpted from "Teen Vegans" The Vegan Society, http://www.sumgai.co.uk/vegansociety/html/info/info07.html, 1997. Reprinted with permission. Reviewed in April, 2002, by Dr. David A. Cooke, MD, Diplomate, American Board of Internal Medicine.

You will also be pleased to know that there are a wide variety of foods that can be used as an alternative to meat and dairy products, e.g. soya milk, ice-cream, margarine and cream, veggie sausages, sausage rolls and pies. You can even buy vegan chocolate.

There are also many cookery books around now that will give you ideas for meals. The recipes are usually easy to follow and the ingredients can be found in most shops.

Family Meal

Make your family a vegan meal once a week to show them you mean business. They will be impressed with your initiative and enjoy the meal too!

Quick Nutrition Guide

Aim to eat a varied whole food diet and choose foods from the following food groups on a daily basis:

- Cereals: barley, rice, wheat (bread, pasta), oats, shredded wheat, millet, corn, bulgur, couscous

- Pulses: beans, peas, lentils (cooked or sprouted)

- Nuts and seeds: all types of nuts, nut butters (peanut butter, cashew nut butter, etc.), pumpkin, sunflower, sesame seeds and tahini (sesame seed spread). Also, sprouted seeds such as alfalfa and mustard.

- Vegetables (cooked and/or raw): deep yellow and dark green leafy vegetables including carrots, green peppers, broccoli, spinach, endive, and kale. Other vegetables include bean sprouts, potatoes, tomatoes, lettuce, cabbage, sweet corn, celery, onions, cucumbers, beetroot, marrows, courgettes, and cauliflower

- Fruits (fresh, dried and canned): bananas, oranges, tangerines, grapefruit, apples, mangoes, cherries, grapes, apricots, pear, paw paws, kiwis, berries, currants, lemons, and plums.

Some Vegan Sources of Key Nutrients

Protein

Whole grains (e.g. whole wheat flour and bread, brown rice), nuts (e.g. hazels, cashews, brazils, almonds, cob nuts), seeds (sunflower, sesame, pumpkin), pulses (e.g. peas, beans, lentils), soya flour, soya milk, tofu.

Carbohydrate

Whole grains (e.g. wheat, oats, barley, rice), whole wheat bread, pasta, and other flour products, lentils, beans, potatoes, dried and fresh fruit.

Fats

Nuts and seeds, nut and seed oils, vegan margarine, avocados. Two polyunsaturated fatty acids not made by the body are the essential fatty acids linoleic acid (omega 6 group) and alpha linolenic acid (omega 3 group). Good sources of these fatty acids include: 1) linoleic acid—safflower, sunflower, corn, evening primrose and soya oils, 2) alpha-linolenic acid—linseed, pumpkin seed, walnut, soya and rape-seed oils.

Vitamins

- A: carrots, spinach, pumpkins, tomatoes, dark green leafy vegetables, vegan margarines
- B: nuts, whole grains, oats, muesli, pulses, yeast extract (e.g. Marmite), leafy green vegetables, potatoes, mushrooms, and dried fruit
- B_{12}: fortified yeast extracts (e.g. Marmite) and soya milks (e.g. Plamil), vegan margarines, packeted 'veggie burger' mixes, some cereals (e.g. Kellogg's Fruit and Fibre, Common Sense Oat Bran Flakes)
- C: citrus fruits (e.g. oranges, lemons, grapefruit), red and black currants, berries, green vegetables, and potatoes
- D: sunlight, some soya milks, and vegan margarines
- E: nuts, seeds, whole grains and flours, vegetable oils
- Folate: wheat germ, raw or lightly-cooked green leafy vegetables (e.g. watercress, broccoli, spinach), yeast, yeast extracts, nuts, peas, runner beans, oranges, dates, avocados, whole grains

Minerals

- Calcium: molasses, seeds, nuts, carob, pulses, miso (fermented soya bean curd), parsley, figs (dried), sea vegetables, grains, fortified soya milk (several varieties are fortified with calcium)

- Iron: seeds, nuts, pulses, miso, grains, dried fruit, molasses, sea vegetables, parsley, green leafy vegetables, using cast-iron cookware

- Zinc: wheat germ, whole grains, nuts, pulses, tofu, soya protein, miso, peas, parsley, bean sprouts

Quick 5-Day Meal Plan

Monday

- Breakfast: wholemeal toast, Marmite or peanut butter, cereal with soya milk

- Lunch: vegetable pasta and mixed salad, apple or banana, muesli bar or shortbread

- Dinner: spaghetti bolognese topped with grated soya cheese, fruit salad and soya cream

Tuesday

- Breakfast: large bowl of porridge with soya milk and added dried fruit and nuts

- Lunch: baked beans on toast, fresh fruit salad

- Dinner: cashew nut roast, potatoes, broccoli, carrots and peas, apple pie and soya dessert

Wednesday

- Breakfast: wholemeal toast with tahini and Marmite

- Lunch: bread rolls filled with salad and vegetable pate, packet of chips, banana or apple

Thursday

- Breakfast: porridge oats made with soya milk and added nuts and dried fruit, wholemeal toast and jam

- Lunch: sandwiches with hummus and salad, vegan yogurt, biscuits, orange, or banana

- Dinner: vegetable curry with rice and popadoms, sliced mango, and soya cream

Friday

- Breakfast: wholemeal toast with fried mushrooms, fresh sliced tomatoes, and baked beans
- Lunch: large pastry filled with soya cheese, pickle and salad, slice of homemade chocolate cake, apple, or banana
- Dinner: vegetable stir fry including tofu marinated in soya sauce, mushrooms, onions, green and red peppers, sweet corn and bean sprouts on a bed of brown rice, fresh fruit salad and soya ice cream

Packed Lunches

There are lots of things you can take to school or college. Here are just a few ideas:

- any fresh or dried fruit
- soup in a flask
- soya sausage rolls
- vegetable samosas
- vegetable spring rolls
- vegetable pakoras
- onion bhajis
- vegetable pasties
- single cartons of fruit juice
- single cartons of soya milk
- pita bread with salad
- salted and unsalted nuts
- crackers and chips

Vegan Drinks

Such as tea and coffee (with soya milk of course!), herbal tea, cocoa, fruit juice, mineral water, tap water, soft drinks, coffee substitutes, and soya milk shakes (chocolate, strawberry, and vanilla flavors available or make your own).

A lot of people like soya milk in their tea or coffee. You can buy a calcium-enriched version for extra calcium or an organic sugar free version. If you don't like the taste of soya milk (I can't believe this!) try disguising the taste by using it in muesli, porridge, custard and rice puddings. You can cook soya milk just like dairy milk so it's a good way of getting extra helpings of calcium, vitamin D, and B$_{12}$. There are lots of different soya milks around—try them all until you find one you like.

Is It Going to Be Expensive?

Vegan foods don't have to be expensive. In fact, if you buy mostly unprocessed foods it will be a lot cheaper. If, however, you want lots of processed foods like sausage rolls and soya cheeses, be prepared to pay.

Nutrition or Know Your Onions

Energy

You must make sure you eat enough each day to get plenty of energy. Don't skip meals, don't go hungry and don't fill up with lots of fizzy, sugary drinks and sweets. You can get energy from all foods, but those high in carbohydrates (bread, pasta, potatoes, dried fruit, fruit juice) and fat (vegetable oils, margarine, nuts and seeds) are especially good.

Fat should not contribute more than 35% of the total energy intake of adults and older children.

Estimated average requirements for energy in calories (kcal)/day:

- 4–14 yrs (boys) 1715–2220
- 4–14 yrs (girls) 1545–1845
- 15–18 yrs (boys) 2755
- 15–18 yrs (girls) 2110
- 19+ yrs (boys) 2550–2100
- 19+ yrs (girls) 1940–1810

The calorie content of processed foods are listed on the packaging. Foods high in sugar and fat are high in calories.

Protein

It is very easy to obtain enough protein during the teenage years. In fact unless you are not eating enough calories each day, in other words starving yourself, then you are unlikely to be lacking in protein. And you don't require huge amounts of protein either. Protein requirement/day:

- 11–14 yrs (boys) 42.1 g
- 11–14 yrs (girls) 41.2 g
- 15–18 yrs (boys) 55.2 g
- 15–18 yrs (girls) 45.0 g

Examples of the amount of food providing 10 g of protein:

- 39 g peanuts
- 109 g wholemeal bread
- 159 g boiled peas
- 256 g baked potatoes

Eat all the above in one day and you will have eaten 55 g of protein. Easy! Even better, you will also be getting energy, vitamins, and minerals which are also contained in these foods.

Vitamins

Vitamin A

Vitamin A or retinol is found naturally only in animal foods. But the carotenes (beta carotene or pro-vitamin A is the most important) are found in orange and green leafy vegetables. Not only is beta-carotene the only natural source of vitamin A for vegans, it is also one of the prime sources for omnivores!

Requirement for vitamin A through to adult (one microgram of retinol is equivalent to 6 μg of beta-carotene)

- girls 350 μg–600 μg
- boys 350 μg–700 μg

Examples of the amount of beta-carotene in different foods per 100 g:

- 4300–11000 μg carrots (boiled)
- 3375 μg curly kale (boiled)
- 300–3000 μg mango (raw)
- 640 μg tomato (raw)

B Vitamins

While each B vitamin is unique, they have features in common and tend to be found in the same types of foods such as whole grains and pulses (except B_{12}—see below).

The daily requirements for each B vitamin for all teenagers is as follows.

- 0.7–1.1 mg B_1 (Thiamine)
- 1.1–1.3 mg B_2 (Riboflavin)
- 12–18 mg B_3 (Niacin)
- 1–1.5 mg B_6 (Pyridoxine)
- 200 μg Folate
- 3–7 mg Pantothenic Acid
- 1.2–1.5 μg B_{12}
- Biotin—No optimal consumption for biotin but the Dept. of Health estimates that intakes between 10–200 μg are safe and adequate.

Example of the range of B vitamins in 100 g Wholemeal bread:

- 0.34 mg B_1 (Thiamine)
- 0.09 mg B_2 (Riboflavin)
- 4.1 mg B_3 (Niacin)
- 0.12 mg B_6 (Pyridoxine)
- 39 μg Folate
- 0.6 mg Pantothenic Acid
- 6 μg Biotin
- 0 μg B_{12}

Example of the range of B vitamins in 100 g of frozen (and boiled) peas:

- 0.26 mg B_1 (Thiamine)
- 0.00 mg B_2 (Riboflavin)
- 1.6 mg B_3 (Niacin)
- 0.09 mg B_6 (Pyridoxine)
- 47 μg Folate
- 0.14 mg Pantothenic Acid

- 0.4 μg Biotin
- 0 μg B$_{12}$

B_{12}

A lot of worry has been generated over getting enough B$_{12}$, and dietary deficiency of B$_{12}$ in vegans is rare.

B$_{12}$ is made by bacteria and was traditionally obtained from fresh garden vegetables and fermented foods. Now, however, due to the intensive processing of fruit and vegetables in the food industry, these foods can no longer be relied upon as adequate B$_{12}$ sources. Some people may obtain B$_{12}$ from lightly washed home-grown vegetables. However, foods fortified with B$_{12}$ are a more reliable source. Try to include B$_{12}$ in your diet at least 2–3 times per week. Foods containing B$_{12}$ include fortified soya milk, fortified vegan margarines, yeast extracts, and some breakfast cereals (e.g. many Kellogg's cereals are suitable for vegans and contain B$_{12}$).

Vitamin C

Almost all the vitamin C in the human diet comes from vegetables and fruit, especially potatoes, green leafy vegetables, citrus fruits, and tomatoes. Teenagers require 35 mg of vitamin C per day.

Examples of the amount of vitamin C in different fruits per 100 g:

- 150–230 mg black currants
- 44–79 mg oranges
- 59 mg kiwi
- 54 mg clementine

Vitamin D

Few foods naturally contain vitamin D and those which do are animal products (vitamin D$_3$ or cholecalciferol). Dietary sources of vitamin D are relatively unimportant as most people obtain vitamin D from the action of ultra-violent B light on sterols in the skin (in other words sunlight on the skin). Winter time supply of vitamin D depends on the previous summer's exposure creating adequate stores in the liver, or on dietary sources. The exact requirement of vitamin D is unknown. Vegan sources of vitamin D (D$_2$ or ergocalciferol) include some fortified soya milks, vegan margarine. If you don't get much sunshine, if you go out with your skin covered up, or if you do not eat foods fortified with vitamin D, then you should consider taking a supplement (vitamin tablet).

Vitamin E

Vitamin E is found in many plant foods such as vegetable oils, nuts, seeds, and whole grains. The Dept. of Health has not set a recommended intake of vitamin E but says that 3–4 mg daily is adequate.

Examples of the amount of vitamin E in different foods per 100 g:

- 37.77 mg sunflower seeds
- 4.99 mg peanut butter
- 40.68 mg safflower oil

Minerals

Calcium

Calcium isn't only found in cow's milk and cheese (despite what the adverts imply). A lot of people don't realize which types of foods contain calcium and are under the impression that milk is the only useful source. To make things clearer we have compared the calcium in milk to the calcium contained in vegetables. Be amazed. Be very amazed.

For extra calcium each day use a calcium-enriched soya milk in your drinks and for cooking.

Examples of the amount of calcium in different foods per 100 g:

- 115 mg whole milk
- 240 mg almonds
- 680 mg tahini
- 130 mg white french stick
- 100 mg wholemeal crackers

Iron

If you were to listen to scare stories you would think every vegan was anemic. Well, it just isn't true and there is plenty of iron in a vegan diet. Iron obtained from meat is better absorbed than iron obtained from plant sources. However, vitamin C helps the absorption and vegans eat a lot of this. If you drink a glass of fruit juice with your meals, you will enhance your iron intake.

The Dept. of Health recommends a daily intake of 11.3–14.8 mg for teenagers.

Examples of the amount of iron in different foods per 100 g:

- 3.5 mg wholemeal rolls
- 1.4 mg baked beans
- 2.2 mg dried mixed fruit
- 4.2 mg dried figs
- 3.0 mg almonds
- 10.6 mg tahini

Still worried about iron? Well, take a look at the iron content of meat and milk—100 g of grilled lamb cutlets contains 1.9 mg of iron. And cow's milk is a very poor source of iron. In fact 100 g of skimmed milk contains 0.06mg of iron.

Zinc

The Dept. of Health recommends a daily intake of 9 mg of zinc for teenagers.

Examples of the amount of zinc in different foods per 100 g:

- 4.2 mg brazil nuts
- 3.3 mg dry roasted peanuts
- 5.4 mg tahini
- 1.8 mg wholemeal bread

Hint: Nutrition is a complex subject and different nutrients interact with each other to keep your body healthy. Eat lots of different foods throughout the day, making sure you don't rely heavily on one particular food (e.g. chips).

Chapter 29

Vegetarian Diets and Athletes

It decreases the risk of heart disease, stroke, atherosclerosis, diabetes, hypertension, obesity and cancer. No, it isn't the latest pharmaceutical wonder or a breakthrough supplement being hawked on late-night infomercials. You may be surprised to learn that this mystery elixir is actually a vegetarian diet!

It wasn't so long ago that such a diet conjured up images of tie-dyed hippies in some remote commune crunching on fruits, nuts, and granola. Now people from all walks of life are jumping on the vegetable bandwagon. In fact, 7 percent of the American population, or 12.4 million people, are currently vegetarians. Many who are recreational or competitive athletes may have already made the dietary switch or may be considering doing so in the future.

When people start trading in their hamburgers for veggie burgers, they worry about meeting their nutrient needs. New evidence shows that a properly planned vegetarian diet can be healthful and nutritionally sound. But what about athletes who have unique and additional strength and stamina needs? This article will show how, with a little planning and lots of variety, vegetarian diets can not only meet an athlete's nutrient needs but also improve athletic performance.

From "Vegetarianism and the Athlete" by Catherine Reade, *IDEA Health & Fitness Source*, February 2000. Reproduced with permission of IDEA Health & Fitness Association, (800) 999-IDEA or (858) 535-8979, www.IDEAfit.com. Original article, including references, can be found at http://www.findarticles. com/cf_0/m0BTW/2_18/59360952/print.jhtml.

You'll learn why high-carbohydrate, low-fat vegetarian diets just happen to be the perfect recipe to fuel working muscles.

Supplementation

While there is no substitute for a varied and well-balanced diet, both Grandjean and Messina recommend that vegetarian athletes take a basic one-a-day type of vitamin and mineral supplement that meets the RDAs. However, clients should avoid supplements that contain iron unless medical tests confirm the need for additional iron. Too much iron can increase the risk of cancer and heart disease.

Don't Forget Fluids

Water is essential for good health, peak energy levels, athletic performance, and life itself! Water helps keep athletes cool through the process of perspiration. To prevent dehydration, water must be consumed regularly throughout the day. Dehydration can lead to early fatigue, muscle cramping, heat exhaustion, and life-threatening heatstroke.

The recommended intake for sedentary individuals is a minimum of eight to ten 8-ounce glasses of fluid daily, with at least four of those glasses as water. Athletes need to drink this amount plus enough to make up for the fluids lost in exercise. Because thirst is not a good indicator of dehydration, athletes need to schedule drinks throughout the day for optimal sports performance. A good strategy is to keep a water bottle at arm's length and sip from it constantly.

The American College of Sports Medicine recommends consuming sports drinks when exercise lasts 60 minutes or longer. These products contain electrolytes, which enhance fluid absorption and boost energy by maintaining blood sugar levels. A drink containing 5 to 8 percent carbohydrate is ideal for quick energy and is easy on the gastrointestinal system.

(Carbohydrate should be in the form of glucose, a glucose polymer, or sucrose; fructose is absorbed more slowly and may cause gastrointestinal distress.) Sports drinks typically supply 50 to 80 calories per 8-ounce serving; those that supply less than 40 calories in the same serving size are ineffective. Vegetarian athletes need to drink fluids before, during, and after exercise. See below for guidelines.

The Vegetarian Diet in a Nutshell

Whether vegetarian athletes are recreational cyclists or triathletes in training, it is important they consume a variety of foods and meet calorie needs. In general, a vegetarian diet for prime performance contains approximately 60 percent carbohydrate, 12 to 15 percent protein and 30 percent or less fat. However, as Messina points out, "There is room for flexibility within the overall diet. The point is to get adequate but not excessive protein and to keep fat intake moderate but not too restricted." Grandjean cautions that "exercise performance itself needs to be evaluated. If an athlete is feeling early fatigue, carbohydrate intake should be assessed. If muscle building is not happening, check total protein intake."

Catherine Reader, MS, RD, created and runs HealthFull Living, a nutrition consulting company in Littleton, Colorado, that specializes in nutrition for sports performance, weight management and wellness. She is also an ACE (American Certification on Exercise)-certified group fitness instructor who has been designing and teaching personalized nutrition and fitness programs for more than 10 years.

Sample Menu Plan

The meal plan in Table 29.1 lists suggested foods to meet the nutrient needs for two fictitious vegetarians: Karen, a 135-pound part-time group fitness instructor and Julie, a 135-pound marathon runner. Karen is estimated to have a light activity level and needs approximately 2,160 calories per day. Julie has a heavy activity level and needs approximately 2,700 calories per day. The diets are for lacto-ovo-vegetarians, as many clients fall into this category.

In general, the more restrictive the diet and the higher the energy demands, the more planning is needed to meet nutritional requirements. Consuming adequate calories is the first nutritional challenge that must be met for peak performance.

Meeting Caloric Needs

To best meet energy demands, athletes should consume six to eight meals per day. Small frequent feedings help supply a steady energy source and are easier on the body's digestive system than three large meals per day. If an athlete on a vegetarian diet consistently loses weight, the caloric density of meals and snacks should be increased by adding more legumes, dried fruits, fruit smoothies (soy or milk based), grains (breads, cereals, pasta, rice), potatoes, and foods that are a little higher in fat (avocados, nuts, seeds, and foods prepared with canola or olive oil). Fruit smoothies and juices, liquid meal replacements, and sports bars can also be used to boost caloric intake.

Table 29.1. Sample Meal Plan. (continued on next page)

Meal	Karen	Calories
Breakfast1 cup (c)	millet rice cereal	160
	1 c nonfat milk	90
	banana	60
	3/4 c orange juice	60
Snack	1 ounce (oz) cashews	180
	1/4 c dried papaya	60
Lunch	bean burrito	355
	1 ½ oz grated cheddar cheese	150
	shredded lettuce, tomato, and salsa	25
	1 c brown rice	160
	8 oz nonfat yogurt	90
Snack	2 oz soy baloney	75
	8 baby carrots	25
Dinner	2 ½ c whole wheat pasta with tomatoes, artichokes, and black beans	415
	2 tbs grated Parmesan cheese	45
	1 oz Italian bread	80
	1 c fruit salad	120
Total Calories:		2,150

Conversely, if too much weight is gained, portion sizes of calorie-dense foods should be decreased and more fruits and vegetables introduced. Any attempt at weight loss should be made slowly (no more than 0.5–1 pound per week) and healthfully. When caloric restriction is too severe and weight loss occurs rapidly, energy decreases, fatigue sets in early, the risk of injury increases, metabolism slows and exercise performance suffers.

Many low-body-weight athletes like gymnasts and wrestlers (especially women) are at the highest risk for not consuming ample calories. When inadequate calories are consumed, the body burns its own protein stores and compromises muscle building. It is recommended that calories not dip below 2,000 daily. When intake drops below this

Table 29.1. Sample Meal Plan. (continued from previous page)

Meal	Julie	Calories
Breakfast	4 whole grain waffles	320
	2 tablespoons (tbs) maple syrup	100
	½ cup strawberries	60
	1 ½ c orange juice	120
Snack	1 slice whole wheat bread	80
	2 tbs peanut butter	180
Lunch	1 c minestrone soup	123
	4 oz soy turkey	150
	seven-grain bread	160
	tomato and lettuce	13
	thin slice Swiss cheese	75
	8 oz apricot-mango nonfat yogurt	90
Snack	2 c sports drink (during run)	160
	After run:	
	1 ½ oz soy nuts	173
	8 baby carrots	25
	1 ½ c pineapple juice	120
Dinner	1 ½ c vegetarian chili	278
	1 ½ oz cheddar cheese	150
	2 oz corn bread	160
	1 c mixed green salad	25
	with ½ cup mandarin oranges	60
	1 teaspoon flaxseed oil dressing	45
Total Calories:		2,757

threshold, it is difficult to meet nutrient needs, especially for iron and calcium.

Carbohydrate Considerations

Carbohydrates are the cornerstone of vegetarian diets, supplying the highest-quality body fuel. They are easy for the body to break down and convert into glucose (energy) for working muscles and the brain—two vital components for peak performance! Carbohydrates supply glucose for energy via the blood stream; glucose is stored in the muscles and liver as glycogen. Glycogen stores are limited in the body, and a lack of glucose can result in fatigue. It is important that all athletes consume a diet rich in carbohydrates (about 60% of total calories) to replenish and optimize glycogen stores and fuel endurance exercise.

There are basically two types of carbohydrates: simple and complex. Simple carbohydrates are sugars, such as table sugar, soda, and hard candy; they are an instant form of energy. Complex carbohydrates are starches, or sugars linked in chains, such as vegetables, legumes, and whole grains; they take slightly longer to produce energy. Note that fruits, though technically considered simple carbohydrates, are actually more nutritionally similar to complex carbohydrates, since fruits are high in vitamins, minerals, and fiber.

Not all complex carbohydrates are considered equal; some have a superior nutritional value because they contain more fiber. For example, whole-grain breads, cereals, rice, and pasta contain more vitamins, minerals, and health-protective phytochemicals than their white, refined counterparts. The higher fiber content allows glucose to be broken down and absorbed more slowly, maintaining a steady stream of blood sugar for a longer time.

Table 29.2. Guidelines for Fluids and Exercise. The following list provides guidelines for fluid replacement when exercising.

When	Cups	Why
2 hours before	at least 2–3	"Water loading" hydrates the body and allows the kidneys 60–90 minutes to process excess liquid.
15 minutes before	1–2	Fluid is available to replace sweat loss and lower body core temperature.
every 15–20 minutes	at least ½ –1	Fluid prevents dehydration; appropriate amount depends on climate, body size, exercise duration, and intensity.
after	as much as possible	Every pound lost should be replaced with 16 ounces of fluid; urine should be pale.

Meeting Carbohydrate Needs

On a daily basis, the majority of carbohydrates vegetarian athletes consume should come from the nutritionally superior, higher-fiber carbohydrates, such as whole grains, legumes, fruits, and vegetables. Many experts recommend a daily carbohydrate intake of 5 to 10 grams per kilogram of body weight (g/kg BW), or 2.3 to 4.5 g/pound.

At the International Center of Sports Nutrition, Grandjean estimates vegetarian athletes' carbohydrate needs based on activity level, as follows:

Moderate Amount: 5 g/kg BW, or 2.3 g/pound—Activities that require moderate amounts of carbohydrates include plyometrics, drills, sprints, weight lifting, skill training, and any aerobic training (running or biking) lasting less than 60 minutes.

Heavy Amount: 8 to 10 g/kg BW, or 3.6 to 4.5 g/pound—Activities that require heavy amounts of carbohydrates include aerobic training lasting longer than 60 minutes.

Using this formula for the case examples cited earlier, Karen, the part-time group fitness instructor has moderate carbohydrate needs calculated as 135 pounds x 2.3 g/pound, which equals approximately 311 g of carbohydrate daily. Marathon runner Julie, on the other hand, has heavy carbohydrate needs calculated as 135 pounds x 3.6 g/pound, which equates to 486 g of carbohydrate daily.

Vegetarian athletes also need to consider their carbohydrate needs immediately prior to and after competing in an athletic event. Experts recommend that athletes consume about 100 g of complex carbohydrates two to three hours prior to an athletic event. Refined grains like bagels and white-flour pasta are the preferred choice since they break down rapidly, supplying glucose more quickly to the body. To replenish glycogen stores after an event, any type of carbohydrate should be consumed as soon as possible (40–60 g per hour during the first 5 hours after the event).

Carbohydrate food sources include breads, cereals, pasta, rice, grains (amaranth, barley, buckwheat, bulgur, corn, kamut, millet, quinoa, rye, spelt, whole wheat), fruits, and vegetables. Legumes, soy, and dairy products supply both carbohydrates and protein.

Protein Pointers

For the athlete, protein is most notably involved in building muscle. Protein is also needed to produce hemoglobin, which carries oxygen to working muscles, and to produce enzymes and hormones involved in metabolism. Additionally, protein serves as a last-resort energy source when carbohydrate consumption is inadequate. In general, protein should make up about 12 to 15 percent of a vegetarian athlete's diet. Protein requirements will vary based on exercise type, duration and intensity; fitness level; and energy intake. However, despite the fact that the current Recommended Dietary Allowance (RDA) for protein is 0.8 g/kg BW, the body of literature overwhelmingly indicates this amount is inadequate to support an athlete's protein needs, since physical training increases the metabolism of amino acids.

While no specific RDA is currently available for athletes, a reasonable daily protein intake for vegetarians would range from 1.5 to 1.8 g/kg BW and possibly even a little higher. Some experts recommend 1.2 to 1.4 g/kg BW for endurance exercisers and 1.7 to 1.8 g/kg BW for strength athletes, whereas the American Dietetic Association (ADA) and the Canadian Dietetic Association both recommend 1.5 g/kg BW. Grandjean concurs with the ADA recommendation but adds the caveat that 65 to 70 percent of that protein should be in the form of animal protein and calories should not be restricted.

Due to the lower digestibility of plant protein (about 85% versus 95% for animal protein), requirements are somewhat higher for vegetarians than nonvegetarians. Virginia Messina, MPH, RD, is a Port Townsend, Washington, based nutrition consultant and author of five books on the nutritional needs of vegetarians. "Depending on the level of exercise, protein needs for nonvegetarians could be as high as 1.5 g/kg BW," she says. "If that is true, we have to assume that some vegans could [need] as much as 1.8 g/kg BW." This recommendation is in keeping with recent research that suggests elite Japanese track and field athletes who consume a plant-based diet may require more than 2 g/kg BW.

Here's how to calculate the protein needs for Karen, the group fitness instructor, and Julie, the marathon runner, using the range of 1.5 to 1.8 g/kg BW (note that 1 kg = 2.2 pounds):

- Karen: 135 pounds = 61 kg x 1.5 g/kg = approx. 92 g protein per day

- Julie: 135 pounds = 61 kg x 1.8 g/kg = approx. 110 g protein per day

Meeting Protein Needs

Proteins are made up of 20 amino acids, nine of which are essential amino acids (EAAs), meaning they must be obtained through diet since our bodies cannot manufacture them. Proteins are labeled either "complete" or "incomplete," based on the number and amount of EAAs present. Animal protein—found in meat, eggs and dairy—is often referred to as complete, since it contains all nine EAAs in amounts that closely match human needs. Thus, vegetarians who consume eggs or dairy products are obtaining complete protein. According to Messina, many plant proteins, such as grains, legumes and nuts, also contain all nine EAAs but because one or more of the EAAs is in short supply, they are considered incomplete.

Protein is the macronutrient most likely to be deficient in vegetarian diets, especially in those that don't contain any animal products. Athletes who follow a lacto-ovo-vegetarian diet usually consume an ample amount of protein, since their diet includes dairy products and eggs. With the exception of fruits, most foods contribute some protein to the diet.

Athletes who adhere to the stricter, vegan diet may not get enough protein to meet their performance needs. According to Messina, Vegan diets tend to be about 10 to 11 percent protein, and this may not meet needs for those athletes whose energy needs are moderate. For example, an 80 kg strength athlete might need about 120 g of protein or more. If he were consuming a typical vegan diet and eating 3,500 calories per day, his protein intake might be only about 96 g pet day. So this athlete would need to make some adjustments by choosing more servings of protein-rich plant food. An athlete with higher protein needs should choose fewer servings of grains and proportionally more of higher-protein foods like legumes.

To meet protein needs, vegan diets require a bit of planning. Vegans can ensure they obtain complete protein by simply combining any legume or bean dish with any grain, nut or seed. Examples of combinations that form complete protein include many ethnic dishes, such as rice and beans; pita bread and hummus; pasta with tomatoes and cannellini beans; and a peanut butter sandwich. To make matters even simpler, these items don't need to be consumed at the same time, just over the course of a day (e.g., oatmeal at breakfast and beans for lunch). If low protein intake is an issue, soy protein shakes can be added.

Soy Stats

A great addition to any vegetarian diet is soy, because of its outstanding protein profile. The protein-packed soybean contains all nine EAAs, with only one EAA, methionine, in short supply. This makes soy a high-quality protein almost equivalent to animal products.

Vegetarian athletes should try to consume one or more servings of soy on a daily basis. It has never been easier to include soy: It can be consumed as soy milk, soy cheese, soy meat analogs (soy dogs, turkey, ham, sausage, pepperoni, etc.), tofu, tempeh, soy nuts or butter, soy flour, soy cereal or soy yogurt; and as textured vegetable protein. Whenever possible, it is best to choose organic products since soy is sometimes heavily treated with agricultural chemicals.

Focus on Fat

Like their meat-eating counterparts, vegetarians should consume approximately 30 percent or less of their daily nutrients from fat. The greatest contribution fat makes to sports performance is as a concentrated energy source. Although it is not yet clear how the different types of fat specifically affect sports performance, there is plenty of evidence indicating how particular fats affect health. Saturated fat and trans fat should be kept to a minimum due to their negative impact on heart health.

In vegetarian diets, saturated fats can be found in whole-milk dairy products, butter, palm oil, and coconut oil. In lacto-ovo-vegetarian diets, whole-milk dairy products should be replaced with reduced-fat varieties. Trans fat is found in margarines and in processed and prepared foods made with "hydrogenated" vegetable oils; it should be avoided whenever possible.

The good news is that vegetarian diets, particularly vegan diets, are naturally low in fat and contain mostly the unsaturated fats found in plant foods. There are two types of essential fats that need to be taken in through the diet: omega-3 and omega-6. Most people consume more omega-6 fats (found in polyunsaturated vegetable oils like corn, safflower, and sunflower) than omega-3 fats (found in fish, flaxseed, hemp oil, walnuts, canola oil and dark green, leafy vegetables). Research seems to indicate that the ratio of these two essential fatty acids is vital and typically out of balance in most diets. Therefore, it is recommended that people on all types of diets strive to include more omega-3 fats and fewer omega-6 fats. Vegetarians in particular should try replacing polyunsaturated vegetable oils (and products that contain them) with monounsaturated fats like olive and canola oils; vegetarians should also eat a handful of nuts—particularly walnuts—regularly. While not to everyone's taste, ground flaxseeds can be added to fruit juice or yogurt, and flaxseed oil dressing can be used to top a salad. (Start with one teaspoon of freshly ground flax and gradually build up to one to two tablespoons daily. Drink lots of water too!)

Micronutrients That Play Hard to Get

When any food group is excluded from the diet, other foods need to replace the lost nutrients to ensure a healthful balance. Since vegetarians exclude meat and vegans exclude all animal products and dairy, vegetarian diets can potentially be deficient in calcium, iron, zinc, and vitamins D and B$_{12}$.

Iron

Iron is especially important to the vegetarian athlete since it helps to shuttle oxygen as hemoglobin in the blood and as myoglobin in the muscle. Iron is also heavily involved in the enzyme systems within the cells that produce energy. Two forms of iron are found in food: heme and non-heme. Heme iron is found primarily in meat, chicken, and fish; this form is more easily absorbed than the non-heme iron found primarily in plants. Certain substances, such as plant phytates and fiber, tannins (found in coffee and tea) and calcium, can inhibit iron absorption.

Despite a diet high in non-heme plant products, vegetarians are not prone to iron deficiency. In fact, many research studies confirm that vegetarians with a well-balanced diet have adequate iron stores. Vegetarians seem to experience physiological adaptations (such as excreting less feral iron) that increase the efficiency of iron absorption. Without severe caloric restriction, vegetarians can easily consume the RDA of 10 milligrams [mg] per day for men and postmenopausal women or 15 mg per day for women of childbearing age. Those at greatest risk for iron deficiency are female vegetarians who restrict calories.

Vegetarian diets tend to be rich in vitamin C, which boosts iron absorption. By adding a vitamin C source to meals or snacks—for example, adding strawberries to cereal or tomatoes to a spinach salad—clients can further increase the amount of iron they take in. Some vegetables, like broccoli and bok choy, pack a double whammy: They are high in both iron and vitamin C. Vegetarians can further increase the iron content of foods, especially acidic ones like tomatoes, by simply cooking in cast-iron pans. To maximize iron absorption, vegetarians should also avoid drinking coffee, tea and calcium-rich milk (cow or soy) and taking calcium supplements when eating plant foods rich in iron.

The iron content of packaged foods is listed as a percent "DV," or Daily Value, and is based on an iron requirement of 18 mg. If a food product states "30% DV," a serving contains 6 mg of iron.

The B Vitamins

The B vitamins are essential for sports performance because they help produce energy from carbohydrate, protein, and fat. Most B vitamins are easily obtained through a varied diet since small amounts exist in many animal and plant foods. The exception is vitamin B_{12}.

Vitamin B_{12} is essential for a healthy nervous system and for the production of red blood cells. This vitamin is naturally found only in animal products. Vegetarian diets that include dairy, eggs, or some other animal products will provide adequate amounts of vitamin B_{12}. Since it is stored in the body, only small amounts are needed. The RDA for adults is 2 micrograms (mcg).

Vegetarians who avoid dairy, eggs, and all other animal products need to find other sources of vitamin B_{12}. Messina recommends that "all vegan athletes should have a vitamin B_{12} supplement or consume foods that are fortified with this nutrient." Food sources that are fortified with vitamin B_{12} include Red Star (T-6635) brand nutritional yeast; some soy milks and meat analogs; and certain cereals, like Grapenuts. Clients should be advised to check labels for B_{12} fortification.

Antioxidants and Exercise

Vegetarian athletes may inadvertently be the beneficiaries of yet another physiological function. Recent research suggests that the antioxidant trio—vitamins C and E and beta carotene—may protect against exercise-induced "oxidative stress." When exercising, the body takes in and utilizes oxygen at a higher rate, promoting cellular oxidation. This, in turn, promotes the production of free radicals (unstable molecules), which can destroy other cells. Any brave molecule that intervenes and squelches free radicals is dubbed an "antioxidant."

Although there is little evidence that increasing antioxidant intake can improve exercise performance, consuming more antioxidants does appear to decrease muscle damage and enhance immune function. Many researchers believe there are no known risks and may possibly be long-term benefits to taking the antioxidant trio in amounts exceeding the RDAs. While these antioxidants also show promise for enhancing recovery from exercise, more research is needed in this area. One thing is sure: all athletes should consume plenty of fruits and vegetables that are naturally rich in antioxidants—for example, strawberries, tangerines, broccoli, carrots, and tomatoes. Vegetarian athletes may have the competitive edge here since their diet is already rich in antioxidants.

Chapter 30

Veganism for the Elderly

Introduction

A vegan diet can provide a nutritionally adequate diet at all times of life. General nutritional studies on elderly people have revealed that intakes of various vitamins and minerals, e.g. vitamin C, folate, riboflavin, vitamin D, iron, potassium and fiber, are lower than desirable. Although no studies have been carried out specifically on the nutritional status of elderly vegans, vegan diets generally contain the above mentioned nutrients in levels similar to the general population. There is a lack of data for deriving specific dietary requirements for the elderly due to the diversity of this population group. The requirements of each individual will depend on eating habits, health, and activity levels.

General Guidelines

Choose a varied diet and strive for a minimum of 5 daily servings of fruits and vegetables, complementing them with generous portions of grains and legumes. A nutritionally balanced diet helps to maintain and boost the immune response—focus on whole grains, green leafy vegetables and vegetable oils—such as safflower, sunflower and rapeseed.

Excerpted from "Veganism for the Over 60s," The Vegan Society, 1997. Reprinted with permission. The full text of this document, including references, can be found at http://www.vegansociety.com/html/info/info05.html.

Detailed below are nutrients that dietitians and nutritionists have pinpointed as being of main concern in the elderly population. The term "elderly" generally refers to men and women of pensionable age. The term "very elderly" is often used for those over 75 years of age.

Vitamin D

Vitamin D is very important to keep bones healthy. Although it can be found in margarine and breakfast cereals (D_3 is animal-derived; D_2 is vegan). Consequently, the main source of vitamin D is from exposure of the skin to sunlight. Low levels have been recorded where individuals have spent long periods in residential homes and hospitals, with little exposure to sunlight. Therefore, try to sit out in the summer—even if you only uncover your hands, face, and neck for short (but regular) sessions. Use a sun screen cream to keep your skin from burning. Even sitting in light shade will help your skin manufacture vitamin D.

Iron

The elderly may be at risk of poor iron status but there is no data to quantify specific requirements. Iron from plant sources is absorbed less efficiently than iron from animal sources. However, vitamin C (e.g. from citrus fruits and fruit juices) greatly enhances the absorption of iron from foods whereas tannins (e.g. found in tea), phytate, and fiber inhibit absorption. Studies have shown that the iron status of vegans is usually normal and iron deficiency is no more common than in the general population.

Calcium

The desirable calcium intake for the elderly is a source of continuing debate. The COMA (Committee on Medical Aspects of Food Policy) panel felt that there was no conclusive evidence that a high calcium intake in the elderly would prevent bone loss—although members suggested it might be prudent for those at risk of osteoporosis (porous or fragile bones) to consume a high calcium diet. However, there does not appear to be a direct link between an older adult's bone density and their current calcium intake. Nevertheless vegans should ensure they consume calcium-containing foods such as almonds, tofu (made with calcium sulphate), fortified soya milk, bread, green vegetables, and pulses. Calcium absorption is more efficient in the presence of vitamin D.

Zinc

Zinc deficiency has been associated with delayed wound healing, decreased taste acuity, and anorexia in old age. Vegan diets usually contain less zinc than non-vegan diets. Plant foods rich in this mineral include nuts, seeds, and whole grain cereals.

Potassium

Potassium is present in nearly all foods. Foods high in potassium include whole grain cereals, fruit, nuts and vegetables. Potassium depletion has been recorded in diets high in refined foods and excess sugar intake.

Folate (Folic Acid)

Folate deficiency is more common in the elderly due to poor intake. In the general elderly population sources of folate, such as vegetables and fruit, are frequently avoided. Vegans, however, generally meet or exceed recommended intakes.

Riboflavin (Vitamin B$_2$)

The *Manual of Dietetics* states "Riboflavin deficiency is rarely reported in Western countries but is common in countries with low intakes of meat and dairy products. Those most likely to be at risk in the UK are vegans." However, there have been no reports of riboflavin deficiency in vegans [in the UK]. Vegan sources of riboflavin include yeast extract, wheat bran, peas, whole cereals, pulses, nuts, mushrooms and avocados.

Vitamin B$_{12}$

Research has shown that vitamin B$_{12}$ deficiency is rare in vegans and when it does occur it is more likely to be as a result of malabsorption rather than dietary deficiency. There is no evidence for an increased requirement for this vitamin in old age.

Vitamin B$_{12}$ is produced by bacteria in the human gut but distal to the site where it can be absorbed. Therefore it is recommended that this vitamin is included in the diet. For vegans, B$_{12}$ fortified foods include yeast extracts, some vegetable stocks, Textured Vegetable Protein (TVP), certain soya milks and margarines, and some breakfast cereals.

Fiber

Fiber is important for providing bulk to enable food to pass through the gut easily. Constipation is a common problem in the elderly which is often due to a low fiber diet. However, vegan diets are generally rich in fiber ensuring the digestive system stays healthy, active, and regular. Transit time in the elderly is no different than for the younger population. Good sources of fiber include fruits, dark leafy vegetables, grains, and legumes.

Fluid

Some elderly people may have a fading sense of thirst which can lead to dehydration. Dehydration can cause mental confusion, headaches, and irritability and so it is important that fluid intake is checked. Recommendations are for a minimum 6–8 glasses of water or liquids per day. For those concerned about nocturnal incontinence, extra fluids can be taken earlier in the day.

A Varied Diet

Aim to eat a varied whole food diet and choose foods from the following food groups on a daily basis:

- Cereals: Barley, rice, wheat (bread, pasta), oats, shredded wheat, millet, corn, bulgur, couscous

- Pulses: Beans, peas, lentils (cooked or sprouted)

- Nuts and seeds: All types of nuts, nut butters (peanut butter, cashew nut butter, etc.), pumpkin, sunflower and sesame seeds and tahini (sesame seed spread). Also, sprouted seeds such as alfalfa and mustard

- Vegetables (cooked and/or raw): Deep yellow and dark green leafy vegetables including carrots, green peppers, broccoli, spinach, endive, and kale. Other vegetables include bean sprouts, potatoes, tomatoes, lettuce, cabbage, sweet corn, celery, onions, cucumbers, beetroot, marrows, courgettes, and cauliflower

- Fruits (fresh, dried and tinned): Bananas, oranges, tangerines, grapefruit, apples, mangoes, cherries, grapes, apricots, pear, paw paws, kiwis, berries, currants, lemons and plums

Some Vegan Sources of Key Nutrients

- Protein: Whole grains (e.g. whole wheat flour and bread, brown rice), nuts (e.g. hazels, cashews, brazils, almonds, cob nuts), seeds (sunflower, sesame, pumpkin), pulses (e.g. peas, beans, lentils), soya flour, soya milk, tofu

- Carbohydrate: Whole grains (e.g. wheat, oats, barley, rice), whole wheat bread, pasta and other flour products, lentils, beans, potatoes, dried and fresh fruit

- Fats: Nuts and seeds, nut and seed oils, vegan margarine, avocados. Two polyunsaturated fatty acids not made by the body are the essential fatty acids linoleic acid (omega 6 group) and alpha linolenic acid (omega 3 group). Good sources of these fatty acids include:
  - linoleic acid—safflower, sunflower, corn, evening primrose and soya oils
  - alpha-linolenic acid—linseed, pumpkin seed, walnut, soya and rapeseed oils

Vitamins

- A: Carrots, spinach, pumpkins, tomatoes, dark green leafy vegetables, vegan margarines

- B: Nuts, whole grains, oats, muesli, pulses, yeast extract (e.g. Marmite), leafy green vegetables, potatoes, mushrooms and dried fruit

- B_{12}: Fortified yeast extracts (e.g. Marmite) and soya milks, vegan margarines, packeted "veggie burger" mixes, some cereals (e.g. Kellogg's Fruit & Fiber, Frosties, Common Sense Oat Bran Flakes). Possibly: fermented foods (e.g. tamari, miso and tempeh, sea vegetables (e.g. hijiki, wakame and spirulina).

- C: Citrus fruits (e.g. oranges, lemons, grapefruit), red and black currants, berries, green vegetables and potatoes

- D: Sunlight, some soya milks, and vegan margarines

- E: Nuts, seeds, whole grains and flours, vegetable oils

- Folate: Wheat germ, raw or lightly-cooked green leafy vegetables (e.g. watercress, broccoli, spinach), yeast, yeast extracts, nuts, peas, runner beans, oranges, dates, avocados, whole grains.

Minerals

- Calcium: Molasses, seeds, nuts, carob, pulses, miso (fermented soya bean curd), parsley, figs (dried), sea vegetables, grains, fortified soya milk (several varieties are fortified with calcium)

- Iron: Seeds, nuts, pulses, miso, grains, dried fruit, molasses, sea vegetables, parsley, green leafy vegetables, using cast-iron cookware

- Zinc: Wheat germ, whole grains, nuts, pulses, tofu, soya protein, miso, peas, parsley, bean sprouts

Exercise and Lifestyle

Exercise is important to improve/maintain strength, suppleness, balance, stamina, and memory. It helps protect against heart disease, osteoporosis, and many other chronic conditions. Try and mix aerobic exercise—e.g. walking and swimming, with simple activities that strengthen muscle—e.g. lifting and carrying. As we age we lose important muscle tissue and muscle strength. Research shows it is never too late to rebuild and strengthen muscle with the right kind of activity and exercise. Muscle mass also determines our basal metabolism which directly affects the appetite. More muscle means a heartier appetite which translates into more nutrients for our bodies.

Research shows without doubt that good nutrition, together with an active lifestyle, can have a beneficial effect on the health of almost all older people and is the best way to retard and even reverse the process of aging.

Medical Problems

The above information is only relevant to relatively healthy individuals; nutritional requirements will be altered by disease and therapeutic drugs. [In such a case, please contact your health care provider regarding maintaining your vegan diet.]

Part Five

Vegetarian Philosophy and Controversies

Chapter 31

Does Vegetarianism Help the Environment?

Chapter Contents

Section 31.1

Environmental Reasons for Vegetarianism

This section contains text from "U.S. could feed 800 million people with grain that livestock eat, Cornell ecologist advises animal scientists" and "Eight Meaty Facts about Animal Food (from *Livestock Production: Energy Inputs and the Environment*, by David Pimentel)," a press release available at http://www. news.cornell.edu/releases/Aug97/livestock.hrs.html, 1997, and "'Ecological Integrity' Tax on eaters at top of food chain would aid environmental sustainability, Cornell ecologist proposes in new book," www.news.cornell.edu/releases/Jan01/ pimentel_book.hrs.html, 2001, Roger Segelken, Cornell University, reprinted with permission. Despite the age of first document, readers seeking information about environmental reasons for vegetarianism will find this information useful.

U.S. Could Feed 800 Million People with Grain that Livestock Eat

From one ecologist's perspective, the American system of farming grain-fed livestock consumes resources far out of proportion to the yield, accelerates soil erosion, affects world food supply, and will be changing in the future.

"If all the grain currently fed to livestock in the United States were consumed directly by people, the number of people who could be fed would be nearly 800 million," David Pimentel, professor of ecology in Cornell University's College of Agriculture and Life Sciences, reported at a meeting of the Canadian Society of Animal Science in Montreal. Or, if those grains were exported, it would boost the U.S. trade balance by $80 billion a year, Pimentel estimated.

With only grass-fed livestock, individual Americans would still get more than the recommended daily allowance (RDA) of meat and dairy protein, according to Pimentel's report, "Livestock Production: Energy Inputs and the Environment."

An environmental analyst and longtime critic of waste and inefficiency in agricultural practices, Pimentel depicted grain-fed livestock farming as a costly and nonsustainable way to produce animal protein. He distinguished grain-fed meat production from pasture-raised livestock, calling cattle-grazing a more reasonable use of marginal land.

Animal protein production requires more than eight times as much fossil-fuel energy than production of plant protein while yielding animal protein that is only 1.4 times more nutritious for humans than the comparable amount of plant protein, according to the Cornell ecologist's analysis.

Tracking food animal production from the feed trough to the dinner table, Pimentel found broiler chickens to be the most efficient use of fossil energy, and beef, the least. Chicken meat production consumes energy in a 4:1 ratio to protein output; beef cattle production requires an energy input to protein output ratio of 54:1. (Lamb meat production is nearly as inefficient at 50:1, according to the ecologist's analysis of U.S. Department of Agriculture statistics. Other ratios range from 13:1 for turkey meat and 14:1 for milk protein, to 17:1 for pork and 26:1 for eggs.)

Animal agriculture is a leading consumer of water resources in the United States, Pimentel noted. Grain-fed beef production takes 100,000 liters of water for every kilogram of food. Raising broiler chickens takes 3,500 liters of water to make a kilogram of meat. In comparison, soybean production uses 2,000 liters per kilogram of food produced; rice, 1,912; wheat, 900; and potatoes, 500 liters. "Water shortages already are severe in the western and southern United States and the situation is quickly becoming worse because of a rapidly growing U.S. population that requires more water for all of its needs, especially agriculture," Pimentel observed.

Livestock are directly or indirectly responsible for much of the soil erosion in the United States, the ecologist determined. On lands where feed grain is produced, soil loss averages 13 tons per hectare per year. Pasture lands are eroding at a slower pace, at an average of 6 tons per hectare per year. But erosion may exceed 100 tons on severely overgrazed pastures, and 54 percent of U.S. pasture land is being overgrazed.

"More than half the U.S. grain and nearly 40 percent of world grain is being fed to livestock rather than being consumed directly by humans," Pimentel said. "Although grain production is increasing in total, the per capita supply has been decreasing for more than a decade. Clearly, there is reason for concern in the future."

Eight Meaty Facts about Animal Food

The following points are from Pimentel's *Livestock Production: Energy Inputs and the Environment*.

- Where's the grain? The 7 billion livestock animals in the United States consume five times as much grain as is consumed directly by the entire American population.

- Herbivores on the hoof. Each year an estimated 41 million tons of plant protein is fed to U.S. livestock to produce an estimated 7 million tons of animal protein for human consumption. About 26 million tons of the livestock feed comes from grains and 15 million tons from forage crops. For every kilogram of high-quality animal protein produced, livestock are fed nearly 6 kg of plant protein.

- Fossil fuel to food fuel. On average, animal protein production in the U.S. requires 28 kilocalories (kcal) for every kcal of protein produced for human consumption. Beef and lamb are the most costly, in terms of fossil fuel energy input to protein output at 54:1 and 50:1, respectively. Turkey and chicken meat production are the most efficient (13:1 and 4:1, respectively). Grain production, on average, requires 3.3 kcal of fossil fuel for every kcal of protein produced. The U.S. now imports about 54 percent of its oil; by the year 2015, that import figure is expected to rise to 100 percent.

- Thirsty production systems. U.S. agriculture accounts for 87 percent of all the fresh water consumed each year. Livestock directly use only 1.3 percent of that water. But when the water required for forage and grain production is included, livestock's water usage rises dramatically. Every kilogram of beef produced takes 100,000 liters of water. Some 900 liters of water go into producing a kilogram of wheat. Potatoes are even less thirsty, at 500 liters per kilogram.

- Home on the range. More than 302 million hectares of land are devoted to producing feed for the U.S. livestock population—about 272 million hectares in pasture and about 30 million hectares for cultivated feed grains.

- Disappearing soil. About 90 percent of U.S. crop land is losing soil—to wind and water erosion—at 13 times above the sustainable rate. Soil loss is most severe in some of the richest farming areas; Iowa loses topsoil at 30 times the rate of soil formation. Iowa has lost one-half its topsoil in only 150 years of farming—soil that took thousands of years to form.

- Plenty of protein. Nearly 7 million tons (metric) of animal protein is produced annually in the U.S.—enough to supply every American man, woman and child with 75 grams of animal protein a day. With the addition of 34 grams of available plant protein, a total of 109 grams of protein is available per capita. The RDA (recommended daily allowance) per adult per day is 56 grams of protein for a mixed diet.

- Out to pasture. If all the U.S. grain now fed to livestock were exported and if cattlemen switched to grass-fed production systems, less beef would be available, and animal protein in the average American diet would drop from 75 grams to 29 grams per day. That, plus current levels of plant-protein consumption, would still yield more than the RDA for protein.

'Ecological Integrity'

Applying the polluter pays principle, a Cornell University ecologist and author suggests a way to improve the environmental sustainability of agriculture: Levy taxes according to food-chain ranking so that products with the worst environmental impact cost the most.

"We should internalize the costs of dietary preferences. If one chooses to eat high-impact food, one should pay the full costs of such a choice," says David Pimentel, the professor of ecology and agricultural science who is a co-editor and co-author of the newly published book *Ecological Integrity: Integrating Environment, Conservation, and Health*.

At the top of the ecologist's tax table—and highest in his ranking of foods that require the most resources to produce while wreaking more environmental degradation—are meats from factory-farmed mammals, such as beef, pork, and eggs. The same foods are the least healthy when consumed in excess, Pimentel notes.

To be taxed the least are products at the bottom of humans' food chain—foods that are more efficiently grown while causing less environmental impact—such as legumes, grains, vegetables, starch crops, fruits and nuts. People eating plant-based diets generally consume fewer health-care resources, the author maintains.

Pimentel's beef with beef and other mammalian food products at the top of the food chain centers on efficiencies of production and their true costs, including long-term degradation of the environment.

Pimentel notes that "a powerful trend to eat lower on the food chain" has started in many developed nations. U.S. beef consumption, after peaking at 95 pounds per person a year in 1976, has dropped to around 65 pounds today. Beef consumption in Europe and the United Kingdom never reached those levels and is now falling even faster than in the United States.

261

"But the countervailing trend is for people in developing nations to eat more meat as they become richer," Pimentel says, noting that China's pork consumption jumped 14 percent in 1995 alone. Pimentel and Goodland called on international aid agencies such as the World Bank to phase out investments in intensive livestock production in Third World countries, "especially grain-fed livestock, and leave it to the private sector." Such groups, they write, "should ensure that good economics prevail, including accounting for full environmental and social costs."

The authors would make exceptions in their tax plan for small-scale meat and milk production, such as natural range-fed cattle, the family cow or pig and scrap-fed chickens. But they know where the food chain tax collection should focus for the greatest bureaucratic efficiency. In the United States, they write, "beef sales are the single-largest revenue source within the whole agriculture sector. Only four meatpackers in the United States hold 82 percent of the market, suggesting a low-cost place to tax."

Section 31.2

American Council on Science and Health Disagrees

Excerpted from American Council on Science and Health (ACSH), "The Beef Controversy" http://www.acsh.org/publications/reports/beefcont.pdf, August 1993. Revised in April 2002, by Dr. David A. Cooke, MD, Diplomate, American Board of Internal Medicine. Full document including references can be found at the URL above. Reprinted with permission of American Council on Science and Health (ACSH), 1995 Broadway, 2nd Floor, New York, NY 10023-5800. To learn more about ACSH, visit www.acsh.org. Although this article is responding to specific claims made by the Beyond Beef coalition, many of the issues raised here will be of interest to those seeking information about vegetarianism and the environment.

Introduction

With good management, cattle production need not ruin land or pollute the environment. Well managed grazing can actually improve the quality of pastureland and rangeland. Manure, when properly handled, is a valuable fertilizer rather than a damaging pollutant. The methane produced by cattle is only a very minor contributor to the so-called greenhouse effect. Cattle graze primarily on poor quality lands that cannot be used for crop production. On a worldwide basis, grazing more than doubles the land area that can be used to produce food for humans. Reducing beef production would lead to a decrease in the demand for feed grain, but it does not necessarily follow that the grain would become available to the world's hungry people. The more likely outcome is that farmers would not grow the grain because there would be no market demand for it, or it would be diverted to other uses. Grain typically constitutes only 15 to 20 percent of the total feed consumed by beef cattle in the U.S. The remainder consists of grasses and other cellulose-rich materials that humans and non-ruminant animals cannot digest. The raising of ruminant animals is the only way to transform these plant materials into food for human consumption.

Contrary to allegations made by Beyond Beef and others, there is little relationship between fast food hamburger consumption in the U.S. and the destruction of rainforests in Central and South America. Only about 0.6 percent of the beef consumed in the U.S. comes from Latin American rainforest areas, and much of that is imported as cooked, canned products, rather than as ground beef.

Lean beef, in reasonable serving sizes, can be included in a healthful diet that meets current dietary guidelines. Beef makes positive nutritional contributions to the diet; its iron and zinc content is especially important.

Residues of pesticides, antibiotics and hormones in beef are well within acceptable limits and do not pose a risk to the health of the American public.

As with all raw foods of animal origin, raw beef can be contaminated with bacteria that cause food borne diseases. Adequate cooking kills these bacteria, making the meat safe to eat. With current technology, it is not possible for producers to guarantee that all meat sold to the public will be free from disease-causing bacteria. Therefore, food service personnel and consumers must do their part to prevent food borne illness by handling foods in a sanitary manner and cooking them properly.

The U.S. Department of Agriculture now requires labels on all packages of meat and poultry which gives instructions for safe handling and cooking. This labeling program is worthwhile, but it should be extended to include eggs, fish and shellfish, as well as meat and poultry. All of these foods require thorough cooking to destroy microorganisms which may be present in the raw products.

The Beef Controversy

The Beyond Beef coalition has raised a wide variety of arguments in support of its goal of drastically reducing beef consumption. Some, including animal rights issues and the desirability of small versus large-scale agricultural operations, are matters of personal philosophy and are outside the scope of this scientific report. Other arguments, to be described in detail below, focus on the effect of beef production on the environment and the world food supply.

Beef Production and the Environment

Desertification

During most of their lives, beef cattle graze on pastureland and rangeland. Beyond Beef claims that cattle are "hoofed locusts" that destroy millions of acres of grazing land in the U.S. each year. It is true that uncontrolled grazing can damage grasslands. Properly managed grazing, however, is not destructive. In fact, because cattle fertilize land by depositing manure, they can enrich grasslands rather than destroy them.

Most of the 600 million acres of pastureland and rangeland in the U.S. are unsuitable for crop cultivation. Their only possible agricultural use is the grazing of ruminant animals (cattle or sheep). The same is true in other parts of the world; cattle graze primarily on poor quality lands that cannot be used for crop production. On a worldwide basis, grazing more than doubles the land area that can be used to produce food for humans. If the demand for ruminant animal products ceased, these vast lands would make no contribution to feeding the people of the world.

Do Cattle Steal Food from People?

Perhaps the most disturbing charge raised is that cattle production is a major contributor to world hunger. The coalition contends that a billion people go hungry because precious grain is fed to cattle and other livestock. It claims that if everyone stopped eating beef, this grain could be used to feed the world's hungry people.

Beyond Beef apparently assumes that the problem of world hunger could be solved simply by increasing the amount of food available for consumption. This is an oversimplified, outdated view. The best current evidence indicates that world hunger is not caused by a simple scarcity of food. Experts believe that hunger is attributable primarily to economic and political factors and problems of distribution, rather than to an insufficient food supply. Hunger is caused by a lack of access to adequate food, rather than a shortage of food per se.

Even emergency situations of widespread starvation, such as the crisis in Somalia, are generally not due to a simple lack of food. Most of the major famines in this century have been caused by war, political or economic disruption, or unwise government policies, rather than by acts of nature such as drought, flood, or disease. Efforts to provide food aid to victims of modern famines have been hampered not by a shortage of food, but by the difficulties of wartime intervention and by problems of distribution that prevent food from reaching the people who need it most.

If people stopped eating meat, the grain now fed to livestock would not necessarily become available to the world's hungry people. Those very poor people cannot afford to buy the grain or transport it from the U.S. to their homes. Farmers might donate a small amount of the grain to relief organizations, but they would not be able to stay in business if they gave away a substantial proportion of their crops. The more likely outcome is that farmers would not grow the grain if there were no market demand for it, or it would be diverted to other uses, such as the production of alcohol for fuel.

It is also important to point out that only a small proportion of the feed consumed by beef cattle consists of grain. In the system of beef production currently used in the U.S., cattle consume grain only during the latter part of their lives, when they are housed in feedlots. Grain typically constitutes 15 to 20 percent of the total feed consumed by the animals at all stages of their life cycle. Less than five pounds of feed grains are used to produce one pound of beef. The remainder of the animals' intake consists of grasses and other cellulose-rich materials that humans and non-ruminant animals cannot digest. The raising of ruminant animals is the only way to transform these plant materials into foods for human consumption.

Cattle can be raised entirely on grass, with no grain at all. This is the custom in many developing areas. In the U.S., however, it makes good economic sense to finish cattle on grain because it is readily available at a reasonable price. Despite Beyond Beef's frequent references to precious grain, there is a surplus rather than a shortage of grain in the U.S. Many American farmers who could not otherwise make a profit by growing grain are able to stay in business because they can sell their crops to livestock producers.

Cattle as a Source of Pollution

Beyond Beef argues that organic waste from livestock is a massive source of pollution. But as with the destruction of grasslands, this is a matter of management rather than an inevitable consequence of meat production. Manure is indeed a harmful pollutant if it ends up in the wrong places. In the right places, however, it is a valuable fertilizer.

The manure produced by grazing cattle is recycled naturally into the soil and plants of the grazing lands. Most of the manure produced in feedlots is removed and applied to soil as a fertilizer. When used in this way, animal wastes are not a source of pollution; instead, they replenish the organic matter and nutrients in soil and enhance plant growth. Federal and state laws prohibit the discharge of livestock manure into surface or groundwaters. Beyond Beef also contends that cattle production is responsible for the release of large quantities of methane, a greenhouse gas which is thought to contribute to global-warming, into the atmosphere.

Cattle do produce methane as a byproduct of their ruminant digestion, but the impact of cattle flatulence on global warming is far smaller than Beyond Beef claims. One expert has calculated that driving six miles each way to buy a hamburger would result in 100 times as much greenhouse gas as the production of the hamburger. Another has pointed out that the amount of methane emitted by one cow in a year has the same effect on global warming as the fuel burned to power a single 75-watt light bulb. The major sources of methane are wetlands, rice paddies, biomass burning, drilling for oil, landfills and coal mines, not cattle. In fact, the National Academy of Sciences has calculated that all ruminant animals, both wild and domesticated (including sheep, goats, deer, buffalo, giraffes and camels, as well as cattle) account for only five percent of total greenhouse gas production.

Destroying Nature

Beyond Beef argues that cattle are causing "the extinction of plant and animal species" and "the purposeful extermination of millions of predators." More succinctly, they claim that cattle are destroying nature.

The problem here is not with the facts but with their interpretation. In discussing these issues, Beyond Beef ignores the needs of people and the ways in which people must modify nature if they are to earn a living and feed themselves. The productive use of land inevitably changes the types of plants and animals that live on it. If humans left all of the earth's land in its natural state, there would be no food for the human population.

In his book, Rifkin claims that, "The elimination of beef will be accompanied by an ecological renaissance, a grand restoration of nature on every continent... Ancient rivers will flow... Streams and springs will come to life... Predator species will thrive... Buffalo will once again roam the West." This is a romantic view, not a realistic one.

Rainforest Destruction

The destruction of tropical rainforests is an issue of concern to many Americans. The idea, raised by Beyond Beef and others, that Americans can help to preserve the rainforests by reducing their consumption of beef (particularly fast food hamburgers) has great emotional appeal. In actuality, however, there is little relationship between U.S. beef consumption and the fate of Central and South American rainforests.

The U.S. is not dependent on foreign sources for its beef supply. About 94 percent of the beef consumed in the U.S. is produced domestically; only six percent is imported. Central America and Brazil account for only about 10 percent of the imports. Thus, about 0.6 percent of all beef consumed in the U.S. comes from rainforest areas. No beef from Brazil ends up in fast food hamburgers, because Brazil exports only cooked or canned beef products (such as canned corned beef) to the U.S.

Central American beef may be used in hamburgers, but it constitutes no more than 0.35 percent of all beef consumed in the U.S. Most hamburger imports come from Australia and New Zealand, rather than tropical rainforest areas.

Chapter 32

Are Humans Natural Omnivores?

Human dentition [teeth] is adapted for a generalized diet composed of both plant and animal foods, and human populations show amazing variability in their plant-to-animal food subsistence ratios. However, it is important to recognize that hominids have evolved important metabolic and biochemical adaptations which are indicative of an increasing physiological dependence upon animal-based foods. Further, comprehensive compilations of hunter-gatherer subsistence strategies indicate that whenever it is ecologically possible, humans will almost always consume more animal food than plant food.

Background: Hunter-Gatherer Plant/Animal Subsistence Ratios.

Our laboratory has recently compiled the plant/animal-food subsistence ratio data in the Ethnographic Atlas for all worldwide hunter-gatherer populations which have been studied either historically or

This material is reprinted with permission from, "Metabolic Evidence of Human Adaptation to Increased Carnivory," by Loren Cordain, Ph.D., and is posted on the website, www.beyondveg.com. © 1998 Loren Cordain. All Rights reserved. Loren Cordain, Ph.D. is a professor in the Department of Health and Exercise Science at Colorado State University. Additional information about the concepts introduced in this article can be found in *The Paleo Diet: Lose Weight and Get Healthy by Eating the Food You Were Designed to Eat*, by Loren Cordain, Ph.D. (John Wiley and Sons, 2001). Full text of this document, including references, can be found at http://www.beyondveg.com/cordain-l/metab-carn/metabolic-carnivory-1a.shtml.

by contemporary anthropologists. The analysis shows that in the majority (61.3%) of worldwide hunter-gatherers, gathered plant food represents 35% or less of the total food utilized. Only 2.2% of the world's hunter-gatherers derive 66% or more of their total foods from plants. Further, not a single hunter-gather population derives 86% or more of its total calories from plant foods.

The most frequently occurring (mode) plant/animal subsistence ratio for worldwide hunter-gatherers is 16–25% plant/75–84% animal, and the median value is 26–35% plant/65–74% animal. These values corroborate five careful modern studies of hunter-gatherers showing a mean energy (caloric) intake from animal-food sources to be 59%.

Comparing the Human Gut with Ape Guts and Biochemical Adaptations of Carnivores

Pongids (the primates that humans are most closely related to), because their diet is largely plant-based, must maintain large and metabolically active guts to process the fibrous plant foods which compose over 93% or greater of their dietary intake. In contrast, the human gut is much smaller and less metabolically active than the ape gut. Presumably this adaptation (reduction in gut size and metabolic activity) evolved in humans because the inclusion of nutrient-dense, animal-based foods by our early hominid ancestors allowed the selective pressure for a large, metabolically active gut to be relaxed.

In addition to the smaller gut that humans maintain relative to apes, there are other metabolic and biochemical clues which point to increased utilization of animal food by humans over our evolutionary history. By evaluating the metabolic and biochemical dietary adaptations of cats (obligate carnivores) and those in humans (omnivores), it becomes apparent that evolution has shaped both hominid and feline metabolic machinery towards a diet in which animal food was predominant.

Obligate carnivores, such as cats, must obtain all of their nutrients from the flesh of other animals and have therefore evolved certain biochemical adaptations which are indicative of their total dietary dependence upon animal-based foods. Most of these biochemical adaptations involve either the loss (or reduced activity) of certain enzymes required for the synthesis of essential nutrients. These adaptations generally occurred because the evolutionary selection pressure to maintain these metabolic pathways was relaxed as cats gradually increased the amount of animal food in their diet as they evolutionarily progressed from omnivory into obligate carnivory.

Taurine

Taurine is an amino acid which is not found in any plant-based food and which is an essential nutrient in all mammalian cells. Herbivores are able to synthesize taurine from precursor amino acids derived from plants, whereas cats have completely lost the ability to synthesize taurine. Since all animal-based foods (except cow's milk) are rich sources of taurine, cats have been able to relax the selective pressure required for taurine synthesis because they obtain all of this nutrient that they need from their exclusive meat-based diet.

Humans, unlike cats, still maintain the ability to synthesize taurine in the liver from precursor substances; however, this ability is quite limited and inefficient when compared to herbivores. Vegan vegetarians following diets devoid of animal products display low levels of both plasma and urinary taurine—levels which are indicative of the poor ability of humans to synthesize taurine. Similar to cats, this inability to efficiently synthesize taurine has come about because the selective pressure to produce this amino acid has been gradually reduced due to humankind's long reliance upon animal food, a food which is quite high in taurine.

20- and 22-Carbon Fatty Acid Requirements

Plant-based foods contain 18-carbon fatty acids of both the omega-3 and omega-6 families, but are virtually devoid of the 20- and 22-carbon fatty acids that are required for the normal functioning of all mammalian cells, whether the mammal is an herbivore or carnivore. Herbivores have evolved hepatic (liver) enzymes (desaturases and elongases) which allow these precursor, plant-based 18-carbon fatty acids to be chain-elongated and desaturated to their 20- and 22-carbon products.

Cats have extremely low levels of the enzymes required to make 20- and 22-carbon fatty acids from 18-carbon fatty acids. Again, the selection pressure to synthesize 20- and 22-carbon lipids (fatty acids) has been almost entirely removed because cats obtain sufficient quantities of these long-chain fatty acids by eating animal tissues which are rich sources of these lipids. Humans, though not as inefficient as the cat, also have relatively inefficient elongase and desaturase enzymes. Again, this metabolic change has occurred largely because the need to desaturate and chain-elongate 18-carbon plant fatty acids to their 20- and 22-carbon products has been reduced because humans, like cats, have obtained a large portion of their 20- and 22-carbon lipids directly by eating other animal tissues.

271

Vitamin A Synthesis

All animals, whether herbivore or carnivore, require vitamin A. Vitamin A is not found in any plant-based food; consequently, herbivores must synthesize it in the liver from beta-carotene consumed from plant-based foods. Cats have lost the ability to synthesize vitamin A from beta-carotene, and must obtain all of their vitamin A from the organs (liver, kidney) of their prey. Again, cats have lost the ability to synthesize vitamin A because the selective pressure (need) to provide adaptive energy for the synthesis of proteins to catalyze the production of vitamin A was reduced as cats progressively increased the amount of animal foods in their diets.

Recently, it has been shown that humans have a limited capacity to absorb beta-carotene in plants (the bioavailability of beta-carotene from plants is low for humans compared to its bioavailability from other sources), presumably because humans, like cats, have consumed vitamin A-rich animal food sources for eons and are in a transitional state from omnivory to obligate carnivory.

Vitamin B_{12}

Vitamin B_{12} is an essential nutrient for both herbivorous and carnivorous mammals. Because B_{12} is not found in higher plants, herbivorous mammals must solely rely upon absorption of B_{12} from bacteria that synthesize it in their gut. Cats can neither synthesize B_{12} nor absorb it from their gut; consequently they have become wholly dependent upon animal flesh as their source for this essential nutrient.

Humans, like cats, cannot depend on the absorption of bacterially produced vitamin B_{12} from the gut, and are reliant upon animal-based sources of this essential vitamin, since it does not occur in a biologically active form in any of the plant foods which humans normally eat. While some viable B_{12} is synthesized in the human colon, the site of absorption is at the ileum, which is "upstream" from the colon at the lower end of the small intestine; thus for humans, B_{12} synthesized in the colon is unavailable and must come from the food eaten. Regarding possible B_{12} synthesis in the small intestine above the ileum, the consensus of scientific literature indicates any amounts that may potentially be produced are not significant or reliable enough to serve as a dependable or sole source for most individuals.

Additionally, while most cases of B_{12} deficiency in omnivores are due to problems of impaired absorption rather than a deficiency of nutritional intake, the opposite situation prevails in vegetarians eating only minimal amounts of animal by-products.

Further, studies in vegans have shown that despite physiological recycling and conservation mechanisms that become increasingly efficient as B_{12} intake falls below normal daily requirements—so that very little is lost from the body—the likelihood is high that B_{12} deficiency will eventually develop (after 20 years or more) in pure vegans who refrain without fail from ingesting any animal-based products or do not take B_{12} supplements.

Recent work has delineated four stages of inadequate B_{12} levels in strict vegetarians. Vegans in early Stage I depletion—prior to ongoing depletion of stores and the declining blood levels of Stage II, biochemical deficiency and impaired DNA synthesis of Stage III, and clinical deficiencies of Stage IV—are able to maintain normal serum B_{12} levels. However, this occurs by drawing from stored reserves in the liver and elsewhere which gradually become depleted, eventually to the point where actual deficiency develops many years later in those who maintain strict habits.

It is this negative metabolic B_{12} balance which occurs soon after exogenous B_{12} ceases to be ingested in appreciable quantities, many years prior to actual deficiency, which points to the human requirement for animal-based B_{12} sources if one is to maintain a positive B_{12} balance. One need not show actual cases of deficiency and end-stage megaloblastic anemia, but only the trend of long-term negative B_{12} balance, to demonstrate the human metabolic need for animal-based foods to maintain a neutral or positive homeostatic balance.

It is now possible to determine negative homeostatic B_{12} balance directly by distinguishing and measuring levels of the two forms in which B_{12} is carried in the blood: either bound to the transcobalamin II "delivery" molecule (called TCII, for short), or bound to the haptocorrin molecule which is a form of "circulating storage." Haptocorrin maintains equilibrium with body stores, meaning that haptocorrin levels reflect current reserve stores of B_{12}. TCII, however, being the "delivery" molecule for B_{12}, transports and gives up its B_{12} to cells that are actively using B_{12} in DNA synthesis, and has a half-life in the blood of only 6 minutes. Thus, when exogenous intake of B_{12} falls below normal, levels of TCII-carried B_{12} begin to reflect the deficit rapidly, and subnormal levels will show up within one week, demonstrating negative B_{12} balance.

It is probable, therefore, that vegans with long-term normal B_{12} balance are ingesting—inadvertently or otherwise—at least small amounts of B_{12}, if not from supplements, then from unreported animal-based

273

sources in their food or contaminated by such sources. (In one study of vegans for which this has been observed, the cause was due to eating unwashed vegetables that had been grown in gardens containing intentionally manured soils, from which the B_{12} came. Ironically, the manure in this case was their own excrement, which as pointed out above harbors bacteria that produce B_{12} in the human colon—where B_{12} cannot be absorbed. Not unless, of course, it is reingested as in the unintentional coprophagy [ingestion of fecal material] occurring in this instance, so that it can pass back through the small intestine again to the ileum where B_{12} is actually absorbed.)

An indication of the masking effect of previously stored B_{12} reserves in obscuring ongoing negative B_{12} balance can be seen in long-term vegan mothers and their infants. Such mothers may maintain blood levels of haptocorrin B_{12} in the normal range for lengthy periods (years) due to increasingly efficient recycling of B_{12} as their reserve stores become depleted, and in adult vegans with such improved B_{12} reabsorption, such clinical deficiency may take 20–30 years to manifest. However, infants of such mothers are born with almost no reserve stores (little or none are available in the mother's body to pass on to them) and go into clinical deficiency much more rapidly.

In summary, the absence of the ability of humans to absorb bacterially produced B_{12} in the colon, and the evidence that strictly behaving vegans will show negative TCII-carried B_{12} balance even when total serum levels are in the normal range, is indicative of the long evolutionary history of animal-based foods in our diet.

Recap

These metabolic and biochemical adaptations in humans in response to increasingly meat-based diets, as well as the anthropological evidence provided by both contemporary and historical studies of hunter-gatherer diets, provide strong evidence for the central role of meat and animal tissues in the human diet. Although it is true that human populations can survive under broad plant/animal subsistence ratios, the consensus evidence supports the notion that whenever it was ecologically possible, animal calories would have always represented the majority of the total daily energy intake.

Chapter 33

Warning: Vegetarian Diets Can Become Obsessive for Teen Girls

Your daughter's seemingly healthy eating habits could be masking a deadly eating disorder.

At her cousin's wedding, Melissa, 14, looked around at the female guests and imagined what the kids at school would say: What a bunch of porkers. "Right there," says Melissa, who was teased for being slightly overweight in junior high school, "I decided I was going to be different."

As she entered high school, Melissa became a vegetarian to cut the calories and fat that her family's meat and fried food diet was heavy on. People praised her slimmer appearance as well as her self-discipline in following such an apparently strict diet. Melissa continued to lose weight, believing that the slimmer she became, the more she would impress people. But by the following spring, it was obvious to everyone but Melissa that she had crossed a line and become anorexic.

This is not to say that every girl who decides to go veg is headed for an eating disorder. "For most teens, becoming vegetarian is a healthy choice," says Judy Krizmanic, author of *Teen's Vegetarian Cookbook* (Viking, 1999). But as with any significant change a child makes, the parents must be sure she's doing it correctly—and with the right motivation. "Wanting to be healthy, being concerned about the environment or animals are all good reasons," says Nancy Logue,

This article originally appeared as "Vegetarian? Or Anorexic?" by Ann Lien in *Vegetarian Times* (September 1999). 1999 Sabot Publishing. Reprinted with permission.

Ph.D., director of the Renfrew Center, an eating disorder clinic in Philadelphia. "But when a lifestyle is pursued to extremes, or extreme behavior becomes attached to it, there's potential for a serious problem."

Anorexia, a pathological fear of weight gain that leads to excessive weight loss, often manifests itself with an obsessive-compulsive personality. Vegetarianism is not simply a lifestyle choice for an anorexic girl. What and how she eats become the daily yardstick by which she measures her worth. Common beliefs among anorexics include, "If I'm a good person, I can have five extra bites at dinner" and "I'm a strong person because I can eat less than other people. Everyone else is weak."

A report in the *Archives of Pediatric Adolescent Medicine* (August, 1997) analyzed how teens hide eating disorders behind the healthy facade of vegetarianism. The study found that while veg teens ate more fruits and vegetables than their omnivorous peers, they were also twice as likely to diet frequently, four times as likely to diet intensively and eight times as likely to abuse laxatives—all behaviors associated with eating disorders.

The National Association of Anorexia and Associated Disorders estimates that more than 8 million Americans suffer from full-blown eating disorders and that 86 percent of them develop the problem before age 20. While anorexia is relatively rare, occurring in just 3 percent of women, its consequences can be dire. "It has the highest mortality rate among eating disorders," says Monika Woolsey, M.S., R.D., editor of the *After the Diet Newsletter* (www.afterthediet.com).

One reason eating-disorders begin in adolescence is because those years are a time of intense pressure—from friends, parents, teachers, and society. A key developmental issue for teens is identity, and they begin to struggle with questions like "Who am I?" and "Where do I fit in?" According to Amy Tuttle, R.D., L.S.W., director of nutrition services at the Renfrew Center, "Young girls are looking outside of themselves for the first time for guidance on identity, and what do they see? That they are supposed to be thin. That women are supposed to have petite needs." To have a strong appetite—for food, competition or recognition—is still largely considered unfeminine in our culture. For girls, the external pressure to be thin and popular combines with an internal drive to excel and be perfect and makes them especially vulnerable to anorexia. (Not surprisingly, 90 percent of all anorexics are female.) According to the Renfrew Center, 53 percent of American 13-year-old girls are already unhappy with their bodies. And researchers have found negative body images among girls as young as 9.

Growing Needs

Teenage girls usually don't shoot up six inches over a summer the way boys often do, but they still need nearly as much food to fuel their growing bodies. And they need the right mix of calories, notes Tuttle. In general, girls aged 11 to 18 need 2,200 calories a day—more if they're physically active. Of that, 40 to 50 percent should come from carbohydrates, 20 to 30 percent from protein and no more than 30 percent from the good fats found in olive oil, avocados, and nuts. "Teenage girls should also get plenty of calcium, iron, zinc, and vitamins D and B_{12}," says Tuttle. Here's what the National Academy of Sciences recommends your daughter take in every day:

- Calcium: 1,200 to 1,500 milligrams (mg.). Nondairy sources include broccoli, legumes, seeds, leafy greens like kale, collards, mustard and bok choy, and calcium fortified foods.

- Iron: 15 to 18 mg. The best sources are from the dried bean family, which includes lentils, lima, and kidney beans. To enhance absorption, include vitamin C-rich foods like cantaloupe, broccoli, and tomatoes with your meals.

- Vitamin D: 800 international units (IU). Getting 15 minutes of sun exposure without sun screen, two to three times a week, will allow the body to make enough on its own.

- Vitamin B_{12}: 3 micrograms (mcg.). Sources include fortified breakfast cereals, soy milk, veggie burgers, eggs, and dairy products. Although seaweed, algae, spirulina, and fermented products (like tempeh) contain B_{12}, it is a form that is not easily assimilated into the body. Supplements are another good source.

- Zinc: 15 mg. Found in whole grains and whole-grain breads. Grains lose zinc when processed to make refined (white) flour.

A Healthy Start

It's just as important to provide your daughter with a supportive environment as it is to educate her on good nutrition.

Be a good role model. Becoming a vegetarian should be enjoyable. Emphasize that a balanced diet has room for treats and that there's no need to deprive oneself.

Be aware of your own prejudices toward overweight or thin people that may fuel her insecurity. "One of the most effective things we can do is to stop judging people by what they eat and what they look like," says Woolsey.

If other family members eat meat, create vegetarian nights for everyone. Let your daughter decide what the menu will be and let her help you cook it. This will connect her to healthful food and teach her to be responsible for her new lifestyle.

Compliment her on her skills and attributes, not her size or weight.

Don't compare her with others, whether it's about appearance or schoolwork.

Don't refer to foods as either good or bad. That only reinforces the all-or-nothing thinking of an anorexic.

Warning Signs

People often lose some weight when they go veg because they're still learning how to eat healthfully. If you notice some of the following symptoms, however, your daughter may have a problem:

- Continued weight loss after the first two or three months of being vegetarian.

- Distorted body image. She repeatedly comments that she's fat or still needs to lose weight, even if she's thin or of a healthy weight.

- Regularly skipping meals or denying she's hungry.

- Complaints about feeling bloated or nauseated when she eats normal portions.

- Elimination of other foods besides meat, especially those that contain fat, like peanut butter, tofu, soy meat substitutes, breads, pasta, and other nutritious foods.

- Ritualistic behavior. "Anorexics typically eat their food in a specific way, whether it's eating in a circle around the plate or cutting everything into several tiny pieces to make the food last," says Woolsey. "Or they may refuse to eat if food isn't served exactly on time."

- Compulsive calorie- and fat-gram counting. "It's hard to tell the difference between someone who's trying to educate herself and someone who's become obsessive," says Woolsey. But sometimes it's obvious. "One of my patients spent over an hour choosing a salad dressing because she had to read every single bottle in the store."

- Obsessive and/or compulsive behavior. Teens are known for being passionate about whatever interests them at the moment, but it's not normal to spend hours rearranging canned food, setting aside the number of beans she can have that night or brushing her teeth five times a day.

- Frequently weighing herself.

- Thinning hair. She may also grow a layer of downy body hair.

- Complaints of being cold even when room temperature is normal.

The Right Course

If you think your daughter may be anorexic, the last thing you want to do is broach the subject in an accusatory way. "Focus on the specific behavior that can't be debated and how it makes you, as the parent, feel," advises Woolsey. For example, you might say, "When you only eat a banana and an apple for dinner, I'm scared that you aren't getting the important nutrients you need."

Many teens find that vegetarianism is a safe and appropriate way to assert their own identity. Because an anorexic's identity is pathologically connected to her diet, you need to show her that you respect her. Otherwise, she will only hear blame and criticism and shut you out. What else you can do:

- Learn everything you can about eating disorders. Anorexics often go through phases of bulimia (binging and purging), so it's essential to know the warning signs for both.

- Pick a good time and place to discuss your concerns. Make sure it's just the two of you and that there are no distractions (such as a ringing telephone) or lingering tensions from a recent argument.

- Offer her the opportunity to talk with a nutritional therapist, one who understands the emotional aspects of eating. Tell her that you want to make sure she has all the right information, so you'd like to hire an expert to work with her. If teens first build trust with a nutritional therapist, they're usually more receptive when the therapist feels it's time to bring in a doctor and/or a psychiatrist.

- The longer anorexia lasts, the more difficult the recovery. Don't be embarrassed to take your daughter to a physician sooner rather than later. A doctor can determine whether she's developing an eating disorder by checking, among other things, her progress on the growth chart and whether her periods have become irregular.

For the most part, becoming a vegetarian is a great way for teens to explore new foods and gain new experiences. As for Melissa, she got the treatment she needed and today is still a vegetarian. However, she continues to struggle against social pressures to be thin and in control of at least one thing—her body. "It's tempting to become alarmed when you hear the facts," says Krizmanic. "But as long as you talk to your teens and provide them with the skills and the resources they need, becoming a vegetarian should be a positive experience."

Part Six

Additional Help
and Information

Chapter 34

Glossary of Terms Related to Vegetarianism

antioxidant: An agent that inhibits oxidation; any of numerous chemical substances, including certain natural body products and nutrients, that can neutralize the oxidant effect of free radicals and other substances.

bioavailability: The physiological availability of a given amount of a drug, as distinct from its chemical potency; proportion of the administered dose which is absorbed into the bloodstream.

carnivorous: Flesh-eating; subsisting on animals as food.

cholesterol: The most abundant steroid in animal tissues, especially in bile and gallstones, and present in food, especially food rich in animal fats; circulates in the plasma complexed to proteins of various densities and plays an important role in the pathogenesis of atheroma formation in arteries.

coprophagia: The eating of excrement.

dentition: The natural teeth, as considered collectively, in the dental arch; may be deciduous, permanent, or mixed.

dietary fiber: the plant polysaccharides and lignin that are resistant to hydrolysis by the digestive enzymes in humans.

This chapter contains terms excerpted from *Stedman's Electronic Medical Dictionary*, copyright 2000 Lippincott Williams & Wilkins. Reprinted with permission.

fat: A greasy, soft-solid material, found in animal tissues and many plants, composed of a mixture of glycerol esters; together with oils they make up the homolipids.

fatty acid: Any acid derived from fats by hydrolysis (e.g., oleic, palmitic, or stearic acids); any long-chain monobasic organic acid; they accumulate in disorders associated with the peroxisomes.

folate: A salt or ester of folic acid.

folic acid: The growth factor for *Lactobacillus casei*, and a member of the vitamin B complex necessary for the normal production of red blood cells. It is a hemopoietic vitamin present in peptide linkages in liver, green vegetables, and yeast; used to treat folate deficiency and megaloblastic anemia, and to assist in lowering homocysteine levels.

gluten: The insoluble protein (prolamines) constituent of wheat and other grains; a mixture of gliadin, glutenin, prolamins, and other proteins; the presence of gluten allows flour to rise.

hepatic: Relating to the liver.

herbivorous: Feeding on plants.

Hominidae: The primate family, which includes modern humans (Homo sapiens) and several fossil groups.

homocystine: The disulfide resulting from the mild oxidation of homocysteine; an analog of cystine.

hydrogenation: Addition of hydrogen to a compound, especially to an unsaturated fat or fatty acid; thus, soft fats or oils are solidified or "hardened."

lacto-ovo-vegetarian: a vegetarian who consumes dairy products and eggs but does not eat animal flesh.

lactose: A disaccharide present in mammalian milk; obtained from cow's milk and used in modified milk preparation, in food for infants and convalescents, and in pharmaceutical preparations; large doses act as an osmotic diuretic and as a laxative. Human milk contains 6.7% lactose.

lactovegetarian: A vegetarian who consumes milk and dairy products but not eggs or meats or seafood.

lipid: "Fat-soluble," an operational term describing a solubility characteristic, not a chemical substance, i.e., denoting substances extracted from animal or vegetable cells by nonpolar solvents; included in the heterogeneous collection of materials thus extractable are fatty acids, glycerides and glyceryl ethers, phospholipids, sphingolipids, long-chain alcohols and waxes, terpenes, steroids, and "fat-soluble" vitamins such as A, D, and E.

lipoprotein: Any complex or compound containing both lipid and protein. Lipoproteins are important constituents of biological membranes and of myelin. Conjugation with protein facilitates transport of lipids, which are hydrophobic, in the aqueous medium of the plasma. The principal classes by density are chylomicrons, which transport dietary cholesterol and triglycerides from the intestine to the liver and other tissues; very low density lipoproteins (VLDL), which transport triglycerides from intestine and liver to muscle and adipose tissue; low density lipoproteins (LDL), which transport cholesterol to tissues other than the liver; and high density lipoproteins (HDL), which transport cholesterol to the liver for excretion in bile. The properties of these and other plasma lipoproteins

metabolism: The sum of the chemical and physical changes occurring in tissue, consisting of anabolism, those reactions that convert small molecules into large, and catabolism, those reactions that convert large molecules into small, including both endogenous large molecules as well as biodegradation of xenobiotics.

obligate: Without an alternative system or pathway.

omnivorous: Living on food of all kinds, upon both animal and vegetable food.

plasma: The proteinaceous fluid (noncellular) portion of the circulating blood, as distinguished from the serum obtained after coagulation.

precursor: That which precedes another or from which another is derived, applied especially to a physiologically inactive substance that is converted to an active enzyme, vitamin, hormone, etc., or to a chemical substance that is built into a larger structure in the course of synthesizing the latter.

protein: Macromolecules consisting of long sequences of α-amino acids [H_2N-CHR-COOH] in peptide (amide) linkage (elimination of H_2O between the α-NH_2 and α-COOH of successive residues). Protein is three-fourths of the dry weight of most cell matter and is involved in structures, hormones, enzymes, muscle contraction, immunologic response, and essential life functions. The amino acids involved are generally the 20 α-amino acids (glycine, L-alanine, etc.) recognized by the genetic code.

saturate: To dissolve a substance up to that concentration beyond which the addition of more results in two phases.

soybean: The bean of the climbing herb *Glycine soja* or *G. hispida* (family *Leguminosae*); a bean rich in protein and containing little starch; it is the source of soybean oil; soybean flour is used in preparing a bread for diabetics, in feeding formulas for infants who are unable to tolerate cow's milk, and for adults allergic to cow's milk.

unsaturated: Not saturated; denoting a solution in which the solvent is capable of dissolving more of the solute.

vitamin: One of a group of organic substances, present in minute amounts in natural foodstuffs, that are essential to normal metabolism; insufficient amounts in the diet may cause deficiency diseases.

Chapter 35

Animal Ingredients and Their Alternatives

People for the Ethical Treatment of Animals' (PETA) list of animal ingredients and their alternatives helps consumers avoid animal ingredients in food, cosmetics, and other products. Please note, however, that it is not all-inclusive. There are thousands of technical and patented names for ingredient variations. Furthermore, many ingredients known by one name can be of animal, vegetable, or synthetic origin. If you have a question regarding an ingredient in a product, call the manufacturer. Good sources of additional information are the *Consumer's Dictionary of Cosmetic Ingredients*, the *Consumer's Dictionary of Food Additives*, or an unabridged dictionary. All of these are available at most libraries.

Adding to the confusion over whether or not an ingredient is of animal origin is the fact that many companies have removed the word animal from their ingredient labels to avoid putting off consumers. For example, rather than use the term *hydrolyzed animal protein*, companies may use another term such as *hydrolyzed collagen*. Simple for them, but frustrating for the caring consumer.

Some animal ingredients do not wind up in the final product but are used in the manufacturing process. For example, in the production of some refined sugars, bone char is used to whiten the sugar; in some wines and beers, isinglass (from the swim bladders of fish) is used as a clearing agent.

From "Animal Ingredients and their Alternatives," a fact sheet produced by People for the Ethical Treatment of Animals (PETA). © PETA. Reprinted with Permission. http://www.peta-online.org/mc/facts/fsm16.html.

Kosher symbols and markings also add to the confusion and are not reliable indicators on which vegans or vegetarians should base their purchasing decisions. This issue is complex, but the *K* or *Kosher* symbols basically mean that the food manufacturing process was overseen by a rabbi, who theoretically ensures that it meets Hebrew dietary laws. The food also may not contain both dairy products and meat, but it may contain one or the other. *P* or *Parve* means the product contains no meat or dairy products but may contain fish or eggs. *D*, as in *Kosher D*, means that the product either contains dairy or was made with dairy machinery. For example, a chocolate and peanut candy may be marked *Kosher D* even if it doesn't contain dairy because the non-dairy chocolate was manufactured on machinery that also made milk chocolate. For questions regarding other symbols, please contact the Orthodox Union (212-563-4000) or other Jewish organizations or publications.

Thousands of products on store shelves have labels that are hard to decipher. It's nearly impossible to be perfectly vegan, but it's getting easier to avoid products with animal ingredients. Our list will give you a good working knowledge of the most common animal-derived ingredients and their alternatives, allowing you to make decisions that will save animals' lives.

Adrenaline: Hormone from adrenal glands of hogs, cattle, and sheep. In medicine. Alternatives: synthetics.

Alanine: (See Amino Acids.)

Albumen: In eggs, milk, muscles, blood, and many vegetable tissues and fluids. In cosmetics, albumen is usually derived from egg whites and used as a coagulating agent. May cause allergic reaction. In cakes, cookies, candies, etc. Egg whites sometimes used in clearing wines. Derivative: Albumin.

Albumin: (See Albumen.)

Alcloxa: (See Allantoin.)

Aldioxa: (See Allantoin.)

Aliphatic Alcohol: (See Lanolin and Vitamin A.)

Allantoin: Uric acid from cows, most mammals. Also in many plants (especially comfrey). In cosmetics (especially creams and lotions) and used in treatment of wounds and ulcers. Derivatives: Alcloxa, Aldioxa. Alternatives: extract of comfrey root, synthetics.

Alligator Skin: (See Leather.)

Alpha-Hydroxy Acids: Any one of several acids used as an exfoliant and in anti-wrinkle products. Lactic acid may be animal-derived (see Lactic Acid). Alternatives: glycolic acid, citric acid, and salicylic acid are plant- or fruit-derived.

Ambergris: From whale intestines. Used as a fixative in making perfumes and as a flavoring in foods and beverages. Alternatives: synthetic or vegetable fixatives.

Amino Acids: The building blocks of protein in all animals and plants. In cosmetics, vitamins, supplements, shampoos, etc. Alternatives: synthetics, plant sources.

Aminosuccinate Acid: (See Aspartic Acid.)

Angora: Hair from the Angora rabbit or goat. Used in clothing. Alternatives: synthetic fibers.

Animal Fats and Oils: In foods, cosmetics, etc. Highly allergenic. Alternatives: olive oil, wheat germ oil, coconut oil, flaxseed oil, almond oil, safflower oil, etc.

Animal Hair: In some blankets, mattresses, brushes, furniture, etc. Alternatives: vegetable and synthetic fibers.

Arachidonic Acid: A liquid unsaturated fatty acid that is found in liver, brain, glands, and fat of animals and humans. Generally isolated from animal liver. Used in companion animal food for nutrition and in skin creams and lotions to soothe eczema and rashes. Alternatives: synthetics, aloe vera, tea tree oil, calendula ointment.

Arachidyl Proprionate: A wax that can be from animal fat. Alternatives: peanut or vegetable oil.

Aspartic Acid: Aminosuccinate Acid. Can be animal or plant source (e.g., molasses). Sometimes synthesized for commercial purposes.

Bee Pollen: Microsporic grains in seed plants gathered by bees then collected from the legs of bees. Causes allergic reactions in some people.

In nutritional supplements, shampoos, toothpastes, deodorants. Alternatives: synthetics, plant amino acids, pollen collected from plants.

Bee Products: Produced by bees for their own use. Bees are selectively bred. Culled bees are killed. A cheap sugar is substituted for their stolen honey. Millions die as a result. Their legs are often torn off by pollen-collection trapdoors.

Beeswax: Honeycomb. Wax obtained from melting honeycomb with boiling water, straining it, and cooling it. From virgin bees. Very cheap and widely used but harmful to the skin. In lipsticks and many other cosmetics (especially face creams, lotions, mascara, eye creams and shadows, face makeups, nail whiteners, lip balms, etc.). Derivatives: Cera Flava. Alternatives: paraffin, vegetable oils, and fats. Ceresin, aka ceresine, aka earth wax. (Made from the mineral ozokerite. Replaces beeswax in cosmetics. Also used to wax paper, to make polishing cloths, in dentistry for taking wax impressions, and in candle-making.) Also, carnauba wax (from the Brazilian palm tree; used in many cosmetics, including lipstick; rarely causes allergic reactions). Candelilla wax (from candelilla plants; used in many cosmetics, including lipstick; also in the manufacture of rubber and phonograph records, in waterproofing and writing inks; no known toxicity). Japan wax (Vegetable wax. Japan tallow. Fat from the fruit of a tree grown in Japan and China.).

Benzoic Acid: In almost all vertebrates and in berries. Used as a preservative in mouthwashes, deodorants, creams, aftershave lotions, etc. Alternatives: cranberries, gum benzoin (tincture) from the aromatic balsamic resin from trees grown in China, Sumatra, Thailand, and Cambodia.

Beta Carotene: (See Carotene.)

Biotin: Vitamin H. Vitamin B Factor. In every living cell and in larger amounts in milk and yeast. Used as a texturizer in cosmetics, shampoos, and creams. Alternatives: plant sources.

Blood: From any slaughtered animal. Used as adhesive in plywood, also found in cheese-making, foam rubber, intravenous feedings, and medicines. Possibly in foods such as lecithin. Alternatives: synthetics, plant sources.

Boar Bristles: Hair from wild or captive hogs. In natural toothbrushes and bath and shaving brushes. Alternatives: vegetable fibers, nylon, the peelu branch or peelu gum (Asian, available in the U.S.; its juice replaces toothpaste).

Bone Char: Animal bone ash. Used in bone china and often to make sugar white. Serves as the charcoal used in aquarium filters. Alternatives: synthetic tribasic calcium phosphate.

Bone Meal: Crushed or ground animal bones. In some fertilizers. In some vitamins and supplements as a source of calcium. In toothpastes. Alternatives: plant mulch, vegetable compost, dolomite, clay, vegetarian vitamins.

Calciferol: (See Vitamin D.)

Calfskin: (See Leather.)

Caprylamine Oxide: (See Caprylic Acid.)

Capryl Betaine: (See Caprylic Acid.)

Caprylic Acid: A liquid fatty acid from cow's or goat's milk. Also from palm and coconut oil, other plant oils. In perfumes, soaps. Derivatives: Caprylic Triglyceride, Caprylamine Oxide, Capryl Betaine. Alternatives: plant sources.

Caprylic Triglyceride: (See Caprylic Acid.)

Carbamide: (See Urea.)

Carmine: Cochineal. Carminic Acid. Red pigment from the crushed female cochineal insect. Reportedly, 70,000 beetles must be killed to produce one pound of this red dye. Used in cosmetics, shampoos, red apple sauce, and other foods (including red lollipops and food coloring). May cause allergic reaction. Alternatives: beet juice (used in powders, rouges, shampoos; no known toxicity); alkanet root (from the root of this herb-like tree; used as a red dye for inks, wines, lip balms, etc.; no known toxicity. Can also be combined to make a copper or blue coloring). (See Colors.)

Carminic Acid: (See Carmine.)

Carotene: Provitamin A. Beta Carotene. A pigment found in many animal tissues and in all plants. Used as a coloring in cosmetics and in the manufacture of vitamin A.

Casein: Caseinate. Sodium Caseinate. Milk protein. In non-dairy creamers, soy cheese, many cosmetics, hair preparations, beauty masks. Alternatives: soy protein, soy milk, and other vegetable milks.

Caseinate: (See Casein.)

Cashmere: Wool from the Kashmir goat. Used in clothing. Alternatives: synthetic fibers.

Castor: Castoreum. Creamy substance with strong odor from muskrat and beaver genitals. Used as a fixative in perfume and incense. Alternatives: synthetics, plant castor oil.

Castoreum: (See Castor.)

Catgut: Tough string from the intestines of sheep, horses, etc. Used for surgical sutures. Also for stringing tennis rackets and musical instruments, etc. Alternatives: nylon and other synthetic fibers.

Cera Flava: (See Beeswax.)

Cerebrosides: Fatty acids and sugars found in the covering of nerves. May include tissue from brain:

Cetyl Alcohol: Wax found in spermaceti from sperm whales or dolphins. Alternatives: Vegetable cetyl alcohol (e.g., coconut), synthetic spermaceti.

Cetyl Palmitate: (See Spermaceti.)

Chitosan: A fiber derived from crustacean shells. Used as a lipid binder in diet products, in hair, oral, and skin care products, antiperspirants, and deodorants. Alternatives: raspberries, yams, legumes, dried apricots, and many other fruits and vegetables.

Cholesterin: (See Lanolin.)

Cholesterol: A steroid alcohol in all animal fats and oils, nervous tissue, egg yolk, and blood. Can be derived from lanolin. In cosmetics, eye creams, shampoos, etc. Alternatives: solid complex alcohols (sterols) from plant sources.

Choline Bitartrate: (See Lecithin.)

Civet: Unctuous secretion painfully scraped from a gland very near the genital organs of civet cats. Used as a fixative in perfumes. Alternatives: (See alternatives to Musk.).

Cochineal: (See Carmine.)

Cod Liver Oil: (See Marine Oil.)

Collagen: Fibrous protein in vertebrates. Usually derived from animal tissue. Can't affect the skin's own collagen. An allergen. Alternatives: soy protein, almond oil, amla oil (see alternative to Keratin), etc.

Colors: Dyes. Pigments from animal, plant, and synthetic sources used to color foods, cosmetics, and other products. Cochineal is from insects. Widely used FD&C and D&C colors are coaltar (bituminous coal) derivatives that are continuously tested on animals due to their carcinogenic properties. Alternatives: grapes, beets, turmeric, saffron, carrots, chlorophyll, annatto, alkanet.

Corticosteroid: (See Cortisone.)

Cortisone: Corticosteroid. Hormone from adrenal glands. Widely used in medicine. Alternatives: synthetics.

Cysteine, L-Form: An amino acid from hair which can come from animals. Used in hair-care products and creams, in some bakery products, and in wound-healing formulations. Alternatives: plant sources.

Cystine: An amino acid found in urine and horsehair. Used as a nutritional supplement and in emollients. Alternatives: plant sources.

Dexpanthenol: (See Panthenol.)

Diglycerides: (See Monoglycerides and Glycerin.)

Dimethyl Stearamine: (See Stearic Acid.)

Down: Goose or duck insulating feathers. From slaughtered or cruelly exploited geese. Used as an insulator in quilts, parkas, sleeping bags, pillows, etc. Alternatives: polyester and synthetic substitutes, kapok (silky fibers from the seeds of some tropical trees) and milkweed seed pod fibers.

Duodenum Substances: From the digestive tracts of cows and pigs. Added to some vitamin tablets. In some medicines. Alternatives: vegetarian vitamins, synthetics.

Dyes: (See Colors.)

Egg Protein: In shampoos, skin preparations, etc. Alternatives: plant proteins.

Elastin: Protein found in the neck ligaments and aortas of cows. Similar to collagen. Can't affect the skin's own elasticity. Alternatives: synthetics, protein from plant tissues.

Emu Oil: From flightless ratite birds native to Australia and now factory farmed. Used in cosmetics and creams. Alternatives: vegetable and plant oils.

Ergocalciferol: (See Vitamin D.)

Ergosterol: (See Vitamin D.)

Estradiol: (See Estrogen.)

Estrogen: Estradiol. Female hormones from pregnant mares. Considered a drug. Can have harmful systemic effects if used by children. Used for reproductive problems and in birth control pills and Premarin, a menopausal drug. In creams, perfumes, and lotions. Has a negligible effect in the creams as a skin restorative; simple vegetable-source emollients are considered better. Alternatives: oral contraceptives and menopausal drugs based on synthetic steroids or phytoestrogens (from plants, especially palm-kernel oil). Menopausal symptoms can also be treated with diet and herbs.

Fats: (See Animal Fats.)

Fatty Acids: Can be one or any mixture of liquid and solid acids such as caprylic, lauric, myristic, oleic, palmitic, and stearic. Used in bubble baths, lipsticks, soap, detergents, cosmetics, food. Alternatives: vegetable-derived acids, soy lecithin, safflower oil, bitter almond oil, sunflower oil, etc.

FD&C Colors: (See Colors.)

Feathers: From exploited and slaughtered birds. Used whole as ornaments or ground up in shampoos. (See Down and Keratin.)

Fish Liver Oil: Used in vitamins and supplements. In milk fortified with vitamin D. Alternatives: yeast extract ergosterol and exposure of skin to sunshine.

Fish Oil: (See Marine Oil.) Fish oil can also be from marine mammals. Used in soap-making.

Fish Scales: Used in shimmery makeups. Alternatives: mica, rayon, synthetic pearl.

Fur: Obtained from animals (usually mink, foxes, or rabbits) cruelly trapped in steel-jaw leghold traps or raised in intensive confinement on fur farms. Alternatives: synthetics. (See Sable Brushes.)

Gel: (See Gelatin.)

Gelatin: Gel. Protein obtained by boiling skin, tendons, ligaments, and/or bones with water. From cows and pigs. Used in shampoos, face masks, and other cosmetics. Used as a thickener for fruit gelatins and puddings (e.g., Jello). In candies, marshmallows, cakes, ice cream, yogurts. On photographic film and in vitamins as a coating and as capsules. Sometimes used to assist in clearing wines. Alternatives: carrageen (carrageenan, Irish moss), seaweeds (algin, agar-agar, kelp used in jellies, plastics, medicine), pectin from fruits, dextrins, locust bean gum, cotton gum, silica gel. Marshmallows were originally made from the root of the marsh mallow plant. Vegetarian capsules are now available from several companies. Digital cameras don't use film.

Glucose Tyrosinase: (See Tyrosine.)

Glycerides: (See Glycerin.)

Glycerin: Glycerol. A byproduct of soap manufacture (normally uses animal fat). In cosmetics, foods, mouthwashes, chewing gum, toothpastes, soaps, ointments, medicines, lubricants, transmission and brake fluid, and plastics. Derivatives: Glycerides, Glyceryls, Glycreth-26, Polyglycerol. Alternatives: vegetable glycerin a byproduct of vegetable oil soap. Derivatives of seaweed, petroleum.

Glycerol: (See Glycerin.)

Glyceryls: (See Glycerin.)

Glycreth-26: (See Glycerin.)

Guanine: Pearl Essence. Obtained from scales of fish. Constituent of ribonucleic acid and deoxyribonucleic acid and found in all animal and plant tissues. In shampoo, nail polish, other cosmetics. Alternatives: leguminous plants, synthetic pearl, or aluminum and bronze particles.

Hide Glue: Same as gelatin but of a cruder impure form. Alternatives: dextrins and synthetic petrochemical-based adhesives. (See Gelatin.)

Honey: Food for bees, made by bees. Can cause allergic reactions. Used as a coloring and an emollient in cosmetics and as a flavoring in foods. Should never be fed to infants. Alternatives: in foods maple syrup, date sugar, syrups made from grains such as barley malt, turbinado sugar, molasses; in cosmetics vegetable colors and oils.

Honeycomb: (See Beeswax.)

Horsehair: (See Animal Hair.)

Hyaluronic Acid: A protein found in umbilical cords and the fluids around the joints. Used in cosmetics: Alternatives: plant oils.

Hydrocortisone: (See Cortisone.)

Hydrolyzed Animal Protein: In cosmetics, especially shampoo and hair treatments. Alternatives: soy protein, other vegetable proteins, amla oil (see alternatives to Keratin).

Imidazolidinyl Urea: (See Urea.)

Insulin: From hog pancreas. Used by millions of diabetics daily. Alternatives: synthetics, vegetarian diet and nutritional supplements, human insulin grown in a lab.

Isinglass: A form of gelatin prepared from the internal membranes of fish bladders. Sometimes used in clearing wines and in foods. Alternatives: bentonite clay, Japanese isinglass, agar-agar (see alternatives to Gelatin), mica, a mineral used in cosmetics.

Isopropyl Lanolate: (See Lanolin.)

Isopropyl Myristate: (See Myristic Acid.)

Isopropyl Palmitate: Complex mixtures of isomers of stearic acid and palmitic acid. (See Stearic Acid.)

Keratin: Protein from the ground-up horns, hooves, feathers, quills, and hair of various animals. In hair rinses, shampoos, permanent wave solutions. Alternatives: almond oil, soy protein, amla oil (from the fruit of an Indian tree), human hair from salons. Rosemary and nettle give body and strand strength to hair.

Lactic Acid: Found in blood and muscle tissue. Also in sour milk, beer, sauerkraut, pickles, and other food products made by bacterial fermentation. Used in skin fresheners, as a preservative, in the formation of plasticizers, etc. Alternative: plant milk sugars, synthetics.

Lactose: Milk sugar from milk of mammals. In eye lotions, foods, tablets, cosmetics, baked goods, medicines. Alternatives: plant milk sugars.

Laneth: (See Lanolin.)

Lanogene: (See Lanolin.)

Lanolin: Lanolin Acids. Wool Fat. Wool Wax. A product of the oil glands of sheep, extracted from their wool. Used as an emollient in many skin care products and cosmetics and in medicines. An allergen with no proven effectiveness. (See Wool for cruelty to sheep.) Derivatives: Aliphatic Alcohols, Cholesterin, Isopropyl Lanolate, Laneth, Lanogene, Lanolin Alcohols, Lanosterols, Sterols, Triterpene Alcohols. Alternatives: plant and vegetable oils.

Lanolin Alcohol: (See Lanolin.)

Lanosterols: (See Lanolin.)

Lard: Fat from hog abdomens. In shaving creams, soaps, cosmetics. In baked goods, French fries, refried beans, and many other foods. Alternatives: pure vegetable fats or oils.

Leather: Suede. Calfskin. Sheepskin. Alligator Skin. Other Types of Skin. Subsidizes the meat industry. Used to make wallets, handbags, furniture and car upholstery, shoes, etc. Alternatives: cotton, canvas, nylon, vinyl, ultrasuede, pleather, other synthetics.

Lecithin: Choline Bitartrate. Waxy substance in nervous tissue of all living organisms. But frequently obtained for commercial purposes from eggs and soybeans. Also from nerve tissue, blood, milk, corn. Choline bitartrate, the basic constituent of lecithin, is in many animal and plant tissues and prepared synthetically. Lecithin can be in eye creams, lipsticks, liquid powders, hand creams, lotions, soaps, shampoos, other cosmetics, and some medicines. Alternatives: soybean lecithin, synthetics.

Linoleic Acid: An essential fatty acid. Used in cosmetics, vitamins. Alternatives: (See alternatives to Fatty Acids.)

Lipase: Enzyme from the stomachs and tongue glands of calves, kids, and lambs. Used in cheese-making and in digestive aids. Alternatives: vegetable enzymes, castor beans.

Lipids: (See Lipoids.)

Lipoids: Lipids. Fat and fat-like substances that are found in animals and plants. Alternatives: vegetable oils.

Marine Oil: From fish or marine mammals (including porpoises). Used in soap-making. Used as a shortening (especially in some margarines), as a lubricant, and in paint. Alternatives: vegetable oils.

Methionine: Essential amino acid found in various proteins (usually from egg albumen and casein). Used as a texturizer and for freshness in potato chips. Alternatives: synthetics.

Milk Protein: Hydrolyzed milk protein. From the milk of cows. In cosmetics, shampoos, moisturizers, conditioners, etc. Alternatives: soy protein, other plant proteins.

Mink Oil: From minks. In cosmetics, creams, etc. Alternatives: vegetable oils and emollients such as avocado oil, almond oil, and jojoba oil.

Monoglycerides: Glycerides. (See Glycerin.) From animal fat. In margarines, cake mixes, candies, foods, etc. In cosmetics. Alternative: vegetable glycerides.

Musk (Oil): Dried secretion painfully obtained from musk deer, beaver, muskrat, civet cat, and otter genitals. Wild cats are kept captive in cages in horrible conditions and are whipped around the genitals to produce the scent; beavers are trapped; deer are shot. In perfumes and in food flavorings. Alternatives: labdanum oil (which comes from various rockrose shrubs) and other plants with a musky scent.

Myristal Ether Sulfate: (See Myristic Acid.)

Myristic Acid: Organic acid in most animal and vegetable fats. In butter acids. Used in shampoos, creams, cosmetics. In food flavorings. Derivatives: Isopropyl Myristate, Myristal Ether Sulfate, Myristyls, Oleyl Myristate. Alternatives: nut butters, oil of lovage, coconut oil, extract from seed kernels of nutmeg, etc.

Myristyls: (See Myristic Acid.)

Natural Sources: Can mean animal or vegetable sources. Most often in the health food industry, especially in the cosmetics area, it means animal sources, such as animal elastin, glands, fat, protein, and oil. Alternatives: plant sources.

Nucleic Acids: In the nucleus of all living cells. Used in cosmetics, shampoos, conditioners, etc. Also in vitamins, supplements. Alternatives: plant sources.

Ocenol: (See Oleyl Alcohol.)

Octyl Dodecanol: Mixture of solid waxy alcohols. Primarily from stearyl alcohol. (See Stearyl Alcohol.)

Oleic Acid: Obtained from various animal and vegetable fats and oils. Usually obtained commercially from inedible tallow. (See Tallow.) In foods, soft soap, bar soap, permanent wave solutions, creams, nail polish, lipsticks, many other skin preparations. Derivatives: Oleyl Oleate, Oleyl Stearate. Alternatives: coconut oil. (See alternatives to Animal Fats and Oils.)

Oils: (See alternatives to Animal Fats and Oils.)

Oleths: (See Oleyl Alcohol.)

Oleyl Alcohol: Ocenol. Found in fish oils. Used in the manufacture of detergents, as a plasticizer for softening fabrics, and as a carrier for medications. Derivatives: Oleths, Oleyl Arachidate, Oleyl Imidazoline.

Oleyl Arachidate: (See Oleyl Alcohol.)

Oleyl Imidazoline: (See Oleyl Alcohol.)

Oleyl Myristate: (See Myristic Acid.)

Oleyl Oleate: (See Oleic Acid.)

Oleyl Stearate: (See Oleic Acid.)

Palmitamide: (See Palmitic Acid.)

Palmitamine: (See Palmitic Acid.)

Palmitate: (See Palmitic Acid.)

Palmitic Acid: From fats, oils (see Fatty Acids). Mixed with stearic acid. Found in many animal fats and plant oils. In shampoos, shaving soaps, creams. Derivatives: Palmitate, Palmitamine, Palmitamide. Alternatives: palm oil, vegetable sources.

Panthenol: Dexpanthenol. Vitamin B-Complex Factor. Provitamin B_5. Can come from animal or plant sources or synthetics. In shampoos, supplements, emollients, etc. In foods. Derivative: Panthenyl. Alternatives: synthetics, plants.

Panthenyl: (See Panthenol.)

Pepsin: In hogs' stomachs. A clotting agent. In some cheeses and vitamins. Same uses and alternatives as Rennet.

Placenta: Placenta Polypeptides Protein. Afterbirth. Contains waste matter eliminated by the fetus. Derived from the uterus of slaughtered animals. Animal placenta is widely used in skin creams, shampoos, masks, etc. Alternatives: kelp. (See alternatives to Animal Fats and Oils.)

Polyglycerol: (See Glycerin.)

Polypeptides: From animal protein. Used in cosmetics. Alternatives: plant proteins and enzymes.

Polysorbates: Derivatives of fatty acids. In cosmetics, foods.

Pristane: Obtained from the liver oil of sharks and from whale ambergris. (See Squalene, Ambergris.) Used as a lubricant and anti-corrosive agent. In cosmetics. Alternatives: plant oils, synthetics.

Progesterone: A steroid hormone used in anti-wrinkle face creams. Can have adverse systemic effects. Alternatives: synthetics.

Propolis: Tree sap gathered by bees and used as a sealant in beehives. In toothpaste, shampoo, deodorant, supplements, etc. Alternatives: tree sap, synthetics.

Provitamin A: (See Carotene.)

Provitamin B$_5$: (See Panthenol.)

Provitamin D$_2$: (See Vitamin D.)

Rennet: Rennin. Enzyme from calves' stomachs. Used in cheese-making, rennet custard (junket), and in many coagulated dairy products. Alternatives: microbial coagulating agents, bacteria culture, lemon juice, or vegetable rennet.

Rennin: (See Rennet.)

Resinous Glaze: (See Shellac.)

Ribonucleic Acid: (See RNA.)

RNA: Ribonucleic Acid. RNA is in all living cells. Used in many protein shampoos and cosmetics. Alternatives: plant cells.

Royal Jelly: Secretion from the throat glands of the honeybee workers that is fed to the larvae in a colony and to all queen larvae. No proven value in cosmetics preparations. Alternatives: aloe vera, comfrey, other plant derivatives.

Sable Brushes: From the fur of sables (weasel-like mammals). Used to make eye makeup, lipstick, and artists' brushes. Alternatives: synthetic fibers.

Sea Turtle Oil: (See Turtle Oil.)

Shark Liver Oil: Used in lubricating creams and lotions. Derivatives: Squalane, Squalene. Alternatives: vegetable oils.

Sheepskin: (See Leather.)

Shellac: Resinous Glaze. Resinous excretion of certain insects. Used as a candy glaze, in hair lacquer, and on jewelry. Alternatives: plant waxes.

Silk: Silk Powder. Silk is the shiny fiber made by silkworms to form their cocoons. Worms are boiled in their cocoons to get the silk. Used in cloth. In silk-screening (other fine cloth can be and is used instead). Taffeta can be made from silk or nylon. Silk powder is obtained from the secretion of the silkworm. It is used as a coloring agent in face powders, soaps, etc. Can cause severe allergic skin reactions and systemic reactions (if inhaled or ingested). Alternatives: milkweed seed-pod fibers, nylon, silk-cotton tree and ceiba tree filaments (kapok), rayon, and synthetic silks.

Snails: In some cosmetics (crushed).

Sodium Caseinate: (See Casein.)

Sodium Steroyl Lactylate: (See Lactic Acid.)

Sodium Tallowate: (See Tallow.)

Spermaceti: Cetyl Palmitate. Sperm Oil. Waxy oil derived from the sperm whale's head or from dolphins. In many margarines. In skin creams, ointments, shampoos, candles, etc. Used in the leather industry. May become rancid and cause irritations. Alternatives: synthetic spermaceti, jojoba oil, and other vegetable emollients.

Sponge (Luna and Sea): A plant-like animal. Lives in the sea. Becoming scarce. Alternatives: synthetic sponges, loofahs (plants used as sponges).

Squalane: (See Shark Liver Oil.)

Squalene: Oil from shark livers, etc. In cosmetics, moisturizers, hair dyes, surface-active agents. Alternatives: vegetable emollients such as olive oil, wheat germ oil, rice bran oil, etc.

Stearamide: (See Stearic Acid.)

Stearamine: (See Stearic Acid.)

Stearamine Oxide: (See Stearyl Alcohol.)

Stearates: (See Stearic Acid.)

Stearic Acid: Fat from cows and sheep and from dogs and cats euthanized in animal shelters, etc. Most often refers to a fatty substance taken from the stomachs of pigs. Can be harsh, irritating. Used in cosmetics, soaps, lubricants, candles, hair spray, conditioners, deodorants, creams, chewing gum, food flavoring. Derivatives: Stearamide, Stearamine, Stearates, Stearic Hydrazide, Stearone, Stearoxytrimethylsilane, Stearoyl Lactylic Acid, Stearyl Betaine, Stearyl Imidazoline. Alternatives: Stearic acid can be found in many vegetable fats, coconut.

Stearic Hydrazide: (See Stearic Acid.)

Stearone: (See Stearic Acid.)

Stearoxytrimethylsilane: (See Stearic Acid.)

Stearoyl Lactylic Acid: (See Stearic Acid.)

Stearyl Acetate: (See Stearyl Alcohol.)

Stearyl Alcohol: Sterols. A mixture of solid alcohols. Can be prepared from sperm whale oil. In medicines, creams, rinses, shampoos, etc. Derivatives: Stearamine Oxide, Stearyl Acetate, Stearyl Caprylate, Stearyl Citrate, Stearyldimethyl Amine, Stearyl Glycyrrhetinate, Stearyl Heptanoate, Stearyl Octanoate, Stearyl Stearate. Alternatives: plant sources, vegetable stearic acid.

Stearyl Betaine: (See Stearic Acid.)

Stearyl Caprylate: (See Stearyl Alcohol.)

Stearyl Citrate: (See Stearyl Alcohol.)

Stearyldimethyl Amine: (See Stearyl Alcohol.)

Stearyl Glycyrrhetinate: (See Stearyl Alcohol.)

Stearyl Heptanoate: (See Stearyl Alcohol.)

Stearyl Imidazoline: (See Stearic Acid.)

Stearyl Octanoate: (See Stearyl Alcohol.)

Stearyl Stearate: (See Stearyl Alcohol.) Steroids. Sterols. From various animal glands or from plant tissues. Steroids include sterols. Sterols are alcohol from animals or plants (e.g., cholesterol). Used in hormone preparation. In creams, lotions, hair conditioners, fragrances, etc. Alternatives: plant tissues, synthetics.

Sterols: (See Stearyl Alcohol and Steroids.)

Suede: (See Leather.)

Tallow: Tallow Fatty Alcohol. Stearic Acid. Rendered beef fat. May cause eczema and blackheads. In wax paper, crayons, margarines, paints, rubber, lubricants, etc. In candles, soaps, lipsticks, shaving creams, other cosmetics. Chemicals (e.g., PCB) can be in animal tallow. Derivatives: Sodium Tallowate, Tallow Acid, Tallow Amide, Tallow Amine, Talloweth-6, Tallow Glycerides, Tallow Imidazoline. Alternatives: vegetable tallow, Japan tallow, paraffin and/or ceresin (see alternatives to Beeswax for all three). Paraffin is usually from petroleum, wood, coal, or shale oil.

Tallow Acid: (See Tallow.)

Tallow Amide: (See Tallow.)

Tallow Amine: (See Tallow.)

Talloweth-6: (See Tallow.)

Tallow Glycerides: (See Tallow.)

Tallow Imidazoline: (See Tallow.)

Triterpene Alcohols: (See Lanolin.)

Turtle Oil: Sea Turtle Oil. From the muscles and genitals of giant sea turtles. In soap, skin creams, nail creams, other cosmetics. Alternatives: vegetable emollients (see alternatives to Animal Fats and Oils).

Tyrosine: Amino acid hydrolyzed from casein. Used in cosmetics and creams. Derivative: Glucose Tyrosinase.

Urea: Carbamide. Excreted from urine and other bodily fluids. In deodorants, ammoniated dentifrices, mouthwashes, hair colorings, hand creams, lotions, shampoos, etc. Used to brown baked goods, such as pretzels. Derivatives: Imidazolidinyl Urea, Uric Acid. Alternatives: synthetics.

Uric Acid: (See Urea.)

Vitamin A: Can come from fish liver oil (e.g., shark liver oil), egg yolk, butter, lemongrass, wheat germ oil, carotene in carrots, and synthetics.

It is an aliphatic alcohol. In cosmetics, creams, perfumes, hair dyes, etc. In vitamins, supplements. Alternatives: carrots, other vegetables, synthetics.

Vitamin B-Complex Factor: (See Panthenol.)

Vitamin B Factor: (See Biotin.)

Vitamin B_{12}: Usually animal source. Some vegetarian B_{12} vitamins are in a stomach base. Alternatives: some vegetarian B_{12}-fortified yeasts and analogs available. Plant algae discovered containing B_{12}, now in supplement form (spirulina). Some nutritionist caution that fortified foods or supplements are essential.

Vitamin D: Ergocalciferol. Vitamin D_2. Ergosterol. Provitamin D_2. Calciferol. Vitamin D_3. Vitamin D can come from fish liver oil, milk, egg yolk, etc. Vitamin D_2 can come from animal fats or plant sterols. Vitamin D_3 is always from an animal source. All the D vitamins can be in creams, lotions, other cosmetics, vitamin tablets, etc. Alternatives: plant and mineral sources, synthetics, completely vegetarian vitamins, exposure of skin to sunshine. Many other vitamins can come from animal sources. Examples: choline, biotin, inositol, riboflavin, etc.

Vitamin H: (See Biotin.)

Wax: Glossy, hard substance that is soft when hot. From animals and plants. In lipsticks, depilatories, hair straighteners. Alternatives: vegetable waxes.

Whey: A serum from milk. Usually in cakes, cookies, candies, and breads. In cheese-making. Alternatives: soybean whey.

Wool: From sheep. Used in clothing. Ram lambs and old wool sheep are slaughtered for their meat. Derivatives: Lanolin, Wool Wax, Wool Fat. Alternatives: cotton, cotton flannel, synthetic fibers, ramie, etc.

Wool Fat: (See Lanolin.)

Wool Wax: (See Lanolin.)

Chapter 36

The Vegetarian
Food Guide Pyramid

The Vegetarian Food Guide Pyramid in this chapter was developed by the Third International Congress on Vegetarian Nutrition as a part of the process of developing a nutritional guide for vegetarians. This Pyramid is meant to serve as a focus for further research and discussion among scientists, health professionals, and vegetarians as guidelines for healthful vegetarian living are refined and developed.

Table 36.1. Summary of questionnaire questions and responses from members of the Third International Congress on Vegetarian Nutrition while developing the Pyramid. (continued on next page)

In developing the guide, which objective is most important?

Develop a guide that:
1) Is applicable to diverse vegetarian practices
2) Helps reduce risk of chronic disease
3) Meets the RDAs for nutrients
4) Helps persons who want to become vegetarian

The information in this chapter is excerpted with permission from "Vegetarian Food Guide Pyramid: A Conceptual Framework," by Ella H. Haddad, Joan Sabaté, and Crystal G. Whitten, *American Journal of Clinical Nutrition*, Volume 70, Number 3, 615S-619S, September 1999. © 1999 American Journal of Clinical Nutrition/The American Society for Clinical Nutrition, Inc.

Table 36.1. Summary of questionnaire questions and responses from members of the Third International Congress on Vegetarian Nutrition while developing the Pyramid. (continued from previous page)

Should the guide be designed for use in developed countries, developing countries, or both?

The guide must be primarily applicable to developed countries.

What influence should epidemiologic data have on the guide's development?

Epidemiologic data should be considered and take precedence over other types of data.

What influence should the RDAs (Recommended Daily Allowances) have on the guide's development?

The RDAs should be met. More recent data must also be considered when available.

What criteria should be used in defining food groups?

Food groups should be categorized the way they usually are.

What food categories should be used?

Grains, legumes, vegetables, fruit, nuts, milk.

Should all types of food items (e.g., whole and processed) be included in the food groups?

Yes, but whole foods should be emphasized.

Should a point system be used to evaluate foods?

No, because it would be too complicated to use on an everyday basis.

What graphic format should be utilized? Pyramid, plate, pie, table of foods, tree, or other?

Pyramid.

Reproduced with permission by the *American Journal of Clinical Nutrition.* © *Am J Clin Nutr.* American Society of Clinical Nutrition.

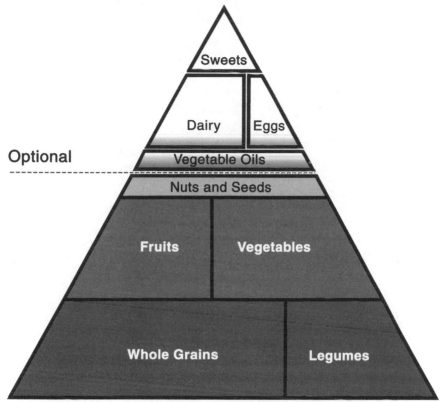

Note: A reliable source of vitamin B_{12} should be included if no dairy or eggs are consumed.

Figure 36.1. The Vegetarian Food Guide Pyramid. Figure reproduced with permission by the American Journal of Clinical Nutrition. © Am J Clin Nutr. American Society of Clinical Nutrition.

Table 36.2. Description of food groups and recommendations for food selection. (continued on next page)

Food group and examples of food items	Recommendations
Whole grains *Grains:* wheat, corn, oats, rice, and millet *Grain products:* bread, pasta, and tortillas	Select whole-wheat and whole-grain products.

Table 36.2. Description of food groups and recommendations for food selection. (continued from previous page)

Legumes
  Beans and peas: soy, pinto, kidney, navy, lima, and garbanzo beans, peas, and lentils
  Soy and soy products: tofu, soy drinks, and texturized protein foods
	Select soy-based milk alternatives fortified with calcium, vitamin D, and vitamin B_{12}.

Vegetables All vegetables	Emphasize leafy, green and yellow vegetables. Eat both cooked and raw vegetables.
Fruit All fruit	Emphasize whole fruit rather than juice.

Nuts and seeds
  Nuts: almonds, walnuts, peanuts, and other nuts
  Seeds: pumpkin, squash, sunflower, and other seeds
  Butters: peanut, almond, and sesame (tahini)
	Eat nuts and seeds raw, dry roasted, or in foods rather than deep-fried.

Vegetable oils *Plant oils*: canola, corn, olive, and sesame	Emphasize oils high in monounsaturated fatty acids such as olive, sesame, and canola. Limit tropical oils (coconut, palm kernel, and palm oil). Avoid hydrogenated fats.
Milk and dairy Milk, yogurt, and cheese	Emphasize nonfat and low-fat products. If dairy is avoided, ensure that adequate reliable sources of calcium, vitamin D, and vitamin B_{12} are consumed.
Eggs	Limit eggs or use egg whites only.
Sweets Honey, syrup (molasses, maple, and carob), sugar, sweeteners, jams, and jellies	Eat sweets in moderation.
Vitamin B_{12} Dietary supplements or fortified foods	A reliable source of B_{12} (cobalamin) should be included if dairy and eggs are avoided.

Reproduced with permission by the *American Journal of Clinical Nutrition.* © *Am J Clin Nutr.* American Society of Clinical Nutrition.

Chapter 37

Other Vegetarian Resources

This chapter lists contact information for some vegetarian and animal-rights organizations, websites, and publications. Information is listed in alphabetical order.

American Soybean Association
12125 Woodcrest Executive Dr.
Suite 100
St. Louis, MO 63141-5009
Toll-Free: 800-688-7692
Phone: 314-576-1770
Fax: 314-576-2786
Website: www.amsoy.org
E-Mail: soygrowers@soy.org

The American Vegan Society
56 Dinshah Lane
P.O. Box 369
Malaga, NJ 08328-0908
Phone: 856-694-2887
Fax: 856-694-2288
Website: www.americanvegan.org

Animal Rights Resources Site
Website:
www.animalconcerns.org
E-Mail:
support@animalconcerns.org

The European Vegetarian Union (EVU)
Website: www.european-vegetarian.org

The Indonesian Vegan Society
Website: www.i-v-s.org

The resources listed in this section were compiled from a wide variety of sources deemed accurate. Contact information was updated and verified in May 2002. Inclusion does not constitute endorsement.

Institute for Plant Based Nutrition
333 Bryn Mawr Avenue
Bala Cynwyd, PA 19004-2606
Website: www.plantbased.org
E-Mail: info@plantbased.org

International Vegetarian Union (IVU)
P.O. Box 9710
Washington, DC 20016
Phone: 202-362-VEGY, Box 3
Website: www.ivu.org
E-Mail: secretary@ivu.org

Issues in Vegetarian Dietetics
Quarterly publication by
Vegetarian Nutrition Dietetic
Practice Group
1307 Sudden Valley
Bellingham, WA 98226
Phone: 360-714-8704
Fax: 360-715-6495
E-mail:
duncveggies@earthlink.net or
KrDuncan@peacehealth.org.

North American Vegetarian Society (NAVS)
P.O. Box 72
Dolgeville, NY 13329
Phone: 568-7970
Fax: 518-568-7979
Website: www.navs-online.org
E-Mail: navs@telnet.net

Online Guide to Vegetarian Restaurants around the World
Website: www.vegdining.com/
Home.cfm

People for the Ethical Treatment of Animals (PETA)
501 Front St.
Norfolk, VA 23510
Phone: 757-622-PETA (7382)
Fax: 757-622-0457
Website: www.peta-online.org
E-Mail: info@peta-online.org

Physician's Committee for Responsible Medicine (PCRM)
5100 Wisconsin Ave., Suite 400
Washington, DC 20016
Phone: 202-686-2210
Fax: 202-686-2216
Website: www.pcrm.org
E-Mail: pcrm@pcrm.org

Rochester Area Vegetarian Society
P.O. Box 20185
Rochester, NY 14602-0185
Phone: 716-234-8750
Website: http://
ravs.enviroweb.org
E-Mail: drveggie@aol.com

Seventh-day Adventist Dietetic Association
One Angwin Avenue
Angwin, CA 94508
Website: www.sdada.org
E-Mail: veggie@sdada.org

Soyfoods Association of North America
1723 U St., N.W.
Washington, DC 20009
Phone: 202-986-5600
Website: www.soyfoods.org
E-Mail: info@soyfoods.org

Soy Stache
P.O. Box 31362
Seattle, WA 98103-1362
Website: www.soystache.com
E-Mail: info@soystache.com

United Soybean Board
16640 Chesterfield Grove Road, Suite 130
Chesterfield, MO 63005
Toll-Free: 800-989-8721
Website:
www.unitedsoybean.org

Vancouver Island Vegan Society
P.O. Box 47077,
750 Goldstream Ave,
Victoria, British Columbia
Canada V9B 5S4
Phone: 250-474-7918

Vegan Action
P.O. Box 4288
Richmond, VA 23220
Phone: 804-254-8346
Website: www.vegan.org
E-Mail: info@vegan.org

Vegan Chef
Website: www.veganchef.com

Vegan Outreach
211 Indian Dr.
Pittsburgh, PA 15238
Phone/Fax: 412-968-0268
Website:
www.veganoutreach.org
E-Mail:
vegan@veganoutreach.org

Vegan Society of Australia
P.O. Box 85
Seaford Vic 3198
Website:
www.veganaustralia.org
E-Mail: info@veganaustralia.org

The Vegetarian Resource Group (VRG)
P.O. Box 1463
Baltimore, MD 21203
Phone: 410-366-8343
Website: www.vrg.org
Email: vrg@vrg.org

The Vegetarian Society of the United Kingdom
Parksdale, Dunham Road
Altrincham, Cheshire WA14 4QG
England
Phone: 0161-925-2000
Fax: 0161-926-9182
Website: www.vegsoc.org
E-Mail: info@vegsoc.org

Vegetarian Times
P.O. Box 420235
Palm Coast, FL 32142-0235
Toll-Free: 877-717-8923
Website:
www.vegetariantimes.com

VegFamily/Vegan Parenting Online
P.O. Box 571961
Tarzana, CA 91357-1961
Website: www.vegfamily.com
E-Mail: info@vegfamily.com

VeggieDate
420 Raymond Ave., Suite 12
Santa Monica, CA 90405
Phone: 310-399-9355
Website: www.veggiedate.org
E-Mail: contact@veggiedate.org

Veggies Unite!
P.O. Box 13038
Fort Wayne, IN 46866-3038
Website: www.vegweb.com
E-Mail: veggie@vegweb.com

VegRD
Virginia Messina
Website: www.vegrd.com
E-Mail: vegRD@yahoo.com

VegSource
P.O. Box 7596
Northridge, CA 91327
Phone: 413-622-9122
Website: www.vegsource.com

The World Animal Network
19 Chestnet Square
Boston, MA 02130
Phone: 617-524-3670
Fax: 617-524-1815
Website: www.worldanimal.net
E-Mail: info@worldanimal.net

Chapter 38

References for Additional Reading

This chapter lists vegetarian cookbooks, books on vegetarian nutrition and lifestyle issues, and other books and articles that may be of interest to people seeking further information.

Cookbooks—General

CalciYum! Delicious, Calcium-Rich, Dairy-Free Vegetarian Recipes, by David and Rochelle Bronfman. Toronto, Ontario, Canada: Bromedia, Inc., 1998. 192 pp.

Cooking Vegetarian: Healthy, Delicious and Easy Vegetarian Cuisine, by Vesanto Melina and Joseph Forest. New York, NY: John Wiley & Sons, 1998. 239 pp.

Great American Vegetarian: Traditional and Regional Recipes for the Enlightened Cook, Nava Atlas. New York, NY: M. Evans and Co., 1998. 256 pp.

Millennium Cookbook: Extraordinary Vegetarian Cuisine, Eric Tucker, John Westerdahl, Sascha Weiss. Berkeley, CA: Ten Speed Press, 1998. 208 pp.

Vegetarian Cooking for Everyone, Deborah Madison. New York, NY: Broadway Books, 1997. 742 pp.

Cookbooks—Low Fat

Delicious Food for a Healthy Heart, Joanne Stepaniak. Summertown, TN: Book Publishing Company, 1999. 172 pp.

Everyday Cooking with Dr. Dean Ornish: 150 Easy, Low-Fat, High Flavor Recipes, Dean Ornish. New York, NY: HarperCollins, 1997. 368 pp.

Steven Raichlen's High-Flavor, Low-Fat Vegetarian Cooking, Steven Raichlen. New York, NY: Penguin USA, 1997. 304 pp.

Stir Crazy! More than 100 Quick, Low-Fat Recipes for Your Wok or Stir-Fry Pan, Susan Jane Cheney. Chicago, IL: NTC/Contemporary Publishing, 1998. 192 pp.

20 Minutes to Dinner: Quick, Low-Fat, Low-Calorie Vegetarian Meals, Bryanna Clark Grogan. Summertown, TN: Book Publishing Company, 1997. 192 pp.

Cookbooks—Featuring Beans and Soy Products

The Complete Soy Cookbook, Paulette Mitchell. New York, NY: Macmillan, 1998. 270 pp.

Soy of Cooking: Easy to Make Vegetarian, Low-fat, Fat-free and Antioxidant-rich Gourmet Recipes, Marie Oser. New York, NY: John Wiley & Sons, 1998. 264 pp.

Tofu and Soyfoods Cookery, Peter Golbitz. Summertown, TN: Book Publishing Company, 1998. 173 pp.

Cookbooks—Ethnic

Delicious Jamaica: Vegetarian Cuisine, Yvonne McCalla Sobers. Summertown, TN: Book Publishing Company, 1996. 160 pp.

Flavors of Korea: Delicious Vegetarian Cuisine, Deborah Coultrip-Davis and Young Sook Ramsay. Summertown, TN: Book Publishing Company, 1998. 192 pp.

Japanese Cooking—Contemporary and Traditional, Miyoko Nishimoto Schinner. Summertown, TN: Book Publishing Company, 1999. 144 pp.

The Lowfat Jewish Vegetarian Cookbook: Healthy Traditions from Around the World, Debra Wasserman. Baltimore, MD: The Vegetarian Resource Group, 1995. 224 pp.

The Meatless Gourmet: Easy Lowfat Favorites, Bobbie Hinman. Rocklin, CA: Prima Publishing, 1996. 512 pp.

Nonna's Italian Kitchen: Delicious Homestyle Vegan Cuisine, Bryanna Clark Grogan. Summertown, TN: Book Publishing Company, 1998. 256 pp.

Books—Nutrition/Lifestyle

Becoming Vegetarian: The Complete Guide to Adopting a Healthy Vegetarian Diet, Vesanto Melina, Brenda Davis, Victoria Harrison. Summertown, TN: Book Publishing Company, 1995. 262 pp.

Being Vegetarian, Suzanne Havala. Chicago, IL: ADA/John Wiley & Sons, 1998. 144 pp.

The Complete Idiot's Guide to Being Vegetarian, Suzanne Havala. New York, NY: Macmillan Publishing Co., 1999. 344 pp.

Simply Vegan: Quick Vegetarian Meals, 3rd ed., Debra Wasserman; Nutrition Section by Reed Mangels. Baltimore, MD: The Vegetarian Resource Group, 1999, 224 pp.

The Tofu Tollbooth, 2nd ed., Elizbeth Zipern and Dar Williams. Woodstock, NY: Ceres Press, 1998. 260 pp.

The Vegetarian Food Guide and Nutrition Counter, Suzanne Havala. New York, NY: Berkley Books, 1997. 176 pp.

Vegetarian Journal's Guide to Natural Foods Restaurants in the US and Canada, 3rd ed., Vegetarian Resource Group. New York, NY: Avery Publishing Group, 1998. 320 pp.

The Vegetarian Way, Virginia Messina and Mark Messina. New York, NY: Crown Trade Paperbacks, 1996. 390 pp.

Books and Cookbooks for Children and Adolescents

Feeding the Healthy Vegetarian Family, Ken Haedrich. New York, NY: Bantam Doubleday Dell Publishing, 1998. 288 pp.

From Animal Crackers to Wild West Beans: Easy and Fun Vegetarian Recipes for Healthy Babies and Children, Carol Timperley. Chicago, IL: Contemporary Publishing, 1998. 144 pp.

Honest Pretzels and 64 Other Amazing Recipes for Cooks Ages 8 and Up, Mollie Katzen. Berkeley, CA: Tricycle Press, 1999. 192 pp.

Leprechaun Cake and Other Tales. A Vegetarian Story-Cookbook, Vonnie Winslow Crist and Debra Wasserman. Baltimore, MD: The Vegetarian Resource Group, 1995. 128 pp.

Pretend Soup and Other Real Recipes: A Cookbook for Preschoolers and Up, Mollie Katzen and Anne Henderson. Berkeley, CA: Tricycle Press, 1994. 95 pp.

A Teen's Guide to Going Vegetarian, Judy Krizmanic. New York, NY: Puffin, 1994. 144 pp.

The Teen's Vegetarian Cookbook, Judy Krizmanic. New York, NY: Viking Press, 1999. 192 pp.

The Vegetarian Child: A Complete Guide for Parents, Lucy Moll. New York, NY: Perigee, 1997. 224 pp.

Miscellaneous Books and Journal Articles

Alternative & Complimentary Nutrition Therapy, L. Kay. Nutrition Dimension Inc., 1999.

Basic Course in Vegetarian and Vegan Nutrition, George L. Eisman. Diet Ethics, 1999.

Becoming Vegan, Brenda Davis, RD & Vesanto Melina, MS, RD, Book Publishing Company, 2000.

Bowes and Church's Food Values of Portions Commonly Used, Jean AT Pennington. 17th edition. Lippincott, 1998.

Carbohydrates: What You Need to Know, The American Dietetic Association, Wiley, 1998.

The Complete Guide to Vegetarian Convenience Foods, Gail Davis. Newspage Press, 1999.

Conveniently Vegan, Debra Wasserman. The Vegetarian Resource Group, 1997.

A Diet for All Reasons: Nutrition Guide & Recipe Collection, Paulette Eisen. Alive Books, 1998.

Dwyer, J. 1999. "Convergence of plant-rich and plant-only diets." *American Journal of Clinical Nutrition*, 70 (3), 620S–2S.

Ecological Integrity: Integrating Environment, Conservation, and Health, edited by David Pimentel. Island Press, 2001.

Food Finder: Food Sources of Vitamins and Minerals, Elizabeth Hands. 3rd edition. ESHA Research, 1995.

Harman, S. K., & Parnell, W. R. 1998. "The nutritional health of New Zealand vegetarian and non-vegetarian Seventh-Day Adventists: Selected vitamin, mineral and lipid levels." *New Zealand Medical Journal*, 111 (1062), 91–4.

Herbs of Choice, Varro E. Tyler. Pharmaceutical Products Press, 1999

Hunt, J. R., et al. 1998. "Zinc absorption, mineral balance and blood lipids in women consuming controlled lacto-ovo-vegetarian and omnivorous diets for 8 weeks." *American Journal of Clinical Nutrition*, 67 (3), 421–30.

Hunt, J. R., et al. 1999. "Nonheme iron absorption, fecal ferritin excretion and blond indexes of iron status in women consuming controlled lacto-ovo-vegetarian diets for 8 weeks." *American Journal of Clinical Nutrition*, 69 (5), 944–52.

Itoh, R., et al. 1998. "Dietary protein intake and urinary excretion of calcium: A cross-sectional study in a healthy Japanese population." *American Journal of Clinical Nutrition*, 69 (4), 742–3.

Klausner, A. 1999. "EN's guide to calcium in unexpected places." *Environmental Nutrition*, 22 (5), 5.

Nieman, D. C. 1999. "Physical fitness and vegetarian diets: Is there a relation?" *American Journal of Clinical Nutrition*, 70 (3), 570S–5S.

The Occasional Vegetarian, Karen Lee and Diane Porter. Warner Books, 1995

The Peaceful Palate, Jennifer Raymond. Book Pub Co, 1996.

Pregnancy Nutrition: Good Health for You and Your Baby, The American Dietetic Association. Wiley, 1998.

Sanders, T. A. 1999. "The nutritional adequacy of plant-based diets." *Proceedings of the Nutrition Society*, 58 (2), 265–9.

The Simple Soybean and Your Health, Mark Messina, Virginia Messina (Contributor), Ken Setchell, Kenneth Setchell. Avery Publishing Group, 1994.

Vegan & Vegetarian FAQ, Davida Gypsy Breier and Reed Mangels, PhD, RD. The Vegetarian Resource Group, 2001.

Vegan Handbook, edited by Debra Wasserman and Reed Mangels PhD, RD. The Vegetarian Resource Group, 1996.

Index

Index

M

Health Reference Series
COMPLETE CATALOG

Adolescent Health Sourcebook

Basic Consumer Health Information about Common Medical, Mental, and Emotional Concerns in Adolescents, Including Facts about Acne, Body Piercing, Mononucleosis, Nutrition, Eating Disorders, Stress, Depression, Behavior Problems, Peer Pressure, Violence, Gangs, Drug Use, Puberty, Sexuality, Pregnancy, Learning Disabilities, and More

Along with a Glossary of Terms and Other Resources for Further Help and Information

Edited by Chad T. Kimball. 658 pages. 2002. 0-7808-0248-9. $78.

■

AIDS Sourcebook, 1st Edition

Basic Information about AIDS and HIV Infection, Featuring Historical and Statistical Data, Current Research, Prevention, and Other Special Topics of Interest for Persons Living with AIDS

Along with Source Listings for Further Assistance

Edited by Karen Bellenir and Peter D. Dresser. 831 pages. 1995. 0-7808-0031-1. $78.

"One strength of this book is its practical emphasis. The intended audience is the lay reader ... useful as an educational tool for health care providers who work with AIDS patients. Recommended for public libraries as well as hospital or academic libraries that collect consumer materials."
— Bulletin of the Medical Library Association, Jan '96

"This is the most comprehensive volume of its kind on an important medical topic. Highly recommended for all libraries." — Reference Book Review, '96

"Very useful reference for all libraries."
— Choice, Association of College and Research Libraries, Oct '95

"There is a wealth of information here that can provide much educational assistance. It is a must book for all libraries and should be on the desk of each and every congressional leader. Highly recommended."
— AIDS Book Review Journal, Aug '95

"Recommended for most collections."
— Library Journal, Jul '95

■

AIDS Sourcebook, 2nd Edition

Basic Consumer Health Information about Acquired Immune Deficiency Syndrome (AIDS) and Human Immunodeficiency Virus (HIV) Infection, Featuring Updated Statistical Data, Reports on Recent Research and Prevention Initiatives, and Other Special Topics of Interest for Persons Living with AIDS, Including New Antiretroviral Treatment Options, Strategies for Combating Opportunistic Infections, Information about Clinical Trials, and More

Along with a Glossary of Important Terms and Resource Listings for Further Help and Information

Edited by Karen Bellenir. 751 pages. 1999. 0-7808-0225-X. $78.

"Highly recommended."
— American Reference Books Annual, 2000

"Excellent sourcebook. This continues to be a highly recommended book. There is no other book that provides as much information as this book provides."
— AIDS Book Review Journal, Dec-Jan 2000

"Recommended reference source."
— Booklist, American Library Association, Dec '99

"A solid text for college-level health libraries."
— The Bookwatch, Aug '99

Cited in Reference Sources for Small and Medium-Sized Libraries, American Library Association, 1999

■

Alcoholism Sourcebook

Basic Consumer Health Information about the Physical and Mental Consequences of Alcohol Abuse, Including Liver Disease, Pancreatitis, Wernicke-Korsakoff Syndrome (Alcoholic Dementia), Fetal Alcohol Syndrome, Heart Disease, Kidney Disorders, Gastrointestinal Problems, and Immune System Compromise and Featuring Facts about Addiction, Detoxification, Alcohol Withdrawal, Recovery, and the Maintenance of Sobriety

Along with a Glossary and Directories of Resources for Further Help and Information

Edited by Karen Bellenir. 613 pages. 2000. 0-7808-0325-6. $78.

"This title is one of the few reference works on alcoholism for general readers. For some readers this will be a welcome complement to the many self-help books on the market. Recommended for collections serving general readers and consumer health collections."
— E-Streams, Mar '01

"This book is an excellent choice for public and academic libraries."
— American Reference Books Annual, 2001

"Recommended reference source."
— Booklist, American Library Association, Dec '00

"Presents a wealth of information on alcohol use and abuse and its effects on the body and mind, treatment, and prevention." — SciTech Book News, Dec '00

"Important new health guide which packs in the latest consumer information about the problems of alcoholism." — Reviewer's Bookwatch, Nov '00

SEE ALSO Drug Abuse Sourcebook, Substance Abuse Sourcebook

Allergies Sourcebook, 1st Edition

Basic Information about Major Forms and Mechanisms of Common Allergic Reactions, Sensitivities, and Intolerances, Including Anaphylaxis, Asthma, Hives and Other Dermatologic Symptoms, Rhinitis, and Sinusitis

Along with Their Usual Triggers Like Animal Fur, Chemicals, Drugs, Dust, Foods, Insects, Latex, Pollen, and Poison Ivy, Oak, and Sumac; Plus Information on Prevention, Identification, and Treatment

Edited by Allan R. Cook. 611 pages. 1997. 0-7808-0036-2. $78.

■

Allergies Sourcebook, 2nd Edition

Basic Consumer Health Information about Allergic Disorders, Triggers, Reactions, and Related Symptoms, Including Anaphylaxis, Rhinitis, Sinusitis, Asthma, Dermatitis, Conjunctivitis, and Multiple Chemical Sensitivity

Along with Tips on Diagnosis, Prevention, and Treatment, Statistical Data, a Glossary, and a Directory of Sources for Further Help and Information

Edited by Annemarie S. Muth. 598 pages. 2002. 0-7808-0376-0. $78.

■

Alternative Medicine Sourcebook, First Edition

Basic Consumer Health Information about Alternatives to Conventional Medicine, Including Acupressure, Acupuncture, Aromatherapy, Ayurveda, Bioelectromagnetics, Environmental Medicine, Essence Therapy, Food and Nutrition Therapy, Herbal Therapy, Homeopathy, Imaging, Massage, Naturopathy, Reflexology, Relaxation and Meditation, Sound Therapy, Vitamin and Mineral Therapy, and Yoga, and More

Edited by Allan R. Cook. 737 pages. 1999. 0-7808-0200-4. $78.

"Recommended reference source."
 —Booklist, American Library Association, Feb '00

"A great addition to the reference collection of every type of library." *—American Reference Books Annual, 2000*

■

Alternative Medicine Sourcebook, Second Edition

Basic Consumer Health Information about Alternative and Complementary Medical Practices, Including Acupuncture, Chiropractic, Herbal Medicine, Homeopathy, Naturopathic Medicine, Mind-Body Interventions, Ayurveda, and Other Non-Western Medical Traditions

Along with Facts about such Specific Therapies as Massage Therapy, Aromatherapy, Qigong, Hypnosis, Prayer, Dance, and Art Therapies, a Glossary, and Resources for Further Information

Edited by Dawn D. Matthews. 618 pages. 2002. 0-7808-0605-0. $78.

Alzheimer's, Stroke & 29 Other Neurological Disorders Sourcebook, 1st Edition

Basic Information for the Layperson on 31 Diseases or Disorders Affecting the Brain and Nervous System, First Describing the Illness, Then Listing Symptoms, Diagnostic Methods, and Treatment Options, and Including Statistics on Incidences and Causes

Edited by Frank E. Bair. 579 pages. 1993. 1-55888-748-2. $78.

"Nontechnical reference book that provides reader-friendly information."
 —Family Caregiver Alliance Update, Winter '96

"Should be included in any library's patient education section." *—American Reference Books Annual, 1994*

"Written in an approachable and accessible style. Recommended for patient education and consumer health collections in health science center and public libraries." *—Academic Library Book Review, Dec '93*

"It is very handy to have information on more than thirty neurological disorders under one cover, and there is no recent source like it." *—Reference Quarterly, American Library Association, Fall '93*

SEE ALSO *Brain Disorders Sourcebook*

■

Alzheimer's Disease Sourcebook, 2nd Edition

Basic Consumer Health Information about Alzheimer's Disease, Related Disorders, and Other Dementias, Including Multi-Infarct Dementia, AIDS-Related Dementia, Alcoholic Dementia, Huntington's Disease, Delirium, and Confusional States

Along with Reports Detailing Current Research Efforts in Prevention and Treatment, Long-Term Care Issues, and Listings of Sources for Additional Help and Information

Edited by Karen Bellenir. 524 pages. 1999. 0-7808-0223-3. $78.

"Provides a wealth of useful information not otherwise available in one place. This resource is recommended for all types of libraries."
 —American Reference Books Annual, 2000

"Recommended reference source."
 —Booklist, American Library Association, Oct '99

■

Arthritis Sourcebook

Basic Consumer Health Information about Specific Forms of Arthritis and Related Disorders, Including Rheumatoid Arthritis, Osteoarthritis, Gout, Polymyalgia Rheumatica, Psoriatic Arthritis, Spondyloarthropathies, Juvenile Rheumatoid Arthritis, and Juvenile Ankylosing Spondylitis

Along with Information about Medical, Surgical, and Alternative Treatment Options, and Including Strategies for Coping with Pain, Fatigue, and Stress

Edited by Allan R. Cook. 550 pages. 1998. 0-7808-0201-2. $78.

". . . accessible to the layperson."
—Reference and Research Book News, Feb '99

■

Asthma Sourcebook

Basic Consumer Health Information about Asthma, Including Symptoms, Traditional and Nontraditional Remedies, Treatment Advances, Quality-of-Life Aids, Medical Research Updates, and the Role of Allergies, Exercise, Age, the Environment, and Genetics in the Development of Asthma

Along with Statistical Data, a Glossary, and Directories of Support Groups, and Other Resources for Further Information

Edited by Annemarie S. Muth. 628 pages. 2000. 0-7808-0381-7. $78.

"A worthwhile reference acquisition for public libraries and academic medical libraries whose readers desire a quick introduction to the wide range of asthma information." *— Choice, Association of College & Research Libraries, Jun '01*

"Recommended reference source."
— Booklist, American Library Association, Feb '01

"Highly recommended." *— The Bookwatch, Jan '01*

"There is much good information for patients and their families who deal with asthma daily."
— American Medical Writers Association Journal, Winter '01

"This informative text is recommended for consumer health collections in public, secondary school, and community college libraries and the libraries of universities with a large undergraduate population."
— American Reference Books Annual, 2001

■

Attention Deficit Disorder Sourcebook, First Edition

Basic Consumer Health Information about Attention Deficit/Hyperactivity Disorder in Children and Adults, Including Facts about Causes, Symptoms, Diagnostic Criteria, and Treatment Options Such as Medications, Behavior Therapy, Coaching, and Homeopathy

Along with Reports on Current Research Initiatives, Legal Issues, and Government Regulations, and Featuring a Glossary of Related Terms, Internet Resources, and a List of Additional Reading Material

Edited by Dawn D. Matthews. 470 pages. 2002. 0-7808-0624-7. $78.

Back & Neck Disorders Sourcebook

Basic Information about Disorders and Injuries of the Spinal Cord and Vertebrae, Including Facts on Chiropractic Treatment, Surgical Interventions, Paralysis, and Rehabilitation

Along with Advice for Preventing Back Trouble

Edited by Karen Bellenir. 548 pages. 1997. 0-7808-0202-0. $78.

"The strength of this work is its basic, easy-to-read format. Recommended."
— Reference and User Services Quarterly, American Library Association, Winter '97

■

Blood & Circulatory Disorders Sourcebook

Basic Information about Blood and Its Components, Anemias, Leukemias, Bleeding Disorders, and Circulatory Disorders, Including Aplastic Anemia, Thalassemia, Sickle-Cell Disease, Hemochromatosis, Hemophilia, Von Willebrand Disease, and Vascular Diseases

Along with a Special Section on Blood Transfusions and Blood Supply Safety, a Glossary, and Source Listings for Further Help and Information

Edited by Karen Bellenir and Linda M. Shin. 554 pages. 1998. 0-7808-0203-9. $78.

"Recommended reference source."
— Booklist, American Library Association, Feb '99

"An important reference sourcebook written in simple language for everyday, non-technical users."
— Reviewer's Bookwatch, Jan '99

■

Brain Disorders Sourcebook

Basic Consumer Health Information about Strokes, Epilepsy, Amyotrophic Lateral Sclerosis (ALS/Lou Gehrig's Disease), Parkinson's Disease, Brain Tumors, Cerebral Palsy, Headache, Tourette Syndrome, and More

Along with Statistical Data, Treatment and Rehabilitation Options, Coping Strategies, Reports on Current Research Initiatives, a Glossary, and Resource Listings for Additional Help and Information

Edited by Karen Bellenir. 481 pages. 1999. 0-7808-0229-2. $78.

"Belongs on the shelves of any library with a consumer health collection." *— E-Streams, Mar '00*

"Recommended reference source."
— Booklist, American Library Association, Oct '99

SEE ALSO *Alzheimer's, Stroke & 29 Other Neurological Disorders Sourcebook, 1st Edition*

Breast Cancer Sourcebook

Basic Consumer Health Information about Breast Cancer, Including Diagnostic Methods, Treatment Options, Alternative Therapies, Self-Help Information, Related Health Concerns, Statistical and Demographic Data, and Facts for Men with Breast Cancer

Along with Reports on Current Research Initiatives, a Glossary of Related Medical Terms, and a Directory of Sources for Further Help and Information

Edited by Edward J. Prucha and Karen Bellenir. 580 pages. 2001. 0-7808-0244-6. $78.

"Recommended reference source."
—Booklist, American Library Association, Jan '02

"This reference source is highly recommended. It is quite informative, comprehensive and detailed in nature, and yet it offers practical advice in easy-to-read language. It could be thought of as the 'bible' of breast cancer for the consumer." *—E-Streams, Jan '02*

"The broad range of topics covered in lay language make the *Breast Cancer Sourcebook* an excellent addition to public and consumer health library collections."
—American Reference Books Annual 2002

"From the pros and cons of different screening methods and results to treatment options, *Breast Cancer Sourcebook* provides the latest information on the subject."
—Library Bookwatch, Dec '01

"This thoroughgoing, very readable reference covers all aspects of breast health and cancer. . . . Readers will find much to consider here. Recommended for all public and patient health collections."
—Library Journal, Sep '01

SEE ALSO Cancer Sourcebook for Women, 1st and 2nd Editions, Women's Health Concerns Sourcebook

■

Breastfeeding Sourcebook

Basic Consumer Health Information about the Benefits of Breastmilk, Preparing to Breastfeed, Breastfeeding as a Baby Grows, Nutrition, and More, Including Information on Special Situations and Concerns Such as Mastitis, Illness, Medications, Allergies, Multiple Births, Prematurity, Special Needs, and Adoption

Along with a Glossary and Resources for Additional Help and Information

Edited by Jenni Lynn Colson. 388 pages. 2002. 0-7808-0332-9. $78.

SEE ALSO Pregnancy & Birth Sourcebook

■

Burns Sourcebook

Basic Consumer Health Information about Various Types of Burns and Scalds, Including Flame, Heat, Cold, Electrical, Chemical, and Sun Burns

Along with Information on Short-Term and Long-Term Treatments, Tissue Reconstruction, Plastic Surgery, Prevention Suggestions, and First Aid

Edited by Allan R. Cook. 604 pages. 1999. 0-7808-0204-7. $78.

"This is an exceptional addition to the series and is highly recommended for all consumer health collections, hospital libraries, and academic medical centers."
—E-Streams, Mar '00

"This key reference guide is an invaluable addition to all health care and public libraries in confronting this ongoing health issue."
—American Reference Books Annual, 2000

"Recommended reference source."
—Booklist, American Library Association, Dec '99

SEE ALSO Skin Disorders Sourcebook

■

Cancer Sourcebook, 1st Edition

Basic Information on Cancer Types, Symptoms, Diagnostic Methods, and Treatments, Including Statistics on Cancer Occurrences Worldwide and the Risks Associated with Known Carcinogens and Activities

Edited by Frank E. Bair. 932 pages. 1990. 1-55888-888-8. $78.

Cited in *Reference Sources for Small and Medium-Sized Libraries, American Library Association, 1999*

"Written in nontechnical language. Useful for patients, their families, medical professionals, and librarians."
—Guide to Reference Books, 1996

"Designed with the non-medical professional in mind. Libraries and medical facilities interested in patient education should certainly consider adding the *Cancer Sourcebook* to their holdings. This compact collection of reliable information . . . is an invaluable tool for helping patients and patients' families and friends to take the first steps in coping with the many difficulties of cancer."
—Medical Reference Services Quarterly, Winter '91

"Specifically created for the nontechnical reader . . . an important resource for the general reader trying to understand the complexities of cancer."
—American Reference Books Annual, 1991

"This publication's nontechnical nature and very comprehensive format make it useful for both the general public and undergraduate students."
—Choice, Association of College and Research Libraries, Oct '90

■

New Cancer Sourcebook, 2nd Edition

Basic Information about Major Forms and Stages of Cancer, Featuring Facts about Primary and Secondary Tumors of the Respiratory, Nervous, Lymphatic, Circulatory, Skeletal, and Gastrointestinal Systems, and Specific Organs; Statistical and Demographic Data; Treatment Options; and Strategies for Coping

Edited by Allan R. Cook. 1,313 pages. 1996. 0-7808-0041-9. $78.

"An excellent resource for patients with newly diagnosed cancer and their families. The dialogue is simple, direct, and comprehensive. Highly recommended for patients and families to aid in their understanding of cancer and its treatment."

— Booklist Health Sciences Supplement, American Library Association, Oct '97

"The amount of factual and useful information is extensive. The writing is very clear, geared to general readers. Recommended for all levels." *— Choice, Association of College & Research Libraries, Jan '97*

■

Cancer Sourcebook, 3rd Edition

Basic Consumer Health Information about Major Forms and Stages of Cancer, Featuring Facts about Primary and Secondary Tumors of the Respiratory, Nervous, Lymphatic, Circulatory, Skeletal, and Gastrointestinal Systems, and Specific Organs

Along with Statistical and Demographic Data, Treatment Options, Strategies for Coping, a Glossary, and a Directory of Sources for Additional Help and Information

Edited by Edward J. Prucha. 1,069 pages. 2000. 0-7808-0227-6. $78.

"This title is recommended for health sciences and public libraries with consumer health collections."

— E-Streams, Feb '01

". . . can be effectively used by cancer patients and their families who are looking for answers in a language they can understand. Public and hospital libraries should have it on their shelves."

— American Reference Books Annual, 2001

"Recommended reference source."

— Booklist, American Library Association, Dec '00

■

Cancer Sourcebook for Women, 1st Edition

Basic Information about Specific Forms of Cancer That Affect Women, Featuring Facts about Breast Cancer, Cervical Cancer, Ovarian Cancer, Cancer of the Uterus and Uterine Sarcoma, Cancer of the Vagina, and Cancer of the Vulva; Statistical and Demographic Data; Treatments, Self-Help Management Suggestions, and Current Research Initiatives

Edited by Allan R. Cook and Peter D. Dresser. 524 pages. 1996. 0-7808 0076-1. $78.

". . . written in easily understandable, non-technical language. Recommended for public libraries or hospital and academic libraries that collect patient education or consumer health materials."

— Medical Reference Services Quarterly, Spring '97

"Would be of value in a consumer health library. . . . written with the health care consumer in mind. Medical jargon is at a minimum, and medical terms are explained in clear, understandable sentences."

— Bulletin of the Medical Library Association, Oct '96

"The availability under one cover of all these pertinent publications, grouped under cohesive headings, makes this certainly a most useful sourcebook." *— Choice, Association of College & Research Libraries, Jun '96*

"Presents a comprehensive knowledge base for general readers. Men and women both benefit from the gold mine of information nestled between the two covers of this book. Recommended."

— Academic Library Book Review, Summer '96

"This timely book is highly recommended for consumer health and patient education collections in all libraries." *— Library Journal, Apr '96*

SEE ALSO *Breast Cancer Sourcebook, Women's Health Concerns Sourcebook*

■

Cancer Sourcebook for Women, 2nd Edition

Basic Consumer Health Information about Gynecologic Cancers and Related Concerns, Including Cervical Cancer, Endometrial Cancer, Gestational Trophoblastic Tumor, Ovarian Cancer, Uterine Cancer, Vaginal Cancer, Vulvar Cancer, Breast Cancer, and Common Non-Cancerous Uterine Conditions, with Facts about Cancer Risk Factors, Screening and Prevention, Treatment Options, and Reports on Current Research Initiatives

Along with a Glossary of Cancer Terms and a Directory of Resources for Additional Help and Information

Edited by Karen Bellenir. 604 pages. 2002. 0-7808-0226-8. $78.

SEE ALSO *Breast Cancer Sourcebook, Women's Health Concerns Sourcebook*

■

Cardiovascular Diseases & Disorders Sourcebook, 1st Edition

Basic Information about Cardiovascular Diseases and Disorders, Featuring Facts about the Cardiovascular System, Demographic and Statistical Data, Descriptions of Pharmacological and Surgical Interventions, Lifestyle Modifications, and a Special Section Focusing on Heart Disorders in Children

Edited by Karen Bellenir and Peter D. Dresser. 683 pages. 1995. 0-7808-0032-X. $78.

". . . comprehensive format provides an extensive overview on this subject." *— Choice, Association of College & Research Libraries, Jun '96*

". . . an easily understood, complete, up-to-date resource. This well executed public health tool will make valuable information available to those that need it most, patients and their families. The typeface, sturdy non-reflective paper, and library binding add a feel of quality found wanting in other publications. Highly recommended for academic and general libraries. "

— Academic Library Book Review, Summer '96

SEE ALSO *Healthy Heart Sourcebook for Women, Heart Diseases & Disorders Sourcebook, 2nd Edition*

Caregiving Sourcebook

Basic Consumer Health Information for Caregivers, Including a Profile of Caregivers, Caregiving Responsibilities and Concerns, Tips for Specific Conditions, Care Environments, and the Effects of Caregiving

Along with Facts about Legal Issues, Financial Information, and Future Planning, a Glossary, and a Listing of Additional Resources

Edited by Joyce Brennfleck Shannon. 600 pages. 2001. 0-7808-0331-0. $78.

"Essential for most collections."
—Library Journal, Apr 1, 2002

"An ideal addition to the reference collection of any public library. Health sciences information professionals may also want to acquire the *Caregiving Sourcebook* for their hospital or academic library for use as a ready reference tool by health care workers interested in aging and caregiving." *—E-Streams, Jan '02*

"Recommended reference source."
—Booklist, American Library Association, Oct '01

■

Colds, Flu & Other Common Ailments Sourcebook

Basic Consumer Health Information about Common Ailments and Injuries, Including Colds, Coughs, the Flu, Sinus Problems, Headaches, Fever, Nausea and Vomiting, Menstrual Cramps, Diarrhea, Constipation, Hemorrhoids, Back Pain, Dandruff, Dry and Itchy Skin, Cuts, Scrapes, Sprains, Bruises, and More

Along with Information about Prevention, Self-Care, Choosing a Doctor, Over-the-Counter Medications, Folk Remedies, and Alternative Therapies, and Including a Glossary of Important Terms and a Directory of Resources for Further Help and Information

Edited by Chad T. Kimball. 638 pages. 2001. 0-7808-0435-X. $78.

"A good starting point for research on common illnesses. It will be a useful addition to public and consumer health library collections."
— American Reference Books Annual 2002

"Will prove valuable to any library seeking to maintain a current, comprehensive reference collection of health resources. . . . Excellent reference."
— The Bookwatch, Aug '01

"Recommended reference source."
— Booklist, American Library Association, July '01

■

Communication Disorders Sourcebook

Basic Information about Deafness and Hearing Loss, Speech and Language Disorders, Voice Disorders, Balance and Vestibular Disorders, and Disorders of Smell, Taste, and Touch

Edited by Linda M. Ross. 533 pages. 1996. 0-7808-0077-X. $78.

"This is skillfully edited and is a welcome resource for the layperson. It should be found in every public and medical library." *—Booklist Health Sciences Supplement, American Library Association, Oct '97*

■

Congenital Disorders Sourcebook

Basic Information about Disorders Acquired during Gestation, Including Spina Bifida, Hydrocephalus, Cerebral Palsy, Heart Defects, Craniofacial Abnormalities, Fetal Alcohol Syndrome, and More

Along with Current Treatment Options and Statistical Data

Edited by Karen Bellenir. 607 pages. 1997. 0-7808-0205-5. $78.

"Recommended reference source."
— Booklist, American Library Association, Oct '97

SEE ALSO *Pregnancy & Birth Sourcebook*

■

Consumer Issues in Health Care Sourcebook

Basic Information about Health Care Fundamentals and Related Consumer Issues, Including Exams and Screening Tests, Physician Specialties, Choosing a Doctor, Using Prescription and Over-the-Counter Medications Safely, Avoiding Health Scams, Managing Common Health Risks in the Home, Care Options for Chronically or Terminally Ill Patients, and a List of Resources for Obtaining Help and Further Information

Edited by Karen Bellenir. 618 pages. 1998. 0-7808-0221-7. $78.

"Both public and academic libraries will want to have a copy in their collection for readers who are interested in self-education on health issues."
—American Reference Books Annual, 2000

"The editor has researched the literature from government agencies and others, saving readers the time and effort of having to do the research themselves. Recommended for public libraries."
— Reference and User Services Quarterly, American Library Association, Spring '99

"Recommended reference source."
— Booklist, American Library Association, Dec '98

■

Contagious & Non-Contagious Infectious Diseases Sourcebook

Basic Information about Contagious Diseases like Measles, Polio, Hepatitis B, and Infectious Mononucleosis, and Non-Contagious Infectious Diseases like Tetanus and Toxic Shock Syndrome, and Diseases Occurring as Secondary Infections Such as Shingles and Reye Syndrome

Along with Vaccination, Prevention, and Treatment Information, and a Section Describing Emerging Infectious Disease Threats

Edited by Karen Bellenir and Peter D. Dresser. 566 pages. 1996. 0-7808-0075-3. $78.

Death & Dying Sourcebook

Basic Consumer Health Information for the Layperson about End-of-Life Care and Related Ethical and Legal Issues, Including Chief Causes of Death, Autopsies, Pain Management for the Terminally Ill, Life Support Systems, Insurance, Euthanasia, Assisted Suicide, Hospice Programs, Living Wills, Funeral Planning, Counseling, Mourning, Organ Donation, and Physician Training

Along with Statistical Data, a Glossary, and Listings of Sources for Further Help and Information

Edited by Annemarie S. Muth. 641 pages. 1999. 0-7808-0230-6. $78.

"Public libraries, medical libraries, and academic libraries will all find this sourcebook a useful addition to their collections."
— American Reference Books Annual, 2001

"An extremely useful resource for those concerned with death and dying in the United States."
— Respiratory Care, Nov '00

"Recommended reference source."
—Booklist, American Library Association, Aug '00

"This book is a definite must for all those involved in end-of-life care." *— Doody's Review Service, 2000*

■

Depression Sourcebook

Basic Consumer Health Information about Unipolar Depression, Bipolar Disorder, Postpartum Depression, Seasonal Affective Disorder, and Other Types of Depression in Children, Adolescents, Women, Men, the Elderly, and Other Selected Populations

Along with Facts about Causes, Risk Factors, Diagnostic Criteria, Treatment Options, Coping Strategies, Suicide Prevention, a Glossary, and a Directory of Sources for Additional Help and Information

Edited by Karen Belleni. 625 pages. 2002. 0-7808-0611-5. $78.

■

Diabetes Sourcebook, 1st Edition

Basic Information about Insulin-Dependent and Non-insulin-Dependent Diabetes Mellitus, Gestational Diabetes, and Diabetic Complications, Symptoms, Treatment, and Research Results, Including Statistics on Prevalence, Morbidity, and Mortality

Along with Source Listings for Further Help and Information

Edited by Karen Bellenir and Peter D. Dresser. 827 pages. 1994. 1-55888-751-2. $78.

". . . very informative and understandable for the layperson without being simplistic. It provides a comprehensive overview for laypersons who want a general understanding of the disease or who want to focus on various aspects of the disease."
— Bulletin of the Medical Library Association, Jan '96

Diabetes Sourcebook, 2nd Edition

Basic Consumer Health Information about Type 1 Diabetes (Insulin-Dependent or Juvenile-Onset Diabetes), Type 2 (Noninsulin-Dependent or Adult-Onset Diabetes), Gestational Diabetes, and Related Disorders, Including Diabetes Prevalence Data, Management Issues, the Role of Diet and Exercise in Controlling Diabetes, Insulin and Other Diabetes Medicines, and Complications of Diabetes Such as Eye Diseases, Periodontal Disease, Amputation, and End-Stage Renal Disease

Along with Reports on Current Research Initiatives, a Glossary, and Resource Listings for Further Help and Information

Edited by Karen Bellenir. 688 pages. 1998. 0-7808-0224-1. $78.

"An invaluable reference." *— Library Journal, May '00*

Selected as one of the 250 "Best Health Sciences Books of 1999." *— Doody's Rating Service, Mar-Apr 2000*

"This comprehensive book is an excellent addition for high school, academic, medical, and public libraries. This volume is highly recommended."
—American Reference Books Annual, 2000

"Provides useful information for the general public."
— Healthlines, University of Michigan Health Management Research Center, Sep/Oct '99

". . . provides reliable mainstream medical information . . . belongs on the shelves of any library with a consumer health collection." *— E-Streams, Sep '99*

"Recommended reference source."
— Booklist, American Library Association, Feb '99

■

Diet & Nutrition Sourcebook, 1st Edition

Basic Information about Nutrition, Including the Dietary Guidelines for Americans, the Food Guide Pyramid, and Their Applications in Daily Diet, Nutritional Advice for Specific Age Groups, Current Nutritional Issues and Controversies, the New Food Label and How to Use It to Promote Healthy Eating, and Recent Developments in Nutritional Research

Edited by Dan R. Harris. 662 pages. 1996. 0-7808-0084-2. $78.

"Useful reference as a food and nutrition sourcebook for the general consumer." *— Booklist Health Sciences Supplement, American Library Association, Oct '97*

"Recommended for public libraries and medical libraries that receive general information requests on nutrition. It is readable and will appeal to those interested in learning more about healthy dietary practices."
— Medical Reference Services Quarterly, Fall '97

"An abundance of medical and social statistics is translated into readable information geared toward the general reader." *— Bookwatch, Mar '97*

"With dozens of questionable diet books on the market, it is so refreshing to find a reliable and factual reference book. Recommended to aspiring professionals, librari-

ans, and others seeking and giving reliable dietary advice. An excellent compilation." — *Choice, Association of College and Research Libraries, Feb '97*

SEE ALSO *Digestive Diseases & Disorders Sourcebook, Gastrointestinal Diseases & Disorders Sourcebook*

■

Diet & Nutrition Sourcebook, 2nd Edition

Basic Consumer Health Information about Dietary Guidelines, Recommended Daily Intake Values, Vitamins, Minerals, Fiber, Fat, Weight Control, Dietary Supplements, and Food Additives

Along with Special Sections on Nutrition Needs throughout Life and Nutrition for People with Such Specific Medical Concerns as Allergies, High Blood Cholesterol, Hypertension, Diabetes, Celiac Disease, Seizure Disorders, Phenylketonuria (PKU), Cancer, and Eating Disorders, and Including Reports on Current Nutrition Research and Source Listings for Additional Help and Information

Edited by Karen Bellenir. 650 pages. 1999. 0-7808-0228-4. $78.

"This book is an excellent source of basic diet and nutrition information." — *Booklist Health Sciences Supplement, American Library Association, Dec '00*

"This reference document should be in any public library, but it would be a very good guide for beginning students in the health sciences. If the other books in this publisher's series are as good as this, they should all be in the health sciences collections."
— *American Reference Books Annual, 2000*

"This book is an excellent general nutrition reference for consumers who desire to take an active role in their health care for prevention. Consumers of all ages who select this book can feel confident they are receiving current and accurate information." — *Journal of Nutrition for the Elderly, Vol. 19, No. 4, '00*

"Recommended reference source."
— *Booklist, American Library Association, Dec '99*

SEE ALSO *Digestive Diseases & Disorders Sourcebook, Gastrointestinal Diseases & Disorders Sourcebook*

■

Digestive Diseases & Disorders Sourcebook

Basic Consumer Health Information about Diseases and Disorders that Impact the Upper and Lower Digestive System, Including Celiac Disease, Constipation, Crohn's Disease, Cyclic Vomiting Syndrome, Diarrhea, Diverticulosis and Diverticulitis, Gallstones, Heartburn, Hemorrhoids, Hernias, Indigestion (Dyspepsia), Irritable Bowel Syndrome, Lactose Intolerance, Ulcers, and More

Along with Information about Medications and Other Treatments, Tips for Maintaining a Healthy Digestive Tract, a Glossary, and Directory of Digestive Diseases Organizations

Edited by Karen Bellenir. 335 pages. 2000. 0-7808-0327-2. $78.

"This title would be an excellent addition to all public or patient-research libraries."
— *American Reference Books Annual, 2001*

"This title is recommended for public, hospital, and health sciences libraries with consumer health collections." — *E-Streams, Jul-Aug '00*

"Recommended reference source."
— *Booklist, American Library Association, May '00*

SEE ALSO *Diet & Nutrition Sourcebook, 1st and 2nd Editions, Gastrointestinal Diseases & Disorders Sourcebook*

■

Disabilities Sourcebook

Basic Consumer Health Information about Physical and Psychiatric Disabilities, Including Descriptions of Major Causes of Disability, Assistive and Adaptive Aids, Workplace Issues, and Accessibility Concerns

Along with Information about the Americans with Disabilities Act, a Glossary, and Resources for Additional Help and Information

Edited by Dawn D. Matthews. 616 pages. 2000. 0-7808-0389-2. $78.

"It is a must for libraries with a consumer health section." — *American Reference Books Annual 2002*

"A much needed addition to the Omnigraphics *Health Reference Series*. A current reference work to provide people with disabilities, their families, caregivers or those who work with them, a broad range of information in one volume, has not been available until now. . . . It is recommended for all public and academic library reference collections." — *E-Streams, May '01*

"An excellent source book in easy-to-read format covering many current topics; highly recommended for all libraries." — *Choice, Association of College and Research Libraries, Jan '01*

"Recommended reference source."
— *Booklist, American Library Association, Jul '00*

"An involving, invaluable handbook."
— *The Bookwatch, May '00*

■

Domestic Violence & Child Abuse Sourcebook

Basic Consumer Health Information about Spousal/Partner, Child, Sibling, Parent, and Elder Abuse, Covering Physical, Emotional, and Sexual Abuse, Teen Dating Violence, and Stalking; Includes Information about Hotlines, Safe Houses, Safety Plans, and Other Resources for Support and Assistance, Community Initiatives, and Reports on Current Directions in Research and Treatment

Along with a Glossary, Sources for Further Reading, and Governmental and Non-Governmental Organizations Contact Information

Edited by Helene Henderson. 1,064 pages. 2001. 0-7808-0235-7. $78.

"This is important information. The Web has many resources but this sourcebook fills an important societal need. I am not aware of any other resources of this type." —*Doody's Review Service, Sep '01*

"Recommended for all libraries, scholars, and practitioners." —*Choice, Association of College & Research Libraries, Jul '01*

"Recommended reference source." —*Booklist, American Library Association, Apr '01*

"Important pick for college-level health reference libraries." —*The Bookwatch, Mar '01*

"Because this problem is so widespread and because this book includes a lot of issues within one volume, this work is recommended for all public libraries." —*American Reference Books Annual, 2001*

■

Drug Abuse Sourcebook

Basic Consumer Health Information about Illicit Substances of Abuse and the Diversion of Prescription Medications, Including Depressants, Hallucinogens, Inhalants, Marijuana, Narcotics, Stimulants, and Anabolic Steroids

Along with Facts about Related Health Risks, Treatment Issues, and Substance Abuse Prevention Programs, a Glossary of Terms, Statistical Data, and Directories of Hotline Services, Self-Help Groups, and Organizations Able to Provide Further Information

Edited by Karen Bellenir. 629 pages. 2000. 0-7808-0242-X. $78.

"Containing a wealth of information, this book will be useful to the college student just beginning to explore the topic of substance abuse. This resource belongs in libraries that serve a lower-division undergraduate or community college clientele as well as the general public." —*Choice, Association of College and Research Libraries, Jun '01*

"Recommended reference source." —*Booklist, American Library Association, Feb '01*

"Highly recommended." —*The Bookwatch, Jan '01*

"Even though there is a plethora of books on drug abuse, this volume is recommended for school, public, and college libraries." —*American Reference Books Annual, 2001*

SEE ALSO Alcoholism Sourcebook, Substance Abuse Sourcebook

■

Ear, Nose & Throat Disorders Sourcebook

Basic Information about Disorders of the Ears, Nose, Sinus Cavities, Pharynx, and Larynx, Including Ear Infections, Tinnitus, Vestibular Disorders, Allergic and Non-Allergic Rhinitis, Sore Throats, Tonsillitis, and Cancers That Affect the Ears, Nose, Sinuses, and Throat

Along with Reports on Current Research Initiatives, a Glossary of Related Medical Terms, and a Directory of Sources for Further Help and Information

Edited by Karen Bellenir and Linda M. Shin. 576 pages. 1998. 0-7808-0206-3. $78.

"Overall, this sourcebook is helpful for the consumer seeking information on ENT issues. It is recommended for public libraries." —*American Reference Books Annual, 1999*

"Recommended reference source." —*Booklist, American Library Association, Dec '98*

■

Eating Disorders Sourcebook

Basic Consumer Health Information about Eating Disorders, Including Information about Anorexia Nervosa, Bulimia Nervosa, Binge Eating, Body Dysmorphic Disorder, Pica, Laxative Abuse, and Night Eating Syndrome

Along with Information about Causes, Adverse Effects, and Treatment and Prevention Issues, and Featuring a Section on Concerns Specific to Children and Adolescents, a Glossary, and Resources for Further Help and Information

Edited by Dawn D. Matthews. 322 pages. 2001. 0-7808-0335-3. $78.

"Recommended for health science libraries that are open to the public, as well as hospital libraries. This book is a good resource for the consumer who is concerned about eating disorders." —*E-Streams, Mar '02*

"This volume is another convenient collection of excerpted articles. Recommended for school and public library patrons; lower-division undergraduates; and two-year technical program students." —*Choice, Association of College & Research Libraries, Jan '02*

"Recommended reference source." —*Booklist, American Library Association, Oct '01*

■

Emergency Medical Services Sourcebook

Basic Consumer Health Information about Preventing, Preparing for, and Managing Emergency Situations, When and Who to Call for Help, What to Expect in the Emergency Room, the Emergency Medical Team, Patient Issues, and Current Topics in Emergency Medicine

Along with Statistical Data, a Glossary, and Sources of Additional Help and Information

Edited by Jenni Lynn Colson. 494 pages. 2002. 0-7808-0420-1. $78.

Endocrine & Metabolic Disorders Sourcebook

Basic Information for the Layperson about Pancreatic and Insulin-Related Disorders Such as Pancreatitis, Diabetes, and Hypoglycemia; Adrenal Gland Disorders Such as Cushing's Syndrome, Addison's Disease, and Congenital Adrenal Hyperplasia; Pituitary Gland Disorders Such as Growth Hormone Deficiency, Acromegaly, and Pituitary Tumors; Thyroid Disorders Such as Hypothyroidism, Graves' Disease, Hashimoto's Disease, and Goiter; Hyperparathyroidism; and Other Diseases and Syndromes of Hormone Imbalance or Metabolic Dysfunction

Along with Reports on Current Research Initiatives

Edited by Linda M. Shin. 574 pages. 1998. 0-7808-0207-1. $78.

"Omnigraphics has produced another needed resource for health information consumers."
— *American Reference Books Annual, 2000*

"Recommended reference source."
— *Booklist, American Library Association, Dec '98*

∎

Environmentally Induced Disorders Sourcebook

Basic Information about Diseases and Syndromes Linked to Exposure to Pollutants and Other Substances in Outdoor and Indoor Environments Such as Lead, Asbestos, Formaldehyde, Mercury, Emissions, Noise, and More

Edited by Allan R. Cook. 620 pages. 1997. 0-7808-0083-4. $78.

"Recommended reference source."
— *Booklist, American Library Association, Sep '98*

"This book will be a useful addition to anyone's library." — *Choice Health Sciences Supplement, Association of College and Research Libraries, May '98*

". . . a good survey of numerous environmentally induced physical disorders . . . a useful addition to anyone's library."
— *Doody's Health Sciences Book Reviews, Jan '98*

". . . provide[s] introductory information from the best authorities around. Since this volume covers topics that potentially affect everyone, it will surely be one of the most frequently consulted volumes in the *Health Reference Series*." — *Rettig on Reference, Nov '97*

∎

Ethnic Diseases Sourcebook

Basic Consumer Health Information for Ethnic and Racial Minority Groups in the United States, Including General Health Indicators and Behaviors, Ethnic Diseases, Genetic Testing, the Impact of Chronic Diseases, Women's Health, Mental Health Issues, and Preventive Health Care Services

Along with a Glossary and a Listing of Additional Resources

Edited by Joyce Brennfleck Shannon. 664 pages. 2001. 0-7808-0336-1. $78.

"Recommended for health sciences libraries where public health programs are a priority."
— *E-Streams, Jan '02*

"Not many books have been written on this topic to date, and the *Ethnic Diseases Sourcebook* is a strong addition to the list. It will be an important introductory resource for health consumers, students, health care personnel, and social scientists. It is recommended for public, academic, and large hospital libraries."
— *American Reference Books Annual 2002*

"Recommended reference source."
— *Booklist, American Library Association, Oct '01*

"Will prove valuable to any library seeking to maintain a current, comprehensive reference collection of health resources. . . . An excellent source of health information about genetic disorders which affect particular ethnic and racial minorities in the U.S."
— *The Bookwatch, Aug '01*

∎

Family Planning Sourcebook

Basic Consumer Health Information about Planning for Pregnancy and Contraception, Including Traditional Methods, Barrier Methods, Hormonal Methods, Permanent Methods, Future Methods, Emergency Contraception, and Birth Control Choices for Women at Each Stage of Life

Along with Statistics, a Glossary, and Sources of Additional Information

Edited by Amy Marcaccio Keyzer. 520 pages. 2001. 0-7808-0379-5. $78.

"Recommended for public, health, and undergraduate libraries as part of the circulating collection."
— *E-Streams, Mar '02*

"Information is presented in an unbiased, readable manner, and the sourcebook will certainly be a necessary addition to those public and high school libraries where Internet access is restricted or otherwise problematic." — *American Reference Books Annual 2002*

"Recommended reference source."
— *Booklist, American Library Association, Oct '01*

"Will prove valuable to any library seeking to maintain a current, comprehensive reference collection of health resources. . . . Excellent reference."
— *The Bookwatch, Aug '01*

SEE ALSO Pregnancy & Birth Sourcebook

∎

Fitness & Exercise Sourcebook, 1st Edition

Basic Information on Fitness and Exercise, Including Fitness Activities for Specific Age Groups, Exercise for People with Specific Medical Conditions, How to Begin a Fitness Program in Running, Walking, Swimming, Cycling, and Other Athletic Activities, and Recent Research in Fitness and Exercise

Edited by Dan R. Harris. 663 pages. 1996. 0-7808-0186-5. $78.

"A good resource for general readers." —*Choice, Association of College and Research Libraries, Nov '97*

"The perennial popularity of the topic . . . make this an appealing selection for public libraries."
—*Rettig on Reference, Jun/Jul '97*

▪

Fitness & Exercise Sourcebook, 2nd Edition

Basic Consumer Health Information about the Fundamentals of Fitness and Exercise, Including How to Begin and Maintain a Fitness Program, Fitness as a Lifestyle, the Link between Fitness and Diet, Advice for Specific Groups of People, Exercise as It Relates to Specific Medical Conditions, and Recent Research in Fitness and Exercise

Along with a Glossary of Important Terms and Resources for Additional Help and Information

Edited by Kristen M. Gledhill. 646 pages. 2001. 0-7808-0334-5. $78.

"This work is recommended for all general reference collections."
—*American Reference Books Annual 2002*

"Highly recommended for public, consumer, and school grades fourth through college."
—*E-Streams, Nov '01*

"Recommended reference source." —*Booklist, American Library Association, Oct '01*

"The information appears quite comprehensive and is considered reliable. . . . This second edition is a welcomed addition to the series."
—*Doody's Review Service, Sep '01*

"This reference is a valuable choice for those who desire a broad source of information on exercise, fitness, and chronic-disease prevention through a healthy lifestyle." —*American Medical Writers Association Journal, Fall '01*

"Will prove valuable to any library seeking to maintain a current, comprehensive reference collection of health resources. . . . Excellent reference."
—*The Bookwatch, Aug '01*

▪

Food & Animal Borne Diseases Sourcebook

Basic Information about Diseases That Can Be Spread to Humans through the Ingestion of Contaminated Food or Water or by Contact with Infected Animals and Insects, Such as Botulism, E. Coli, Hepatitis A, Trichinosis, Lyme Disease, and Rabies

Along with Information Regarding Prevention and Treatment Methods, and Including a Special Section for International Travelers Describing Diseases Such as Cholera, Malaria, Travelers' Diarrhea, and Yellow Fever, and Offering Recommendations for Avoiding Illness

Edited by Karen Bellenir and Peter D. Dresser. 535 pages. 1995. 0-7808-0033-8. $78.

"Targeting general readers and providing them with a single, comprehensive source of information on selected topics, this book continues, with the excellent caliber of its predecessors, to catalog topical information on health matters of general interest. Readable and thorough, this valuable resource is highly recommended for all libraries."
—*Academic Library Book Review, Summer '96*

"A comprehensive collection of authoritative information." —*Emergency Medical Services, Oct '95*

▪

Food Safety Sourcebook

Basic Consumer Health Information about the Safe Handling of Meat, Poultry, Seafood, Eggs, Fruit Juices, and Other Food Items, and Facts about Pesticides, Drinking Water, Food Safety Overseas, and the Onset, Duration, and Symptoms of Foodborne Illnesses, Including Types of Pathogenic Bacteria, Parasitic Protozoa, Worms, Viruses, and Natural Toxins

Along with the Role of the Consumer, the Food Handler, and the Government in Food Safety; a Glossary, and Resources for Additional Help and Information

Edited by Dawn D. Matthews. 339 pages. 1999. 0-7808-0326-4. $78.

"This book is recommended for public libraries and universities with home economic and food science programs." —*E-Streams, Nov '00*

"Recommended reference source."
—*Booklist, American Library Association, May '00*

"This book takes the complex issues of food safety and foodborne pathogens and presents them in an easily understood manner. [It does] an excellent job of covering a large and often confusing topic."
—*American Reference Books Annual, 2000*

▪

Forensic Medicine Sourcebook

Basic Consumer Information for the Layperson about Forensic Medicine, Including Crime Scene Investigation, Evidence Collection and Analysis, Expert Testimony, Computer-Aided Criminal Identification, Digital Imaging in the Courtroom, DNA Profiling, Accident Reconstruction, Autopsies, Ballistics, Drugs and Explosives Detection, Latent Fingerprints, Product Tampering, and Questioned Document Examination

Along with Statistical Data, a Glossary of Forensics Terminology, and Listings of Sources for Further Help and Information

Edited by Annemarie S. Muth. 574 pages. 1999. 0-7808-0232-2. $78.

"Given the expected widespread interest in its content and its easy to read style, this book is recommended for most public and all college and university libraries."
—*E-Streams, Feb '01*

"Recommended for public libraries."
—*Reference & User Services Quarterly, American Library Association, Spring 2000*

"Recommended reference source."
—*Booklist, American Library Association, Feb '00*

"A wealth of information, useful statistics, references are up-to-date and extremely complete. This wonderful collection of data will help students who are interested in a career in any type of forensic field. It is a great resource for attorneys who need information about types of expert witnesses needed in a particular case. It also offers useful information for fiction and nonfiction writers whose work involves a crime. A fascinating compilation. All levels." — *Choice, Association of College and Research Libraries, Jan 2000*

"There are several items that make this book attractive to consumers who are seeking certain forensic data.... This is a useful current source for those seeking general forensic medical answers."
—*American Reference Books Annual, 2000*

■

Gastrointestinal Diseases & Disorders Sourcebook

Basic Information about Gastroesophageal Reflux Disease (Heartburn), Ulcers, Diverticulosis, Irritable Bowel Syndrome, Crohn's Disease, Ulcerative Colitis, Diarrhea, Constipation, Lactose Intolerance, Hemorrhoids, Hepatitis, Cirrhosis, and Other Digestive Problems, Featuring Statistics, Descriptions of Symptoms, and Current Treatment Methods of Interest for Persons Living with Upper and Lower Gastrointestinal Maladies

Edited by Linda M. Ross. 413 pages. 1996. 0-7808-0078-8. $78.

"... very readable form. The successful editorial work that brought this material together into a useful and understandable reference makes accessible to all readers information that can help them more effectively understand and obtain help for digestive tract problems."
— *Choice, Association of College & Research Libraries, Feb '97*

SEE ALSO *Diet & Nutrition Sourcebook, 1st and 2nd Editions, Digestive Diseases & Disorders*

■

Genetic Disorders Sourcebook, 1st Edition

Basic Information about Heritable Diseases and Disorders Such as Down Syndrome, PKU, Hemophilia, Von Willebrand Disease, Gaucher Disease, Tay-Sachs Disease, and Sickle-Cell Disease, Along with Information about Genetic Screening, Gene Therapy, Home Care, and Including Source Listings for Further Help and Information on More Than 300 Disorders

Edited by Karen Bellenir. 642 pages. 1996. 0-7808-0034-6. $78.

"Recommended for undergraduate libraries or libraries that serve the public."
—*Science & Technology Libraries, Vol. 18, No. 1, '99*

"Provides essential medical information to both the general public and those diagnosed with a serious or fatal genetic disease or disorder." —*Choice, Association of College and Research Libraries, Jan '97*

"Geared toward the lay public. It would be well placed in all public libraries and in those hospital and medical libraries in which access to genetic references is limited." —*Doody's Health Sciences Book Review, Oct '96*

■

Genetic Disorders Sourcebook, 2nd Edition

Basic Consumer Health Information about Hereditary Diseases and Disorders, Including Cystic Fibrosis, Down Syndrome, Hemophilia, Huntington's Disease, Sickle Cell Anemia, and More; Facts about Genes, Gene Research and Therapy, Genetic Screening, Ethics of Gene Testing, Genetic Counseling, and Advice on Coping and Caring

Along with a Glossary of Genetic Terminology and a Resource List for Help, Support, and Further Information

Edited by Kathy Massimini. 768 pages. 2001. 0-7808-0241-1. $78.

"Recommended for public libraries and medical and hospital libraries with consumer health collections."
— *E-Streams, May '01*

"Recommended reference source."
— *Booklist, American Library Association, Apr '01*

"Important pick for college-level health reference libraries." — *The Bookwatch, Mar '01*

■

Head Trauma Sourcebook

Basic Information for the Layperson about Open-Head and Closed-Head Injuries, Treatment Advances, Recovery, and Rehabilitation

Along with Reports on Current Research Initiatives

Edited by Karen Bellenir. 414 pages. 1997. 0-7808-0208-X. $78.

■

Headache Sourcebook

Basic Consumer Health Information about Migraine, Tension, Cluster, Rebound and Other Types of Headaches, with Facts about the Cause and Prevention of Headaches, the Effects of Stress and the Environment, Headaches during Pregnancy and Menopause, and Childhood Headaches

Along with a Glossary and Other Resources for Additional Help and Information

Edited by Dawn D. Matthews. 362 pages. 2002. 0-7808-0337-X. $78.

Health Insurance Sourcebook

Basic Information about Managed Care Organizations, Traditional Fee-for-Service Insurance, Insurance Portability and Pre-Existing Conditions Clauses, Medicare, Medicaid, Social Security, and Military Health Care

Along with Information about Insurance Fraud

Edited by Wendy Wilcox. 530 pages. 1997. 0-7808-0222-5. $78.

"Particularly useful because it brings much of this information together in one volume. This book will be a handy reference source in the health sciences library, hospital library, college and university library, and medium to large public library."
— *Medical Reference Services Quarterly, Fall '98*

Awarded "Books of the Year Award"
— *American Journal of Nursing, 1997*

"The layout of the book is particularly helpful as it provides easy access to reference material. A most useful addition to the vast amount of information about health insurance. The use of data from U.S. government agencies is most commendable. Useful in a library or learning center for healthcare professional students."
— *Doody's Health Sciences Book Reviews, Nov '97*

Health Reference Series Cumulative Index 1999

A Comprehensive Index to the Individual Volumes of the Health Reference Series, Including a Subject Index, Name Index, Organization Index, and Publication Index

Along with a Master List of Acronyms and Abbreviations

Edited by Edward J. Prucha, Anne Holmes, and Robert Rudnick. 990 pages. 2000. 0-7808-0382-5. $78.

"This volume will be most helpful in libraries that have a relatively complete collection of the Health Reference Series." — *American Reference Books Annual, 2001*

"Essential for collections that hold any of the numerous *Health Reference Series* titles."
— *Choice, Association of College and Research Libraries, Nov '00*

Healthy Aging Sourcebook

Basic Consumer Health Information about Maintaining Health through the Aging Process, Including Advice on Nutrition, Exercise, and Sleep, Help in Making Decisions about Midlife Issues and Retirement, and Guidance Concerning Practical and Informed Choices in Health Consumerism

Along with Data Concerning the Theories of Aging, Different Experiences in Aging by Minority Groups, and Facts about Aging Now and Aging in the Future; and Featuring a Glossary, a Guide to Consumer Help, Additional Suggested Reading, and Practical Resource Directory

Edited by Jenifer Swanson. 536 pages. 1999. 0-7808-0390-6. $78.

"Recommended reference source."
— *Booklist, American Library Association, Feb '00*

SEE ALSO *Physical & Mental Issues in Aging Sourcebook*

Healthy Heart Sourcebook for Women

Basic Consumer Health Information about Cardiac Issues Specific to Women, Including Facts about Major Risk Factors and Prevention, Treatment and Control Strategies, and Important Dietary Issues

Along with a Special Section Regarding the Pros and Cons of Hormone Replacement Therapy and Its Impact on Heart Health, and Additional Help, Including Recipes, a Glossary, and a Directory of Resources

Edited by Dawn D. Matthews. 336 pages. 2000. 0-7808-0329-9. $78.

"A good reference source and recommended for all public, academic, medical, and hospital libraries."
— *Medical Reference Services Quarterly, Summer '01*

"Because of the lack of information specific to women on this topic, this book is recommended for public libraries and consumer libraries."
— *American Reference Books Annual, 2001*

"Contains very important information about coronary artery disease that all women should know. The information is current and presented in an easy-to-read format. The book will make a good addition to any library." — *American Medical Writers Association Journal, Summer '00*

"Important, basic reference."
— *Reviewer's Bookwatch, Jul '00*

SEE ALSO *Cardiovascular Diseases & Disorders Sourcebook, 1st Edition, Heart Diseases & Disorders Sourcebook, 2nd Edition, Women's Health Concerns Sourcebook*

Heart Diseases & Disorders Sourcebook, 2nd Edition

Basic Consumer Health Information about Heart Attacks, Angina, Rhythm Disorders, Heart Failure, Valve Disease, Congenital Heart Disorders, and More, Including Descriptions of Surgical Procedures and Other Interventions, Medications, Cardiac Rehabilitation, Risk Identification, and Prevention Tips

Along with Statistical Data, Reports on Current Research Initiatives, a Glossary of Cardiovascular Terms, and Resource Directory

Edited by Karen Bellenir. 612 pages. 2000. 0-7808-0238-1. $78.

"This work stands out as an imminently accessible resource for the general public. It is recommended for the reference and circulating shelves of school, public, and academic libraries."
— *American Reference Books Annual, 2001*

"Recommended reference source."
— *Booklist, American Library Association, Dec '00*

"Provides comprehensive coverage of matters related to the heart. This title is recommended for health sciences and public libraries with consumer health collections."
— *E-Streams, Oct '00*

SEE ALSO Cardiovascular Diseases & Disorders Sourcebook, 1st Edition; Healthy Heart Sourcebook for Women

■

Household Safety Sourcebook

Basic Consumer Health Information about Household Safety, Including Information about Poisons, Chemicals, Fire, and Water Hazards in the Home

Along with Advice about the Safe Use of Home Maintenance Equipment, Choosing Toys and Nursery Furniture, Holiday and Recreation Safety, a Glossary, and Resources for Further Help and Information

Edited by Dawn D. Matthews. 606 pages. 2002. 0-7808-0338-8. $78.

■

Immune System Disorders Sourcebook

Basic Information about Lupus, Multiple Sclerosis, Guillain-Barré Syndrome, Chronic Granulomatous Disease, and More

Along with Statistical and Demographic Data and Reports on Current Research Initiatives

Edited by Allan R. Cook. 608 pages. 1997. 0-7808-0209-8. $78.

■

Infant & Toddler Health Sourcebook

Basic Consumer Health Information about the Physical and Mental Development of Newborns, Infants, and Toddlers, Including Neonatal Concerns, Nutrition Recommendations, Immunization Schedules, Common Pediatric Disorders, Assessments and Milestones, Safety Tips, and Advice for Parents and Other Caregivers

Along with a Glossary of Terms and Resource Listings for Additional Help

Edited by Jenifer Swanson. 585 pages. 2000. 0-7808-0246-2. $78.

"As a reference for the general public, this would be useful in any library." — *E-Streams, May '01*

"Recommended reference source."
— *Booklist, American Library Association, Feb '01*

"This is a good source for general use."
— *American Reference Books Annual, 2001*

Injury & Trauma Sourcebook

Basic Consumer Health Information about the Impact of Injury, the Diagnosis and Treatment of Common and Traumatic Injuries, Emergency Care, and Specific Injuries Related to Home, Community, Workplace, Transportation, and Recreation

Along with Guidelines for Injury Prevention, a Glossary, and a Directory of Additional Resources

Edited by Joyce Brennfleck Shannon. 696 pages. 2002. 0-7808-0421-X. $78.

■

Kidney & Urinary Tract Diseases & Disorders Sourcebook

Basic Information about Kidney Stones, Urinary Incontinence, Bladder Disease, End Stage Renal Disease, Dialysis, and More

Along with Statistical and Demographic Data and Reports on Current Research Initiatives

Edited by Linda M. Ross. 602 pages. 1997. 0-7808-0079-6. $78.

■

Learning Disabilities Sourcebook

Basic Information about Disorders Such as Dyslexia, Visual and Auditory Processing Deficits, Attention Deficit/Hyperactivity Disorder, and Autism

Along with Statistical and Demographic Data, Reports on Current Research Initiatives, an Explanation of the Assessment Process, and a Special Section for Adults with Learning Disabilities

Edited by Linda M. Shin. 579 pages. 1998. 0-7808-0210-1. $78.

Named "Outstanding Reference Book of 1999."
— *New York Public Library, Feb 2000*

"An excellent candidate for inclusion in a public library reference section. It's a great source of information. Teachers will also find the book useful. Definitely worth reading."
— *Journal of Adolescent & Adult Literacy, Feb 2000*

"Readable . . . provides a solid base of information regarding successful techniques used with individuals who have learning disabilities, as well as practical suggestions for educators and family members. Clear language, concise descriptions, and pertinent information for contacting multiple resources add to the strength of this book as a useful tool." — *Choice, Association of College and Research Libraries, Feb '99*

"Recommended reference source."
— *Booklist, American Library Association, Sep '98*

"A useful resource for libraries and for those who don't have the time to identify and locate the individual publications." — *Disability Resources Monthly, Sep '98*

Liver Disorders Sourcebook

Basic Consumer Health Information about the Liver and How It Works; Liver Diseases, Including Cancer, Cirrhosis, Hepatitis, and Toxic and Drug Related Diseases; Tips for Maintaining a Healthy Liver; Laboratory Tests, Radiology Tests, and Facts about Liver Transplantation

Along with a Section on Support Groups, a Glossary, and Resource Listings

Edited by Joyce Brennfleck Shannon. 591 pages. 2000. 0-7808-0383-3. $78.

"A valuable resource."
—American Reference Books Annual, 2001

"This title is recommended for health sciences and public libraries with consumer health collections."
— E-Streams, Oct '00

"Recommended reference source."
—Booklist, American Library Association, Jun '00

Lung Disorders Sourcebook

Basic Consumer Health Information about Emphysema, Pneumonia, Tuberculosis, Asthma, Cystic Fibrosis, and Other Lung Disorders, Including Facts about Diagnostic Procedures, Treatment Strategies, Disease Prevention Efforts, and Such Risk Factors as Smoking, Air Pollution, and Exposure to Asbestos, Radon, and Other Agents

Along with a Glossary and Resources for Additional Help and Information

Edited by Dawn D. Matthews. 678 pages. 2002. 0-7808-0339-6. $78.

Medical Tests Sourcebook

Basic Consumer Health Information about Medical Tests, Including Periodic Health Exams, General Screening Tests, Tests You Can Do at Home, Findings of the U.S. Preventive Services Task Force, X-ray and Radiology Tests, Electrical Tests, Tests of Blood and Other Body Fluids and Tissues, Scope Tests, Lung Tests, Genetic Tests, Pregnancy Tests, Newborn Screening Tests, Sexually Transmitted Disease Tests, and Computer Aided Diagnoses

Along with a Section on Paying for Medical Tests, a Glossary, and Resource Listings

Edited by Joyce Brennfleck Shannon. 691 pages. 1999. 0-7808-0243-8. $78.

"Recommended for hospital and health sciences libraries with consumer health collections."
— E-Streams, Mar '00

"This is an overall excellent reference with a wealth of general knowledge that may aid those who are reluctant to get vital tests performed."
— Today's Librarian, Jan 2000

"A valuable reference guide."
—American Reference Books Annual, 2000

Men's Health Concerns Sourcebook

Basic Information about Health Issues That Affect Men, Featuring Facts about the Top Causes of Death in Men, Including Heart Disease, Stroke, Cancers, Prostate Disorders, Chronic Obstructive Pulmonary Disease, Pneumonia and Influenza, Human Immunodeficiency Virus and Acquired Immune Deficiency Syndrome, Diabetes Mellitus, Stress, Suicide, Accidents and Homicides; and Facts about Common Concerns for Men, Including Impotence, Contraception, Circumcision, Sleep Disorders, Snoring, Hair Loss, Diet, Nutrition, Exercise, Kidney and Urological Disorders, and Backaches

Edited by Allan R. Cook. 738 pages. 1998. 0-7808-0212-8. $78.

"This comprehensive resource and the series are highly recommended."
—American Reference Books Annual, 2000

"Recommended reference source."
—Booklist, American Library Association, Dec '98

Mental Health Disorders Sourcebook, 1st Edition

Basic Information about Schizophrenia, Depression, Bipolar Disorder, Panic Disorder, Obsessive-Compulsive Disorder, Phobias and Other Anxiety Disorders, Paranoia and Other Personality Disorders, Eating Disorders, and Sleep Disorders

Along with Information about Treatment and Therapies

Edited by Karen Bellenir. 548 pages. 1995. 0-7808-0040-0. $78.

"This is an excellent new book . . . written in easy-to-understand language."
— Booklist Health Sciences Supplement, American Library Association, Oct '97

". . . useful for public and academic libraries and consumer health collections."
—Medical Reference Services Quarterly, Spring '97

"The great strengths of the book are its readability and its inclusion of places to find more information. Especially recommended." *— Reference Quarterly, American Library Association, Winter '96*

". . . a good resource for a consumer health library."
—Bulletin of the Medical Library Association, Oct '96

"The information is data-based and couched in brief, concise language that avoids jargon. . . . a useful reference source." *— Readings, Sep '96*

"The text is well organized and adequately written for its target audience." *— Choice, Association of College and Research Libraries, Jun '96*

". . . provides information on a wide range of mental disorders, presented in nontechnical language."
—Exceptional Child Education Resources, Spring '96

"Recommended for public and academic libraries."
—Reference Book Review, 1996

Mental Health Disorders Sourcebook, 2nd Edition

Basic Consumer Health Information about Anxiety Disorders, Depression and Other Mood Disorders, Eating Disorders, Personality Disorders, Schizophrenia, and More, Including Disease Descriptions, Treatment Options, and Reports on Current Research Initiatives

Along with Statistical Data, Tips for Maintaining Mental Health, a Glossary, and Directory of Sources for Additional Help and Information

Edited by Karen Bellenir. 605 pages. 2000. 0-7808-0240-3. $78.

"Well organized and well written."
—American Reference Books Annual, 2001

"Recommended reference source."
—Booklist, American Library Association, Jun '00

■

Mental Retardation Sourcebook

Basic Consumer Health Information about Mental Retardation and Its Causes, Including Down Syndrome, Fetal Alcohol Syndrome, Fragile X Syndrome, Genetic Conditions, Injury, and Environmental Sources

Along with Preventive Strategies, Parenting Issues, Educational Implications, Health Care Needs, Employment and Economic Matters, Legal Issues, a Glossary, and a Resource Listing for Additional Help and Information

Edited by Joyce Brennfleck Shannon. 642 pages. 2000. 0-7808-0377-9. $78.

"Public libraries will find the book useful for reference and as a beginning research point for students, parents, and caregivers."
—American Reference Books Annual, 2001

"The strength of this work is that it compiles many basic fact sheets and addresses for further information in one volume. It is intended and suitable for the general public. This sourcebook is relevant to any collection providing health information to the general public."
—E-Streams, Nov '00

"From preventing retardation to parenting and family challenges, this covers health, social and legal issues and will prove an invaluable overview."
—Reviewer's Bookwatch, Jul '00

■

Obesity Sourcebook

Basic Consumer Health Information about Diseases and Other Problems Associated with Obesity, and Including Facts about Risk Factors, Prevention Issues, and Management Approaches

Along with Statistical and Demographic Data, Information about Special Populations, Research Updates, a Glossary, and Source Listings for Further Help and Information

by Wilma Caldwell and Chad T. Kimball. 376
0-7808-0333-7. $78.

"The book synthesizes the reliable medical literature on obesity into one easy-to-read and useful resource for the general public."
—American Reference Books Annual 2002

"This is a very useful resource book for the lay public."
—Doody's Review Service, Nov '01

"Well suited for the health reference collection of a public library or an academic health science library that serves the general population." *—E-Streams, Sep '01*

"Recommended reference source."
—Booklist, American Library Association, Apr '01

" Recommended pick both for specialty health library collections and any general consumer health reference collection." *— The Bookwatch, Apr '01*

■

Ophthalmic Disorders Sourcebook

Basic Information about Glaucoma, Cataracts, Macular Degeneration, Strabismus, Refractive Disorders, and More

Along with Statistical and Demographic Data and Reports on Current Research Initiatives

Edited by Linda M. Ross. 631 pages. 1996. 0-7808-0081-8. $78.

■

Oral Health Sourcebook

Basic Information about Diseases and Conditions Affecting Oral Health, Including Cavities, Gum Disease, Dry Mouth, Oral Cancers, Fever Blisters, Canker Sores, Oral Thrush, Bad Breath, Temporomandibular Disorders, and other Craniofacial Syndromes

Along with Statistical Data on the Oral Health of Americans, Oral Hygiene, Emergency First Aid, Information on Treatment Procedures and Methods of Replacing Lost Teeth

Edited by Allan R. Cook. 558 pages. 1997. 0-7808-0082-6. $78.

"Unique source which will fill a gap in dental sources for patients and the lay public. A valuable reference tool even in a library with thousands of books on dentistry. Comprehensive, clear, inexpensive, and easy to read and use. It fills an enormous gap in the health care literature." *— Reference and User Services Quarterly, American Library Association, Summer '98*

"Recommended reference source."
—Booklist, American Library Association, Dec '97

■

Osteoporosis Sourcebook

Basic Consumer Health Information about Primary and Secondary Osteoporosis and Juvenile Osteoporosis and Related Conditions, Including Fibrous Dysplasia, Gaucher Disease, Hyperthyroidism, Hypophosphatasia, Myeloma, Osteopetrosis, Osteogenesis Imperfecta, and Paget's Disease

Along with Information about Risk Factors, Treatments, Traditional and Non-Traditional Pain Management, a Glossary of Related Terms, and a Directory of Resources

Edited by Allan R. Cook. 584 pages. 2001. 0-7808-0239-X. $78.

"This would be a book to be kept in a staff or patient library. The targeted audience is the layperson, but the therapist who needs a quick bit of information on a particular topic will also find the book useful."
—*Physical Therapy, Jan '02*

"This resource is recommended as a great reference source for public, health, and academic libraries, and is another triumph for the editors of Omnigraphics."
—*American Reference Books Annual 2002*

"Recommended for all public libraries and general health collections, especially those supporting patient education or consumer health programs."
—*E-Streams, Nov '01*

"Will prove valuable to any library seeking to maintain a current, comprehensive reference collection of health resources. . . . From prevention to treatment and associated conditions, this provides an excellent survey."
—*The Bookwatch, Aug '01*

"Recommended reference source."
—*Booklist, American Library Association, July '01*

SEE ALSO *Women's Health Concerns Sourcebook*

■

Pain Sourcebook, 1st Edition

Basic Information about Specific Forms of Acute and Chronic Pain, Including Headaches, Back Pain, Muscular Pain, Neuralgia, Surgical Pain, and Cancer Pain

Along with Pain Relief Options Such as Analgesics, Narcotics, Nerve Blocks, Transcutaneous Nerve Stimulation, and Alternative Forms of Pain Control, Including Biofeedback, Imaging, Behavior Modification, and Relaxation Techniques

Edited by Allan R. Cook. 667 pages. 1997. 0-7808-0213-6. $78.

"The text is readable, easily understood, and well indexed. This excellent volume belongs in all patient education libraries, consumer health sections of public libraries, and many personal collections."
—*American Reference Books Annual, 1999*

"A beneficial reference." —*Booklist Health Sciences Supplement, American Library Association, Oct '98*

"The information is basic in terms of scholarship and is appropriate for general readers. Written in journalistic style . . . intended for non-professionals. Quite thorough in its coverage of different pain conditions and summarizes the latest clinical information regarding pain treatment." —*Choice, Association of College and Research Libraries, Jun '98*

"Recommended reference source."
—*Booklist, American Library Association, Mar '98*

Pain Sourcebook, 2nd Edition

Basic Consumer Health Information about Specific Forms of Acute and Chronic Pain, Including Muscle and Skeletal Pain, Nerve Pain, Cancer Pain, and Disorders Characterized by Pain, Such as Fibromyalgia, Shingles, Angina, Arthritis, and Headaches

Along with Information about Pain Medications and Management Techniques, Complementary and Alternative Pain Relief Options, Tips for People Living with Chronic Pain, a Glossary, and a Directory of Sources for Further Information

Edited by Karen Bellenir. 670 pages. 2002. 0-7808-0612-3. $78.

■

Pediatric Cancer Sourcebook

Basic Consumer Health Information about Leukemias, Brain Tumors, Sarcomas, Lymphomas, and Other Cancers in Infants, Children, and Adolescents, Including Descriptions of Cancers, Treatments, and Coping Strategies

Along with Suggestions for Parents, Caregivers, and Concerned Relatives, a Glossary of Cancer Terms, and Resource Listings

Edited by Edward J. Prucha. 587 pages. 1999. 0-7808-0245-4. $78.

"An excellent source of information. Recommended for public, hospital, and health science libraries with consumer health collections." —*E-Streams, Jun '00*

"Recommended reference source."
—*Booklist, American Library Association, Feb '00*

"A valuable addition to all libraries specializing in health services and many public libraries."
—*American Reference Books Annual, 2000*

■

Physical & Mental Issues in Aging Sourcebook

Basic Consumer Health Information on Physical and Mental Disorders Associated with the Aging Process, Including Concerns about Cardiovascular Disease, Pulmonary Disease, Oral Health, Digestive Disorders, Musculoskeletal and Skin Disorders, Metabolic Changes, Sexual and Reproductive Issues, and Changes in Vision, Hearing, and Other Senses

Along with Data about Longevity and Causes of Death, Information on Acute and Chronic Pain, Descriptions of Mental Concerns, a Glossary of Terms, and Resource Listings for Additional Help

Edited by Jenifer Swanson. 660 pages. 1999. 0-7808-0233-0. $78.

"This is a treasure of health information for the layperson." —*Choice Health Sciences Supplement, Association of College & Research Libraries, May 2000*

"Recommended for public libraries."
—*American Reference Books Annual, 2000*

"Recommended reference source."
—*Booklist, American Library Association, Oct '99*

SEE ALSO *Healthy Aging Sourcebook*

Podiatry Sourcebook

Basic Consumer Health Information about Foot Conditions, Diseases, and Injuries, Including Bunions, Corns, Calluses, Athlete's Foot, Plantar Warts, Hammertoes and Clawtoes, Clubfoot, Heel Pain, Gout, and More

Along with Facts about Foot Care, Disease Prevention, Foot Safety, Choosing a Foot Care Specialist, a Glossary of Terms, and Resource Listings for Additional Information

Edited by M. Lisa Weatherford. 380 pages. 2001. 0-7808-0215-2. $78.

"Recommended reference source."
— Booklist, American Library Association, Feb '02

"There is a lot of information presented here on a topic that is usually only covered sparingly in most larger comprehensive medical encyclopedias."
— American Reference Books Annual 2002

■

Pregnancy & Birth Sourcebook

Basic Information about Planning for Pregnancy, Maternal Health, Fetal Growth and Development, Labor and Delivery, Postpartum and Perinatal Care, Pregnancy in Mothers with Special Concerns, and Disorders of Pregnancy, Including Genetic Counseling, Nutrition and Exercise, Obstetrical Tests, Pregnancy Discomfort, Multiple Births, Cesarean Sections, Medical Testing of Newborns, Breastfeeding, Gestational Diabetes, and Ectopic Pregnancy

Edited by Heather E. Aldred. 737 pages. 1997. 0-7808-0216-0. $78.

"A well-organized handbook. Recommended."
— Choice, Association of College and Research Libraries, Apr '98

"Recommended reference source."
— Booklist, American Library Association, Mar '98

"Recommended for public libraries."
— American Reference Books Annual, 1998

SEE ALSO *Congenital Disorders Sourcebook, Family Planning Sourcebook*

■

Prostate Cancer Sourcebook

Basic Consumer Health Information about Prostate Cancer, Including Information about the Associated Risk Factors, Detection, Diagnosis, and Treatment of Prostate Cancer

Along with Information on Non-Malignant Prostate Conditions, and Featuring a Section Listing Support and Treatment Centers and a Glossary of Related Terms

Edited by Dawn D. Matthews. 358 pages. 2001. 0-7808-0324-8. $78.

"Recommended reference source."
—Booklist, American Library Association, Jan '02

"A valuable resource for health care consumers seeking information on the subject....All text is written in a clear, easy-to-understand language that avoids technical jargon. Any library that collects consumer health resources would strengthen their collection with the addition of the *Prostate Cancer Sourcebook.*"
— American Reference Books Annual 2002

■

Public Health Sourcebook

Basic Information about Government Health Agencies, Including National Health Statistics and Trends, Healthy People 2000 Program Goals and Objectives, the Centers for Disease Control and Prevention, the Food and Drug Administration, and the National Institutes of Health

Along with Full Contact Information for Each Agency

Edited by Wendy Wilcox. 698 pages. 1998. 0-7808-0220-9. $78.

"Recommended reference source."
— Booklist, American Library Association, Sep '98

"This consumer guide provides welcome assistance in navigating the maze of federal health agencies and their data on public health concerns."
— SciTech Book News, Sep '98

■

Reconstructive & Cosmetic Surgery Sourcebook

Basic Consumer Health Information on Cosmetic and Reconstructive Plastic Surgery, Including Statistical Information about Different Surgical Procedures, Things to Consider Prior to Surgery, Plastic Surgery Techniques and Tools, Emotional and Psychological Considerations, and Procedure-Specific Information

Along with a Glossary of Terms and a Listing of Resources for Additional Help and Information

Edited by M. Lisa Weatherford. 374 pages. 2001. 0-7808-0214-4. $78.

"An excellent reference that addresses cosmetic and medically necessary reconstructive surgeries. . . . The style of the prose is calm and reassuring, discussing the many positive outcomes now available due to advances in surgical techniques."
— American Reference Books Annual 2002

"Recommended for health science libraries that are open to the public, as well as hospital libraries that are open to the patients. This book is a good resource for the consumer interested in plastic surgery."
—E-Streams, Dec '01

"Recommended reference source."
—Booklist, American Library Association, July '01

■

Rehabilitation Sourcebook

Basic Consumer Health Information about Rehabilitation for People Recovering from Heart Surgery, Spinal Cord Injury, Stroke, Orthopedic Impairments, Amputation, Pulmonary Impairments, Traumatic Injury, and More, Including Physical Therapy, Occupa-

tional Therapy, Speech/ Language Therapy, Massage Therapy, Dance Therapy, Art Therapy, and Recreational Therapy

Along with Information on Assistive and Adaptive Devices, a Glossary, and Resources for Additional Help and Information

Edited by Dawn D. Matthews. 531 pages. 1999. 0-7808-0236-5. $78.

"This is an excellent resource for public library reference and health collections."
— American Reference Books Annual, 2001

"Recommended reference source."
— Booklist, American Library Association, May '00

Respiratory Diseases & Disorders Sourcebook

Basic Information about Respiratory Diseases and Disorders, Including Asthma, Cystic Fibrosis, Pneumonia, the Common Cold, Influenza, and Others, Featuring Facts about the Respiratory System, Statistical and Demographic Data, Treatments, Self-Help Management Suggestions, and Current Research Initiatives

Edited by Allan R. Cook and Peter D. Dresser. 771 pages. 1995. 0-7808-0037-0. $78.

"Designed for the layperson and for patients and their families coping with respiratory illness. . . . an extensive array of information on diagnosis, treatment, management, and prevention of respiratory illnesses for the general reader."
— Choice, Association of College and Research Libraries, Jun '96

"A highly recommended text for all collections. It is a comforting reminder of the power of knowledge that good books carry between their covers."
— Academic Library Book Review, Spring '96

"A comprehensive collection of authoritative information presented in a nontechnical, humanitarian style for patients, families, and caregivers."
— Association of Operating Room Nurses, Sep/Oct '95

Sexually Transmitted Diseases Sourcebook, 1st Edition

Basic Information about Herpes, Chlamydia, Gonorrhea, Hepatitis, Nongonoccocal Urethritis, Pelvic Inflammatory Disease, Syphilis, AIDS, and More

Along with Current Data on Treatments and Preventions

Edited by Linda M. Ross. 550 pages. 1997. 0-7808-0217-9. $78.

Sexually Transmitted Diseases Sourcebook, 2nd Edition

Basic Consumer Health Information about Sexually Transmitted Diseases, Including Information on the Diagnosis and Treatment of Chlamydia, Gonorrhea, Hepatitis, Herpes, HIV, Mononucleosis, Syphilis, and Others

Along with Information on Prevention, Such as Condom Use, Vaccines, and STD Education; And Featuring a Section on Issues Related to Youth and Adolescents, a Glossary, and Resources for Additional Help and Information

Edited by Dawn D. Matthews. 538 pages. 2001. 0-7808-0249-7. $78.

"Recommended for consumer health collections in public libraries, and secondary school and community college libraries."
— American Reference Books Annual 2002

"Every school and public library should have a copy of this comprehensive and user-friendly reference book."
— Choice, Association of College & Research Libraries, Sep '01

"This is a highly recommended book. This is an especially important book for all school and public libraries." — AIDS Book Review Journal, Jul-Aug '01

"Recommended reference source."
— Booklist, American Library Association, Apr '01

"Recommended pick both for specialty health library collections and any general consumer health reference collection." — The Bookwatch, Apr '01

Skin Disorders Sourcebook

Basic Information about Common Skin and Scalp Conditions Caused by Aging, Allergies, Immune Reactions, Sun Exposure, Infectious Organisms, Parasites, Cosmetics, and Skin Traumas, Including Abrasions, Cuts, and Pressure Sores

Along with Information on Prevention and Treatment

Edited by Allan R. Cook. 647 pages. 1997. 0-7808-0080-X. $78.

". . . comprehensive, easily read reference book."
— Doody's Health Sciences Book Reviews, Oct '97

SEE ALSO Burns Sourcebook

Sleep Disorders Sourcebook

Basic Consumer Health Information about Sleep and Its Disorders, Including Insomnia, Sleepwalking, Sleep Apnea, Restless Leg Syndrome, and Narcolepsy

Along with Data about Shiftwork and Its Effects, Information on the Societal Costs of Sleep Deprivation, Descriptions of Treatment Options, a Glossary of Terms, and Resource Listings for Additional Help

Edited by Jenifer Swanson. 439 pages. 1998. 0-7808-0234-9. $78.

"This text will complement any home or medical library. It is user-friendly and ideal for the adult reader."
—*American Reference Books Annual, 2000*

"A useful resource that provides accurate, relevant, and accessible information on sleep to the general public. Health care providers who deal with sleep disorders patients may also find it helpful in being prepared to answer some of the questions patients ask."
—*Respiratory Care, Jul '99*

"Recommended reference source."
—*Booklist, American Library Association, Feb '99*

Sports Injuries Sourcebook, First Edition

Basic Consumer Health Information about Common Sports Injuries, Prevention of Injury in Specific Sports, Tips for Training, and Rehabilitation from Injury

Along with Information about Special Concerns for Children, Young Girls in Athletic Training Programs, Senior Athletes, and Women Athletes, and a Directory of Resources for Further Help and Information

Edited by Heather E. Aldred. 624 pages. 1999. 0-7808-0218-7. $78.

"While this easy-to-read book is recommended for all libraries, it should prove to be especially useful for public, high school, and academic libraries; certainly it should be on the bookshelf of every school gymnasium."
—*E-Streams, Mar '00*

"Public libraries and undergraduate academic libraries will find this book useful for its nontechnical language."
—*American Reference Books Annual, 2000*

Sports Injuries Sourcebook, Second Edition

Basic Consumer Health Information about the Diagnosis, Treatment, and Rehabilitation of Common Sports-Related Injuries in Children and Adults

Along with Suggestions for Conditioning and Training, Information and Prevention Tips for Injuries Frequently Associated with Specific Sports and Special Populations, a Glossary, and a Directory of Additional Resources

Edited by Joyce Brennfleck Shannon. 614 pages. 2002. 0-7808-0604-2. $78.

Stress-Related Disorders Sourcebook

Basic Consumer Health Information about Stress and Stress-Related Disorders, Including Stress Origins and Signals, Environmental Stress at Work and Home, Mental and Emotional Stress Associated with Depression, Post-Traumatic Stress Disorder, Panic Disorder, Suicide, and the Physical Effects of Stress on the Cardiovascular, Immune, and Nervous Systems

Along with Stress Management Techniques, a Glossary, and a Listing of Additional Resources

Edited by Joyce Brennfleck Shannon. 610 pages. 2002. 0-7808-0560-7. $78.

Substance Abuse Sourcebook

Basic Health-Related Information about the Abuse of Legal and Illegal Substances Such as Alcohol, Tobacco, Prescription Drugs, Marijuana, Cocaine, and Heroin; and Including Facts about Substance Abuse Prevention Strategies, Intervention Methods, Treatment and Recovery Programs, and a Section Addressing the Special Problems Related to Substance Abuse during Pregnancy

Edited by Karen Bellenir. 573 pages. 1996. 0-7808-0038-9. $78.

"A valuable addition to any health reference section. Highly recommended."
—*The Book Report, Mar/Apr '97*

". . . a comprehensive collection of substance abuse information that's both highly readable and compact. Families and caregivers of substance abusers will find the information enlightening and helpful, while teachers, social workers and journalists should benefit from the concise format. Recommended."
—*Drug Abuse Update, Winter '96/'97*

SEE ALSO Alcoholism Sourcebook, Drug Abuse Sourcebook

Surgery Sourcebook

Basic Consumer Health Information about Inpatient and Outpatient Surgeries, Including Cardiac, Vascular, Orthopedic, Ocular, Reconstructive, Cosmetic, Gynecologic, and Ear, Nose, and Throat Procedures and More

Along with Information about Operating Room Policies and Instruments, Laser Surgery Techniques, Hospital Errors, Statistical Data, a Glossary, and Listings of Sources for Further Help and Information

Edited by Annemarie S. Muth and Karen Bellenir. 600 pages. 2002. 0-7808-0380-9. $78.

Transplantation Sourcebook

Basic Consumer Health Information about Organ and Tissue Transplantation, Including Physical and Financial Preparations, Procedures and Issues Relating to Specific Solid Organ and Tissue Transplants, Rehabilitation, Pediatric Transplant Information, the Future of Transplantation, and Organ and Tissue Donation

Along with a Glossary and Listings of Additional Resources

Edited by Joyce Brennfleck Shannon. 628 pages. 2002. 0-7808-0322-1. $78.

Traveler's Health Sourcebook

Basic Consumer Health Information for Travelers, Including Physical and Medical Preparations, Transportation Health and Safety, Essential Information about Food and Water, Sun Exposure, Insect and Snake Bites, Camping and Wilderness Medicine, and Travel with Physical or Medical Disabilities

Along with International Travel Tips, Vaccination Recommendations, Geographical Health Issues, Disease Risks, a Glossary, and a Listing of Additional Resources

Edited by Joyce Brennfleck Shannon. 613 pages. 2000. 0-7808-0384-1. $78.

"Recommended reference source."
   — Booklist, American Library Association, Feb '01

"This book is recommended for any public library, any travel collection, and especially any collection for the physically disabled."
   —American Reference Books Annual, 2001

■

Vegetarian Sourcebook

Basic Consumer Health Information about Vegetarian Diets, Lifestyle, and Philosophy, Including Definitions of Vegetarianism and Veganism, Tips about Adopting Vegetarianism, Creating a Vegetarian Pantry, and Meeting Nutritional Needs of Vegetarians, with Facts Regarding Vegetarianism's Effect on Pregnant and Lactating Women, Children, Athletes, and Senior Citizens

Along with a Glossary of Commonly Used Vegetarian Terms and Resources for Additional Help and Information

Edited byChad T. Kimball. 360 pages. 2002. 0-7808-0439-2. $78.

■

Women's Health Concerns Sourcebook

Basic Information about Health Issues That Affect Women, Featuring Facts about Menstruation and Other Gynecological Concerns, Including Endometriosis, Fibroids, Menopause, and Vaginitis; Reproductive Concerns, Including Birth Control, Infertility, and Abortion, and Facts about Additional Physical, Emotional, and Mental Health Concerns Prevalent among Women Such as Osteoporosis, Urinary Tract Disorders, Eating Disorders, and Depression

Along with Tips for Maintaining a Healthy Lifestyle

Edited by Heather E. Aldred. 567 pages. 1997. 0-7808-0219-5. $78.

"Handy compilation. There is an impressive range of diseases, devices, disorders, procedures, and other physical and emotional issues covered . . . well organized, illustrated, and indexed."   *— Choice, Association of College and Research Libraries, Jan '98*

SEE ALSO *Breast Cancer Sourcebook, Cancer Sourcebook for Women, 1st and 2nd Editions, Healthy Heart Sourcebook for Women, Osteoporosis Sourcebook*

Workplace Health & Safety Sourcebook

Basic Consumer Health Information about Workplace Health and Safety, Including the Effect of Workplace Hazards on the Lungs, Skin, Heart, Ears, Eyes, Brain, Reproductive Organs, Musculoskeletal System, and Other Organs and Body Parts

Along with Information about Occupational Cancer, Personal Protective Equipment, Toxic and Hazardous Chemicals, Child Labor, Stress, and Workplace Violence

Edited by Chad T. Kimball. 626 pages. 2000. 0-7808-0231-4. $78.

"As a reference for the general public, this would be useful in any library."   *—E-Streams, Jun '01*

"Provides helpful information for primary care physicians and other caregivers interested in occupational medicine. . . . General readers; professionals."
   — Choice, Association of College & Research Libraries, May '01

"Recommended reference source."
   —Booklist, American Library Association, Feb '01

"Highly recommended."   *—The Bookwatch, Jan '01*

■

Worldwide Health Sourcebook

Basic Information about Global Health Issues, Including Malnutrition, Reproductive Health, Disease Dispersion and Prevention, Emerging Diseases, Risky Health Behaviors, and the Leading Causes of Death

Along with Global Health Concerns for Children, Women, and the Elderly, Mental Health Issues, Research and Technology Advancements, and Economic, Environmental, and Political Health Implications, a Glossary, and a Resource Listing for Additional Help and Information

Edited by Joyce Brennfleck Shannon. 614 pages. 2001. 0-7808-0330-2. $78.

"Named an Outstanding Academic Title."
   —Choice, Association of College & Research Libraries, Jan '02

"Yet another handy but also unique compilation in the extensive Health Reference Series, this is a useful work because many of the international publications reprinted or excerpted are not readily available. Highly recommended."
   —Choice, Association of College & Research Libraries, Nov '01

"Recommended reference source."
   —Booklist, American Library Association, Oct '01

Teen Health Series

Helping Young Adults Understand, Manage,
and Avoid Serious Illness

Diet Information for Teens
Health Tips about Diet and Nutrition
Including Facts about Nutrients, Dietary Guidelines,
Breakfasts, School Lunches, Snacks, Party Food, Weight
Control, Eating Disorders, and More

Edited by Karen Bellenir. 399 pages. 2001. 0-7808-0441-4. $58.

"Full of helpful insights and facts throughout the book. ... An excellent resource to be placed in public libraries or even in personal collections."
—*American Reference Books Annual 2002*

"Recommended for middle and high school libraries and media centers as well as academic libraries that educate future teachers of teenagers. It is also a suitable addition to health science libraries that serve patrons who are interested in teen health promotion and education." —*E-Streams, Oct '01*

"This comprehensive book would be beneficial to collections that need information about nutrition, dietary guidelines, meal planning, and weight control. ... This reference is so easy to use that its purchase is recommended." —*The Book Report, Sep-Oct '01*

"This book is written in an easy to understand format describing issues that many teens face every day, and then provides thoughtful explanations so that teens can make informed decisions. This is an interesting book that provides important facts and information for today's teens." —*Doody's Health Sciences Book Review Journal, Jul-Aug '01*

"A comprehensive compendium of diet and nutrition. The information is presented in a straightforward, plain-spoken manner. This title will be useful to those working on reports on a variety of topics, as well as to general readers concerned about their dietary health." —*School Library Journal, Jun '01*

Drug Information for Teens
Health Tips about the Physical and Mental Effects of Substance Abuse
Including Facts about Alcohol, Anabolic Steroids, Club
Drugs, Cocaine, Depressants, Hallucinogens, Herbal
Products, Inhalants, Marijuana, Narcotics, Stimulants,
Tobacco, and More

Edited by Karen Bellenir. 472 pages. 2002. 0-7808-0444-9. $58.

Mental Health Information for Teens
Health Tips about Mental Health and Mental Illness
Including Facts about Anxiety, Depression, Suicide,
Eating Disorders, Obsessive-Compulsive Disorders,
Panic Attacks, Phobias, Schizophrenia, and More

Edited by Karen Bellenir. 406 pages. 2001. 0-7808-0442-2. $58.

"In both language and approach, this user-friendly entry in the *Teen Health Series* is on target for teens needing information on mental health concerns." —*Booklist, American Library Association, Jan '02*

"Readers will find the material accessible and informative, with the shaded notes, facts, and embedded glossary insets adding appropriately to the already interesting and succinct presentation."
—*School Library Journal, Jan '02*

"This title is highly recommended for any library that serves adolescents and parents/caregivers of adolescents." —*E-Streams, Jan '02*

"Recommended for high school libraries and young adult collections in public libraries. Both health professionals and teenagers will find this book useful."
—*American Reference Books Annual 2002*

"This is a nice book written to enlighten the society, primarily teenagers, about common teen mental health issues. It is highly recommended to teachers and parents as well as adolescents."
—*Doody's Review Service, Dec '01*

Sexual Health Information for Teens
Health Tips about Sexual Development, Human Reproduction, and Sexually Transmitted Diseases
Including Facts about Puberty, Reproductive Health,
Chlamydia, Human Papillomavirus, Pelvic Inflam-
matory Disease, Herpes, AIDS, Contraception, Preg-
nancy, and More

Edited by Deborah A. Stanley. 400 pages. 2002. 0-7808-0445-7. $58.